Brazilian Ronaldinho celebrates scoring for
Barcelona against Athletic Bilbao, during their
Spanish Liga match, played at the Camp Nou
stadium in Barcelona, Spain.

LONDON, NEW YORK, MUNICH,
MELBOURNE AND DELHI

Senior Designer Guy Harvey
Senior Editor Catherine Saunders
Editor Julia March
Editorial Assistants Jo Casey and Darren Nelson
Designers Jon Hall and Dan Bunyan
Brand Manager Robert Perry
Publishing Manager Simon Beecroft
Category Publisher Alex Allan/Siobhan Williamson
Production Amy Bennett
Production Editor Siu Chan

Body illustration p.28-29 by Medi-Mation
Statistics p.128–147 by Aidan Radnedge

First published in Great Britain in 2008
by Dorling Kindersley Limited,
80 Strand, London WC2R 0RL
A Penguin Company

This edition produced for The Book People Ltd, Hall Wood Avenue,
Haydock, St Helens, WA11 9UL

2 4 6 8 10 9 7 5 3
FD159 – 09/08

© 2008 Dorling Kindersley Ltd.

ISBN: 978-1-85613-122-3

Reproduced by Media Development and Printing Ltd., UK
Printed and bound in China by Hung Hing.

Acknowledgements
The publisher would like to thank Steve Ellis for high res work, Will Jones and Martin Copeland
for picture research, Ann Barrett for the index, Louise Hughes for legal advice and
Dr Robert Marshall for medical expertise.
Discover more at
www.dk.com

*Ecstatic Greek fans celebrate winning the
UEFA European Championship in 2004.
Greece beat the hosts Portugal 1–0.*

FOOTBALL
THE ULTIMATE GUIDE

Written by Martin Cloake, Glenn Dakin,
Adam Powley, Aidan Radnedge
and Catherine Saunders

CONTENTS

Italy celebrate their 5–3 penalty shoot-out victory over France in the 2006 World Cup Final.

A group of children play football barefoot, overlooking Rio de Janeiro, Brazil.

THE BEAUTIFUL GAME

"FOOTBALL IS ONE OF THE WORLD'S BEST MEANS OF COMMUNICATION. IT IS IMPARTIAL, APOLITICAL AND UNIVERSAL. FOOTBALL UNITES PEOPLE AROUND THE WORLD EVERY DAY. YOUNG OR OLD, PLAYERS OR FANS, RICH OR POOR, THE GAME MAKES EVERYONE EQUAL, STIRS THE IMAGINATION, MAKES PEOPLE HAPPY AND MAKES THEM SAD."

FRANZ BECKENBAUER, WORLD CUP
WINNING PLAYER AND COACH

Football, soccer, fussball, futebol, futbol, voetball – whatever we call it, it's the same beautiful game. For many of us it is quite simply the greatest game on Earth. Its popularity has spread across the globe to every tiny island and remote wilderness. It is a game for everybody. The love of the game brings people together – whether it is to play it, watch it or just endlessly debate the referees' decisions! Rich and poor, boys and girls, young and old, everyone can play the game. Best of all, you don't need any fancy equipment. All you need is a ball...

ABOUT THE BOOK

This guide to the beautiful game has it all – from the history of the game to the anatomy of a footballer, the greatest teams to the most famous players, the most prestigious competitions to the die-hard fans. However, football is an ever-changing game: Every effort has been made to verify all facts and statistics – they are correct at time of going to press but may be subject to change at any future time.

ORIGINS OF FOOTBALL

> "SOMEONE SAID 'FOOTBALL IS MORE IMPORTANT THAN LIFE AND DEATH TO YOU' AND I SAID 'LISTEN, IT'S MORE IMPORTANT THAN THAT.'" BILL SHANKLY, FORMER MANAGER OF LIVERPOOL FC

No one can say precisely when, how or even why the game of football developed. Games resembling football can be traced back as far as the ancient Chinese, Greek and Roman civilisations. However, the rules of these games differed widely – from the number of players, to the handling of the ball and the size of the goal. A standard set of rules was needed and eventually the English took on the job. In 1863 the English Football Association was formed and it published the 'Laws of the Game'. This meant that every team could play by the same rules, creating the foundation for the way football is played today, all over the world.

CUJU

The first game believed to have involved players kicking a ball was an ancient Chinese game called cuju. Popular in the 2nd century BCE, the object of cuju was to kick a leather ball through a hole in a piece of silk held up by two 10m (30ft) poles.

DID YOU KNOW?

More countries are members of FIFA than of the United Nations (an organisation which aims to promote international cooperation).

KEMARI

The Japanese sport of kemari developed from the Chinese game cuju. It was first played in about 600 CE but has been revived in modern times. The object of kemari is to keep the ball in the air. The game is unique because all the players must work together, so there are no winners or losers.

MEDIEVAL FOOTBALL

In the Middle Ages football games were popular throughout Europe. However, they were often little more than mass brawls between neighbouring towns or villages. By the 16th century, football was also being played in English public (fee-paying) schools. Although this helped the game to develop, each school had its own set of rules which made it very difficult for them to play each other.

By 1881 some teams had begun to wear co-ordinated kits.

DEVELOPING GAME

By the end of the 19th century, football was growing rapidly in popularity. Once again it was the British who helped to spread the game around the world, firstly to Europe and then on to South America, North America, Africa, Asia and Australasia.

At first footballers were just talented amateurs, but in 1885 they became professionals and therefore could be paid. Organised leagues and cup competitions were formed and games attracted huge crowds. In 1901, more than 110,000 fans watched Tottenham Hotspur and Sheffield United in the English FA Cup Final.

THE MODERN ERA

"THE ONLY THING THAT HAS NEVER CHANGED IN THE HISTORY OF THE GAME IS THE SHAPE OF THE BALL."

DENIS LAW, FORMER SCOTLAND STRIKER

Throughout the 20th century the game of football has continued to develop across the globe and in the last thirty years it has become big business, thanks to worldwide TV coverage and lucrative sponsorship deals. Nowadays, the top players are highly-trained superstars, earning massive salaries for their talents, both on and off the pitch.

It was a very different story for footballers in 1900. Above, West Bromwich Albion players enjoy a training session – a brisk walk in their suits! In 1901 the English FA set the maximum wage for a footballer at £4 a week.

1880s
In the 1880s teams began to wear co-ordinated kits for the first time. They were usually long shorts with knee-length socks and knitted jerseys.

1900s
After 1901 players were allowed to show their knees so shorts became shorter. Striped shirts with collars also became fashionable.

1930s
During the 1930s, shorts became even shorter and also baggier. There was more variation in kit style.

1950s
During the 1950s, football fashions really began to take off. Lightweight shirt fabrics were introduced and kit design became more colourful and daring.

1960s
By the 1960s boots as well as kits were much more lightweight. Surprisingly, during the 1960s plain kits were fashionable as they showed up better under the floodlights.

1970s
During the 1970s, teams began to assert their individuality with distinctive kits. They also began to realise the marketing potential of kit sponsorship and replica shirts.

THE FOOTBALL

The first footballs were inflated pigs' bladders or skins stuffed with straw or sawdust. In the 19th and early 20th centuries, footballs were made of animal bladders wrapped in leather. They often lost their shape during a match and became very heavy in wet conditions. Modern footballs are lighter and are usually made of leather or plastic with a special waterproof coating. Match balls must be 68–70 cm (27–28 in) in circumference and weigh 410–450 g (14–16 oz).

BOOTS

Early footballers nailed studs into their heavy leather work boots and the first football boots were heavy, ankle-high leather boots. Lighter, shorter boots, made of a mixture of leather and synthetic materials were first introduced in the 1960s. Today's boots use the latest technology, They are light, and sleek, with plastic studs.

1980s

During the 1980s kit fabrics became even more lightweight but for many the decade was defined by the players' hairstlyes. Curly perms and the 'mullet' (below) were the height of fashion.

1990s

The 1990s saw a trend for bright colours and crazy patterns. Thankfully this fad had passed by the end of the decade.

1970s

In the 1970s, players began wearing numbers on their shorts. Although with shorts this tiny, it is a wonder they found space...

DREAM TEAM

It's not just the game that has developed over the years, the players and kits have changed too – from the long shorts and perfectly groomed moustaches of the 19th century to the long hair and tight shorts of the 1970s and the high-tech, ever-changing kits of the 21st century. Check out this all-time fantasy eleven of professional footballers through the ages.

2000s

In the 21st century replica football kits and sponsorship deals are even bigger business. Most teams have at least three kits which they change every season.

2000s

Even in the 21st century, footballers still make some serious fashion mistakes. Cameroon's body-hugging one-piece kit in 2004 earned them a fine and a points deduction from FIFA.

WOMEN'S FOOTBALL

"THE FUTURE OF FOOTBALL IS FEMININE."

FIFA CHIEF EXECUTIVE SEPP BLATTER

Today there are more than 26 million female footballers in the world and it is women who have led football's long-awaited advances in the USA and China. Although the first women's professional league collapsed in the USA in 2003, it appears to be only a temporary setback. Semi-professional domestic leagues have sprung up all over the world, and international tournaments such as the Women's World Cup have become compelling fixtures in the football calendar.

No one, man or woman, has scored more international goals than Mia Hamm, with 158.

DICK, KERR'S LADIES

The first ever women's international was played in 1920 between France and a team of factory workers from Lancashire, England who had defeated male players at the Dick, Kerr and Co.'s base in Preston. Dick, Kerr's Ladies became a touring sensation and they used their matches to raise money for injured First World War soldiers. The team played on until 1965 as Preston Ladies, despite many obstacles such as the English FA banning women from using official pitches between 1921 and 1971.

MIA HAMM

USA star player Mia Hamm is more famous than most of her male counterparts. She spearheaded USA victories in the 1991 and 1999 Women's World Cup finals and is her country's top scorer. Now retired, Hamm and her strike partner Michelle Akers were the only women included in Pelé's 2004 list of the 125 greatest living footballers.

China striker Sun Wen has had to settle for several second-place finishes behind US footballers – in the 1999 World Cup, and a series of end-of-year prize-givings. However her goalscoring and passing abilities finally received top billing when FIFA named her the Woman Player of the Century in 2002, although she still had to share the title with America's Michelle Akers.

KARREN BRADY

has proved the sceptics wrong by making a success of Birmingham City since taking over as managing director in 1992, at the age of 23. She has helped to pave the way for other women to work in football as referees and match commentators.

WOMEN'S DREAM TEAM? 1. Bente Nordby (Norway) 2. Kerstin Stegemann (Germany) 3. Sandra Minnert (Germany) 4. Hege Riise (Norway) 5. Carla Werden Overbeck (USA) 6. Steffi Jones (Germany) 7. Kristine Lilly (USA) 8. Michelle Akers (USA) 9. Mia Hamm (USA) 10. Sun Wen (China) 11. Julie Foudy (USA)

BIRGIT PRINZ

Germany forward Birgit Prinz has won an unprecedented hat-trick of FIFA Women's Player of the Year prizes in 2003, 2004 and 2005. Her seven goals helped Germany win the Women's World Cup for the first time in 2003 and she was instrumental in their 2007 victory. In 2005 Prinz and Inka Grings fired Germany to their fourth consecutive UEFA Championship trophy. Italian club Perugia tried in vain to sign her for their men's team in 2003.

Like Birgit Prinz, Sweden's Hanna Ljungberg was wanted by Serie A's Perugia, but turned them down. Ljungberg is a skilful and hard-working forward, but despite talents such as her and Swedish top scorer Pia Sundhage, Sweden's women have had to settle for finishing runners-up in the 2003 World Cup and at two European Championships.

Although England's women are still striving for their big international breakthrough, they have one of the world's most recognised female footballers – star striker Rachel Yankey. Her goals in 2007 helped Arsenal Ladies to the UEFA Women's Cup, two years after she and international team-mate Rachel Unitt won the American W-League with the New Jersey Wildcats.

Women were banned from playing football in Brazil until 1975.

ONE TO WATCH

China forward Ma Xiaoxu made history when she was voted Asia's Young Footballer of the Year in 2006 – ahead of the continent's men. Although she has been nicknamed 'Sun Wen Junior' she names veteran US midfielder Kristine Lilly as her heroine. Ma Xiaoxu's late equaliser and opening spot-kick in the shoot-out helped China to win the 2006 AFC Women's Asian Cup final against Australia.

DID YOU KNOW?

Brazilian Milene Domingues, the ex wife of Ronaldo, is a WAG with a difference. In 1997 she set a women's world ball-juggling record when she kept a football in the air for more than nine hours and six minutes with a total of 55,187 touches! After Ronaldo joined Real Madrid in 2002, she too moved to the Spanish capital – but signed for city rivals Atlético instead in a record £200,000 transfer.

MARTA

Brazilian midfielder Marta Vieira da Silva had her boots imprinted in cement outside Rio's Maracanã Stadium after Brazil beat the USA in the 2007 Pan American Games. FIFA Women's Player of the Year in 2006, Marta plays her club football for Sweden's Umeå IK as there is no women's league in Brazil.

PLAYING BY THE RULES

"MY JOB IS NOT TO CHANGE THE GAME BUT MAKE IT WORK TO EVERYONE'S SATISFACTION."

REFEREE PIERLUIGI COLLINA

Football is a simple game. It is based on 17 laws first agreed in 1863, which have been revised and updated to fit in with the modern game. The rules are the same whether you are playing in your local park or in the World Cup Finals. A match lasts for 90 minutes and is contested by two teams, each with 11 players. One player on each team must be a goalkeeper and the winners are the team who score the most goals. Check out the glossary on p.148–149 for extra information.

Italian Pierluigi Collina was widely considered to be the best referee in the world until he retired from the game in 2005.

MATCH OFFICALS

A referee ensures that the rules of the game are followed. He or she is supported by two assistants, one on each touchline. Assistant referees carry a flag to signal infringements such as offside or a foul. Being a match official is a tough job and requires skills such as physical fitness (match officials must keep up with play at all times), good eyesight and the ability to make split-second decisions while under pressure.

CARDS

Free kicks are awarded for minor fouls and infringements, but for persistent or serious breaches of the rules, referees will show a yellow card. Two yellow cards in a match result in a red card and the player must leave the pitch for the rest of the game. A serious foul will result in an immediate red card.

FOULS

When one of the laws of football is broken, it is generally known as a 'foul'. The most common types of foul are tackles in which the player (deliberately or accidentally) trips or makes contact with the opposition player rather than the ball. Other common fouls are handball, obstruction and dangerous play.

LA Galaxy's Kyle Martino (right) fouls DC United's Fred and earns a red card. If a foul occurs inside the penalty area, a penalty kick will be awarded.

The assistant referee flags to signal that a player is offside.

OFFSIDE

The attacking player is in an offside position if he is closer to the goal line than the ball and the second-to-last opponent. (The last opponent is usually the goalkeeper.) However, offside is judged from the moment the ball is played, not when it is received and it is only an offence if the player gains an advantage, is interfering with play or affecting his opponent.

KEY

1 Goal line
2 Goal
3 Six-yard box
4 Penalty spot
5 Eighteen-yard box
6 Centre spot
7 Centre circle
8 Halfway line
9 Corner arc
10 Touchline

THE PITCH

Above is an illustration of a typical football pitch with the key areas marked. According to the Laws of the Game, not all pitches have to be the same size. They must be rectangular, and between 90 and 120 metres (100 and 130 yards) long and between 45 and 90 metres (50 and 100 yards) wide. One part of the pitch must always be the same size – the goal. It must be 2.44 metres high and 7.32 metres wide (8 feet by 8 yards).

THE LAWS OF FOOTBALL
Here are some key laws of the game.

THE REFEREE
The referee's decision is always final. He or she can only reverse a decision (usually on the advice of the assistant referee) immediately after the incident, if play has not been re-started.

THE PERIOD OF PLAY
A 90-minute match is divided into two equal halves of 45 minutes, with a half-time interval of not more than 15 minutes. Extra time is added on to each half to make up for stoppages such as substitutions and injuries.

IN AND OUT OF PLAY
A ball is only out of play if the whole of the ball has crossed the touchline or goal line, whether it is on the ground or in the air. It is in play if it rebounds off a goalpost, crossbar, corner flag or even the referee, as long as it lands on the field of play.

SCORING
A goal is scored when the whole of the ball crosses the goal line, between the goalposts and underneath the crossbar, as long as none of the Laws of the Game have been infringed. The winning team are the ones who score the most goals. If the score is equal at the end of the match, it is known as a 'draw'.

PENALTIES
Infringements on the attacking team in the penalty area usually result in a penalty kick – a one-on-one shot with the goalkeeper. The ball is placed on the penalty spot and the penalty taker steps forward. The goalkeeper faces the kicker but must remain on the goal line. All other players must stand outside the penalty area, behind the penalty spot. As soon as the penalty is taken the ball is in play but the penalty taker cannot strike the ball again until it has touched another player.

SUBSTITUTIONS
Before a match begins, each team can name a number of substitute players (the number varies between competitions). Of these named substitutes a fixed number (usually three) can be brought on during the course of the match, if the referee consents.

THE CLUB

"EVERYONE PLAYS THEIR PART. IF WE WIN ANYTHING, THEN IT WILL BE TOGETHER, NOT AS INDIVIDUALS."

FORMER PORTO AND CHELSEA MANAGER JOSE MOURINHO

Although the players are the ones who grab the glory, the headlines and the big salaries, a football club is about more than just the team. The club is a business and many people work behind the scenes to ensure that it is profitable off the pitch as well as successful on the pitch. From the people who sell the match day tickets to the people who negotiate big-money sponsorship deals, everyone plays a part in the club's success. Take a look at this pyramid, which shows how the average club is structured and who does what.

BIG MONEY

In the 21st century, football is big business. Russian billionaire Roman Abramovich (right) bought England's Chelsea FC in 2003. With billions of dedicated fans around the globe, lucrative sponsorship deals and potentially enormous revenues from TV, it is hardly surprising that many big companies and wealthy business people are keen to invest in football clubs.

STRUCTURE

Not all clubs are run in exactly the same way. Some are privately owned, while others have shareholders and a Board of Directors. Some have a Director of Football and head coach instead of a manager. However, this illustration should give you some idea of just how many different people are involved in the smooth running of a football club.

THE TEAM
The team is picked from a squad of players. Squad size varies from about 20-30 (there are no set rules) and this system provides cover for injured players.

YOUTH TEAM
Most clubs want to find and keep young footballing talent so many have academies, development programmes and under-18 teams.

RESERVES
Every player in the squad needs to be match fit. Reserve team games give players who are not in the first 11 a chance to play and also help injured players to regain their sharpness.

ASSISTANT MANAGER
The assistant manager works closely with the manager and the team. If a manager is sacked, the assistant may take temporary charge of the team.

MANAGER
A manager or head coach is in charge of the first team. He controls training, picks the team and sets the tactics. At some clubs, he also scouts for new players and handles transfer negotiations.

OTHER COACHES
The reserve and youth teams also have dedicated coaches. They will liaise with the manager and discuss which players may be ready to move into the first team.

KIT MANAGER
Most teams have two or three different kits and it is the kit manager's job to ensure that every member of the squad has a complete set of kit for every match.

PRESS OFFICER
The press officer has the vital job of liaising with the media – TV, newspapers and magazines – to ensure that facts about the club are reported correctly.

GROUND STAFF
A team of expert ground staff ensure that the pitch is in peak condition at all times, from the depths of winter to the height of summer.

HEALTH AND FITNESS
Many different people look after the health and fitness of the players, from team doctors and physiotherapists to fitness and skills coaches.

COMMUNITY LIAISON
A club is a member of its local community. The liaison team organise community events to develop local links and help the club to feel part of the area it represents.

TICKET OFFICE
For most clubs, demand for tickets greatly exceeds the number available, so it is the job of the ticket office to co-ordinate all ticket sales.

STADIUM STAFF
From catering staff and programme sellers to stewards who keep the crowds safe and well behaved, it takes hundreds of staff to run the stadium.

MARKETING AND PUBLICITY
The club's image is very important. The marketing and publicity department handle everything from merchandising to promotional events and campaigns.

BUSINESS STAFF
Some people handle the commercial side of the business. These include accountants, hospitality and events co-ordinators, development managers and administration staff.

NON-EXECUTIVE DIRECTOR
Most football clubs are controlled by a Board of Directors. A non-executive director attends Board meetings and acts as an advisor but is not employed full-time by the club.

EXECUTIVE DIRECTOR
An executive director is employed by the club. He or she is involved in the day-to-day running of the club. A club may have any number of executive and non-executive directors.

CHIEF EXECUTIVE
A Chief Executive or Managing Director deals with the day-to-day running of the whole football club. He or she is answerable to the Chairman and the Board.

CHAIRMAN
The Chairman is the head of the Board of Directors. Some Chairmen are involved in the day-to-day running of the club, while others leave it to a Chief Executive or Managing Director.

VICE CHAIRMAN
The Vice Chairman is the Chairman's second-in-command and will take charge of Board meetings if the Chairman is unable to attend.

FINANCIAL DIRECTOR
Executive Directors are often given responsibility for key areas of the club. A vital role is the Financial Director who must oversee all financial aspects of the club.

FANS
The loyal fans who support their team through good times and bad are the heart and soul of any club.

FANS FANS FANS FANS FANS FANS FANS FANS FANS FANS FANS FANS FANS FANS

THE TEAM

The day-to-day running of a football team is hard work! Keeping a talented squad of individuals fit, healthy, happy, playing well and working together is a tough job. Players might get injured or they might lose their form for a few games; they might have a better offer from another club or they might not fit in with the style or direction in which the manager wishes to take the club. In the modern game expectations are high, but the rewards are even higher.

THE MANAGER

The manager (or sometimes the Head Coach) is the boss of the team. He takes charge of training, picks the team and decides the tactics. It is a high-pressure role and too many bad results can cost a manager his job. Dutch manager Guus Hiddink (above) has an impressive CV which includes PSV Eindhoven, Fenerbahçe, Valencia, Netherlands, Real Madrid, Real Betis, Republic of Korea, Australia and Russia. Manchester United's Sir Alex Ferguson is a rarity in football management – he has been in his job for more than 20 years.

FC Barcelona line up before a pre-season match against Internazionale in 2007.

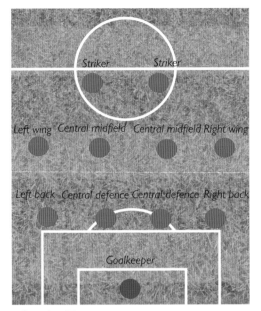

Striker   Striker

Left wing Central midfield Central midfield Right wing

Left back Central defence Central defence Right back

Goalkeeper

4-4-2 This illustration shows a traditional 4–4–2 formation: four defenders, four midfielders and two strikers. There is a flexibility within this formation as midfielders can play deep to provide defensive cover or even sit just behind the strikers in an attacking 4–4–2 formation.

TACTICS

Tactics and formations vary depending on the abilities of the players in the squad, the nature of the opposition and the manager's style of play. They can even be changed during the course of a match to protect a lead or provide more attacking options. There are many different styles of play but here are three of the most common formations.

4-5-1 This formation involves four defenders, a five-man midfield and a lone striker and is primarily used when a team wants to keep possession of the ball and prevent the other team from scoring. It is particularly useful in games when away goals count and the home team need to stop the visitors scoring.

4-3-3 This attacking formation involves four defenders, three midfielders and three strikers. The emphasis is on attack with this style of play so it is only really used against weak opposition or when chasing a goal during a match.

THE CAPTAIN

The manager chooses one player to be the leader on the pitch. Known as the captain or 'skipper', this player is usually one of the oldest or longest-serving members of the team, such as Germany's Oliver Kahn (above). He has no official authority but wearing the captain's armband for club or country is a great honour. Captains must also participate in the pre-match coin toss which decides who plays at which end.

THE FIRST ELEVEN

Players train hard every day in the hope of making it into the team and when they are on the pitch, it is their job to carry the hopes and expectations of the manager, the Board and the fans.

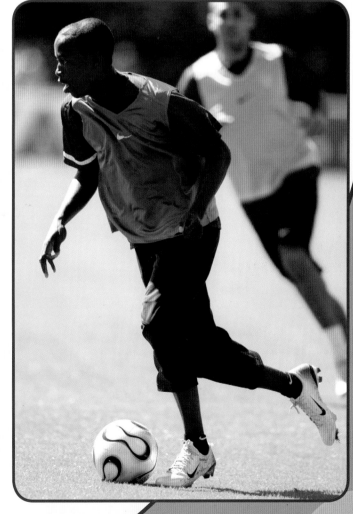

TRAINING

Players such as USA's DaMarcus Beasley (right) work hard in training to stay fit and injury free and also to practise their skills. Training methods vary between clubs, between managers and between individuals.

PUNCHING

The only kind of punch that is allowed in a football match is a punch by the goalkeeper to the ball, in the area. In high-pressure situations, the goalkeeper may not be able to catch the ball cleanly so he must punch it away. It is important to get height and distance on a punch so that the goal threat is cleared. A poor punch can rebound off a player and end up in the back of the net!

Italy's Gianluigi Buffon punches clear of Germany's Miroslav Klose in the 2006 World Cup semi-final.

GOALKEEPERS

"IF YOU'RE A GOALKEEPER, IT DOESN'T MATTER WHAT YOU SAVE THE BALL WITH – IF YOU KEEP IT OUT, IT'S NOT A GOAL."

FORMER REPUBLIC OF IRELAND AND LIVERPOOL DEFENDER MARK LAWRENSON

In some ways goalkeepers are the odd-ones-out of the football team. For a start they wear a different kit (to distinguish them from the rest of the team) and are the only players permitted to handle the ball in open play. Moreover, they are often all that stands in the way of a certain goal – a great save and the goalkeeper is the hero, a clumsy fumble and they are the villain!

DIVING SAVE

Goalkeepers need quick reactions, agility and the courage to put themselves in dangerous situations. If the ball comes at them from a low angle, the goalkeeper must make a diving save, as France keeper Grégory Coupet demonstrates (right).

REACTIONS

Goalkeepers must always be alert and ready to react to goal threats. Sometimes they have to improvise, as Polish keeper Jerzy Dudek does with a point-blank stop against France in a friendly match in 2004.

CATCHING

When catching the ball, it is important to take it firmly and cleanly. Here, USA goalkeeper Kasey Keller (above) clutches the ball safely to his body in a friendly match against Germany in 2006.

DID YOU KNOW?

There have been many spectacular saves, but probably none more inventive than former Colombian goalkeeper René Higuita's famous 'scorpion kick'. It occurred during a friendly match between Colombia and England at Wembley in 2003. Instead of catching an England cross, Higuita performed this acrobatic kick (right).

UNDERARM THROW
Netherlands goalkeeper Edwin van der Sar (above) demonstrates the underarm throw, which is perfect for moving the ball a short distance.

OVERARM THROW
Brazil goalkeeper Dida (above) uses an overarm throw to launch a quick counter-attack. This technique requires accuracy, strength and power.

INDIVIDUAL STYLE
Goalkeepers are famous for their individuality and eccentricities, but probably none more so than former Mexico goalkeeper Jorge Campos. (left). Despite his short stature (1.68 m/5 ft 6 in) Campos was extremely agile and earned 130 caps for his country. He was famous for his eye-catching kits, which he designed himself and his occasional fondness for playing as a striker, all of which helped to make him a cult figure with fans around the world.

DISTRIBUTING THE BALL
As well as being the last line of defence, a goalkeeper can be the launch pad for an attack. He must be able to distribute the ball effectively and accurately whether it is with his hands or his feet. Above, England goalkeeper Paul Robinson aims a massive goal kick up the pitch towards the strikers. Robinson once scored directly from a long-range kick!

PENALTIES
For most goalkeepers, penalties are the ultimate test. This one-on-one situation favours the attacker and gives the goalkeeper very little chance of glory. Even if he correctly guesses which way the attacker will shoot, a well struck penalty is virtually impossible to save. However, some goalkeepers have a reputation for saving penalties, such as Portugal keeper Ricardo (right).

Ricardo saves a penalty from England's Frank Lampard during Portugal's penalty shoot-out victory in the 2006 World Cup quarter-finals.

TACKLING

A tackle is the most direct way of winning the ball back from the opposition and breaking down an attack. Tackles must be from the side or the front, never from behind, and timing is vital to win the ball cleanly and safely.

Chelsea's Ricardo Carvalho makes a sliding tackle on his international team mate, Manchester United's Cristiano Ronaldo.

DEFENCE

"STRIKERS WIN YOU GAMES, BUT DEFENDERS WIN YOU CHAMPIONSHIPS."

FORMER ENGLAND MIDFIELDER AND NOW CLUB MANAGER, JOHN GREGORY

Although strikers and midfielders often steal all the glory, the defence is the backbone of the team. Defenders must be strong, aware, skilful and cool under pressure. However, it is important for every player to know how to defend as during a match any player could find themselves needing to make a goal-saving tackle or goal-line clearance.

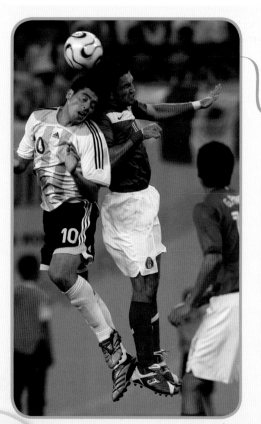

Argentina won the match 2–1 thanks to goals from Hernán Crespo and Maxi Rodríguez.

HEADING

Defenders need to have a strong physical presence, particularly in the air. Here Mexico's José Fonseca (right) rises above Argentina's Juan Riquelme (left) to head the ball during the 2006 World Cup Finals. An effective defensive header should travel as far and as high as possible.

TEAM DEFENDING

An important part of good defending is organisation. Whether it is trapping the attacker offside, marking for a corner or just covering for each other, defenders must work together. Here Ronaldinho of Brazil prepares to take a free kick from just outside the area, but first he must get past England's defensive wall.

WINNING THE BALL

Sometimes a defender doesn't even have to make a tackle to win the ball – by reading the game or marking tightly he can intercept a pass or cheekily steal the ball right off an attacker's toes! Pace and skill can also help the defender to stay one step ahead of the attacking player.

Italy's Fabio Cannavaro (right) beats France's Franck Ribéry (left) to the ball in the 2006 World Cup final.

Fabio Cannavaro lifted the World Cup in 2006 as Italian captain. He was also named World and European Footballer of the Year in 2006.

STRENGTH

Strength and determination are key parts of a defender's game. Winning headers, making tackles and passing under pressure all require strength as well as skill and good technique. Above, France defender Lilian Thuram (right) uses his strength and body size to shield the ball from Spain striker Fernando Torres (left) in a 2006 World Cup Finals match.

MIDFIELD

"THE MIDFIELD IS THE MOST CRUCIAL AREA OF THE GAME, THE ONE WHERE MATCHES ARE WON OR LOST."

MANCHESTER CITY MANAGER SVEN-GÖRAN ERIKSSON

The midfield is the engine of the team. Midfielders provide a vital link between defence and attack, tracking back and making tackles to win the ball and then driving forward with vision and awareness. Some midfielders embody all these attributes while others have more specialist roles. A 'holding' midfielder plays a defensive game, while an attacking midfielder may play just behind the strikers. It is the job of a winger to make runs on the outside of the pitch, beating defenders and supplying accurate crosses.

PACE AND POWER

Attacking midfielders like Spain's Cesc Fàbregas (above, left) need pace to outrun defenders, strength to hold off challenges and the skills to supply accurate passes.

TACKLING

The midfield is a key area of the pitch and winning the ball in this area can quickly turn defence into attack. This means that tackling is often a vital part of a midfielder's role. Here, France midfielder Patrick Vieira (right) stretches beyond Portugal's Luis Figo (left) to win the ball from him.

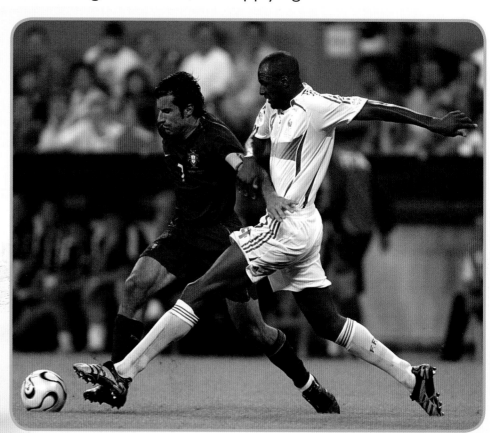

Argentina defensive midfielder Javier Mascherano is admired for his passing and tackling skills.

PASSING

Passing and distribution are also important skills for a midfielder. Whether it is having the vision to play a cross-field pass and set up an attack or calmly passing the ball out of defence, a midfielder needs to blend creativity with coolness under pressure.

DID YOU KNOW?

Many midfielders claim that they work the hardest of out of everyone in the team and they certainly cover the greatest distance. In fact a top level midfielder covers more than 10 km (6.2 miles) per game.

WING PLAY

Wingers play on the far sides of the pitch, making attacking runs, beating defenders and supplying accurate crosses to the strikers. They need speed, strength and versatility plus excellent dribbling and passing skills. Manchester United and Portugal's Cristiano Ronaldo (right) is one of the world's finest wingers.

A prolific goalscorer, Ronaldo is a skilled header of the ball and often takes free kicks.

Ronaldo is versatile and can play on the right or left wing.

Ronaldo is also famous for his step-overs and tricks which bamboozle defenders.

GOALSCORING

Midfielders, especially attacking ones, must also be able to score goals. After a penetrating forward run or fast-paced attack a midfielder can often find himself in a goal-scoring position. Above, France midfielder Franck Ribéry confidently rounds the stranded Spain goalkeeper Iker Casillas to score a goal.

GOAL HUNGRY

The best strikers have a natural instinct for goals. They are always looking to get into goalscoring positions and to create chances. Not all strikers and forward players have the same role – some play deep and link play with the midfield while others play further forward, looking to poach close-range goals at the slightest opportunity.

Dutch striker Dirk Kuyt is a versatile and hard-working striker who can also play on the wing.

ATTACK

"SOMETIMES IN FOOTBALL YOU HAVE TO SCORE GOALS."

FRANCE AND BARCELONA STRIKER
THIERRY HENRY

The object of the game of football is to score goals, so it is often the all-out attacking players such as strikers who grab the headlines and the glory. Strikers need quick reactions, accurate shooting technique and an eye for goal in order to turn chances into goals. However, good attacking play requires more than just the ability to score goals – awareness, positional play, passing and determination are also key attributes.

HEADING

Attacking players also need to be skilled in the air. A good attacking header should be aimed downwards, towards goal or into the path of a team mate. Above, England striker Michael Owen (centre) aims for goal with a header against Albania.

PENALTIES

A penalty is a high-pressure situation so nerves can play a huge part. Most players choose their spot before they strike the ball and hope that the goalkeeper dives the wrong way. Above, France striker David Trézéguet takes a penalty in the 2006 World Cup final but unfortunately hits the crossbar.

SWERVE

Being able to strike the ball in different directions takes great skill. Above, England striker Wayne Rooney turns his body and strikes across the ball to produce a fierce swerve shot. This kind of shot is very difficult for goalkeepers to save.

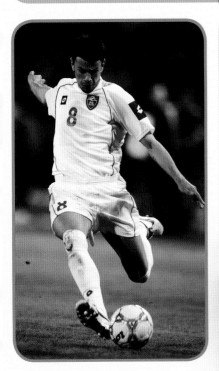

SPECTACULAR GOALS

Scoring a goal is great but scoring a spectacular goal is even better! Powerful shots from distance, strikes conjured from the most impossible angles or impressive solo skill all make fantastic goals. Below, Roma and Italy's Franceso Totti attempts an acrobatic overhead shot with his back to goal.

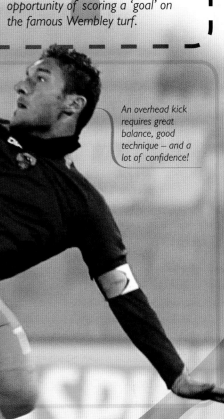

An overhead kick requires great balance, good technique – and a lot of confidence!

PASSING

Whether it is an attacking pass or a shot on goal, timing and accuracy are vital. A pass must be accurately delivered to reach the intended team mate and perfectly timed to reach the target while he is in an onside position. Above, Serbia striker Mateja Kežman launches a long-range attacking pass.

BODY MATTERS

"FOR A PROFESSIONAL SPORTSMAN, BEING INJURED IS LIKE LIVING IN A STRANGER'S BODY."

FORMER FRANCE MIDFIELDER ROBERT PIRÈS

A footballer's body is the tool of his trade so he must look after it. This means working hard in training, eating the right foods and living a healthy lifestyle. Professional footballers won't get far without natural talent, but agility, speed, strength and power are also must-haves for modern players. Take a look inside the body of a super-fit footballer and see how it works, then check out some common footballing injuries. WARNING: SENSITIVE READERS MAY WANT TO SKIP THIS PAGE!

DID YOU KNOW?

In 1998, Republic of Ireland striker, Robbie Keane ruptured his knee cartilage after stretching to pick up his TV remote control.

Arsenal's Steve Morrow broke his collarbone falling off team mate Tony Adams' shoulders while celebrating the 1993 League Cup final win.

When DR Congo striker Lomana LuaLua scored a goal for Portsmouth in 2006, he celebrated with his trademark somersault but sprained his ankle on landing.

Patella (knee cap) · Patellar tendon · Femur · Lateral collateral ligaments · Cartilage · Medial collateral ligament · Tibia · Anterior and posterior cruciate ligaments · Meniscus · Cartilage

WARM-UP

Players train regularly during the football season. They must not only practise their football skills, but also work on their strength and stamina. At the beginning of every training session and before a match, footballers prepare their muscles and increase their heart rate with special warm-up and stretching exercises. Warm-ups prepare the body for more strenuous activity and can help to prevent injury. When the game or trainings session is over, players 'warm down' to allow their bodies to recover gradually.

THE PHYSIO (short for physiotherapist) treats injuries during a match. He or she is only allowed on the pitch if the referee gives permission. The physio also helps players recover from long term injuries using treatments such as massage and specially developed exercise programmes.

KNEE

Sharp turns when all the weight is borne by the knee can damage the meniscus (known as cartilage damage), while turns, awkward landings and over extending can damage the cruciate and medial ligaments.

FOOT

From sprained ankles to broken toes, damaged tendons or severe bruising, the foot and ankle area of the body can take a lot of punishment during a football game. A particularly common injury is the broken metatarsal (right). The five metatarsals are the long bones which attach the toe bones (phalanxes) to the bones near the ankle (collectively known as the tarsals). The metatarsals are usually broken by impact e.g. a mistimed tackle or a bad landing.

FAKING IT

Players might suffer hard or dangerous tackles during a match, but sometimes the reaction can be worse than the foul! What FIFA diplomatically calls 'simulation' is the kind of play acting that belongs on a cinema screen, not a football pitch. Theatrical dives while clutching a supposedly injured body part are designed to fool the referee into penalising the opposition. Unfortunately, it sometimes works...

End of tibia · Talus · Navicular · Cuneiform bones · Broken metatarsal · Phalanx · Cuboid · Calcaneus

Cranium
(skull)

Orbicularis oculi
Closes the eye

Sternocleidomastoid
Tilts and twists neck

Clavicle
(collarbone)

Deltoid
Raises arm away
from body to front,
side and rear

Sternum
(breastbone)

Biceps
Flexes forearm at elbow

Pelvis

Sacrum

Adductors
Rotate and draw thigh
in towards body

Gracilis
Flexes and rotates leg,
draws thigh in towards
body

Femur
(thigh bone)

Tibia
(shin bone)

Peroneus longus
Flexes foot downward
and turns it outward

Fibula
(calf bone)

Retinaculum
Stabilises ankle joint

Trapezius
Rotates and retracts
shoulder blade

Ribs

Rectus abdominus
Flexes spine and draws
pelvis forward

External oblique
abdominal
Flexes and rotates trunk

Pectineus
Flexes and draws
thigh in towards
body

Tensor fasciae latae
Helps to keep knee straight

Sartorius
Flexes thigh at hip and leg at knee; turns
thigh outward

Rectus femoris (quadriceps)
Flexes thigh at hip and helps to
extend knee

Vastus lateralis (quadriceps)
Plays a part in extending knee

Vastus medialis
(quadriceps)
Plays a part in
extending knee

Patella
(kneecap)

Gastrocnemius
Flexes foot
downward

Tendons of foot

Humerus

Semitendinosus

Extensor
retinaculum
Ligamentous band
supporting wrist

HERNIA

Kicking, sprinting and turning all put stress on the groin and pelvis and in extreme cases this can lead to a hernia. Most hernias are like this one (right) and occur when the abdominal wall is ruptured. On the outside of the body it appears as a lump and it is caused by the intestines poking through the abdomen. Surgery is required to cure a hernia.

Abdominal wall

Herniated loop
of intestine

Inguinal ligament

Tear in muscle

Biceps femoris

Semimembranosus

HAMSTRING STRAIN

Football can be tough on a player's muscles so muscle injuries are common. The most frequently injured muscles are the hamstrings, the group of three at the back of the upper leg (above) that are used to extend the thigh, flex the knee and rotate the leg. Muscle injuries usually occur when a player stretches too far. This can tear the muscle (as above) and is known as a 'strain'. A small strain can heal in a matter of days but a larger strain may take months to heal.

ANATOMY OF A FOOTBALLER

A professional footballer's body is a high-tech machine. It is made up of many parts which must work together to give him the power and agility to play for 90 minutes. Bones, muscles and joints enable a footballer to perform a variety of movements such as kicking, running, turning and heading. Take a look at the illustration on the left – identify some key bones and discover how some vital muscles help a footballer to play.

INJURIES

Football is a hard, physical game. Injuries are common, especially to the lower parts of the body – groin, pelvis, hip, thigh, knee, calf and foot. Most happen suddenly in a game, as a result of a collision or awkward landing but others can develop slowly over time. The smaller illustrations show some of the main injuries suffered by footballers.

29

EUROPE

Formed in 1954, the Union of European Football Associations (UEFA) now has 53 members. It is the most powerful of the world football confederations and has 13 World Cup Finals places. Former Soviet countries Georgia, Armenia, Kazakhstan and Azerbaijan are members of UEFA and so is Israel, although they are not technically part of Europe.

"AT A TIME WHEN EUROPE IS SEEKING TO DEFINE ITSELF, NOTHING CONTRIBUTES MORE TO THIS QUEST THAN ITS LOVE FOR OUR SPORT." FIFA PRESIDENT MICHEL PLATINI

Over the years, intensely competitive leagues such as Serie A in Italy, the Premier League in England, La Liga in Spain and the Bundesliga in Germany have produced many top class players. This has made Europe a powerhouse of international football with many strong national teams, even from comparatively small nations such as Portugal and the Czech Republic. Nowadays the money and prestige of European league football attracts the world's greatest stars to the continent.

ICELAND

NORTHERN IRELAND

REPUBLIC OF IRELAND

FANATICS
European fans are increasingly using football as a way of celebrating – and sometimes spoofing – their national stereotypes. While patriotic Norwegians, Swedes and Danes dress as Vikings, many English fans favour the medieval knight look while proud Scottish fans like to dig out their family tartan!

THE ORANJE
Any city that has hosted a major football tournament will remember any visiting Dutch fans. Famous for the crazy orange outfits, these loyal fans often make sure that their team has the brightest and loudest support, both on and off the pitch.

PORTUGAL

SPAIN

31

ENGLAND

"GOD BLESS WHOEVER INVENTED FOOTBALL. IT WAS THE ENGLISH, I THINK. AND WHAT A FANTASTIC IDEA IT WAS." ITALIAN STRIKER, PAOLO ROSSI

The FA was formed in 1863. The official badge features three lions, which are from the royal coat of arms and the Red Rose of Lancaster, the official emblem of England.

Credited as the founders of modern football, England are the oldest international team in the world, alongside Scotland. These two countries played the first ever international match in 1872. England did not play outside the British Isles until 1908 and did not enter the World Cup until 1950. Despite perennially high hopes, the team have only won one major tournament – the 1966 World Cup, in England.

MOMENT OF GLORY

England's finest footballing hour came on 30 July, 1966, at Wembley Stadium. As 98,000 fans roared them on, the team took a famous victory in the World Cup final against West Germany. England won a thrilling game 4–2 after extra time. Some people say that Hurst's second goal (England's third) did not cross the line, but USSR linesman Tofik Bakhramov ruled that it did.

England captain Bobby Moore proudly holds up the Jules Rimet trophy.

Striker Geoff Hurst scored three goals, and remains the only player to have scored a hat-trick in a World Cup final. England's other goal was scored by Martin Peters.

Former England striker Gary Lineker is the only English player to top the scoring charts at a World Cup Finals. His six goals at Mexico '86 included a hat-trick against Poland.

Michael Owen was 18 when he scored a wonder goal against Argentina in the 1998 World Cup Finals. He ran from the centre circle, through the Argentinian defence, and shot into the top corner. England still lost the second round match 4–3 on penalties.

ENGLAND DREAM TEAM? 1. Gordon Banks 2. Alf Ramsey 3. Ray Wilson 4. Glenn Hoddle 5. Bobby Moore 6. Billy Wright 7. Stanley Matthews 8. Bobby Charlton 9. Gary Lineker 10. Jimmy Greaves 11. Tom Finney

ENGLAND HOT SHOT

Wayne Rooney is one of English football's most exciting talents. The versatile striker can play from deep in midfield or on either wing. He has great balance, a powerful shot and immense strength that leaves opposing defenders trailing in his wake. Despite a fiery temper that saw him sent off in the 2006 World Cup quarter-final against Portugal, Rooney looks destined to become a true legend.

Wayne Rooney shoots at goal during England's 2006 World Cup match against Ecuador.

DAVID BECKHAM is possibly the most recognised player in world football. This skilful and inspirational midfielder captained his country for six years, and has played for Manchester United, Real Madrid and LA Galaxy. Famous for his ability to bend free kicks from distance, Beckham's most important goal was a 25-yard free kick in the 90th minute against Greece that helped England qualify for the 2002 World Cup Finals.

KEY MEN

John Terry (left) and Steven Gerrard are two of the current England team's key players. Terry is a brave, powerful central defender whose commanding performances on the pitch have led to him being made captain of his club, Chelsea, as well as his country. Gerrard is a gifted and hard-working midfielder with an eye for creating and scoring goals. His never-say-die attitude makes him a firm favourite with both Liverpool and England fans.

Originally built in 1923, Wembley Stadium is the home of English football. In 2007 a new structure was opened and with 90,000 seats it is the second largest stadium in Europe.

FACT FILE: ENGLAND
NICKNAME
The Three Lions

TOP GOALSCORERS
1. Bobby Charlton 49 (1958–1970)
2. Gary Lineker 48 (1984–1992)
3. Jimmy Greaves 44 (1959–1967)
4. Michael Owen 40 (1998–present)
5. Tom Finney 30 (1946–1958)
= Nat Lofthouse 30 (1950–1958)
= Alan Shearer 30 (1992–2000)

MOST APPEARANCES
1. Peter Shilton 125 (1970–1990)
2. Bobby Moore 108 (1962–1973)
3. Bobby Charlton 106 (1958–1970)
4. Billy Wright 105 (1946–1959)
5. David Beckham 102 (1996–present)

TROPHIES/HONOURS
FIFA WORLD CUP
1966 England 4 West Germany 2 (aet)

DID YOU KNOW?

The legendary Sir Stanley Matthews (see p.125) achieved a series of 'firsts' – he was the first Football Writers' Association Footballer of the Year (in 1948), the first European Footballer of the Year (in 1956), and the first footballer to be knighted (in 1965).

Billy Wright played in 70 consecutive England internationals between October 1951 and May 1959, a national record.

FRANCE

> "WINNING THE WORLD CUP IS THE MOST BEAUTIFUL THING TO HAPPEN TO FRANCE SINCE THE REVOLUTION."
>
> EMMANUEL PETIT, SCORER OF THE THIRD GOAL IN THE '98 FINAL

Famed for skill, flair and entertainment, French football has always placed more emphasis on attack rather than the physical and tactical style favoured by other European nations. Yet for all the undoubted talent of its footballers, France did not lift an international trophy until the 1984 European Championship. However, since then the national side have won the World Cup, and the European Championship for a second time, providing a strong challenge to Brazil's domination of the modern game.

The Fédération Française de Football was founded in 1919, replacing five previous bodies that had competed to control the national game.

MICHEL PLATINI

Arguably France's greatest ever player, midfielder Michel Platini was European Footballer of the Year for three consecutive years – 1983, 1984 and 1985. A club player with Nancy, St Étienne and Juventus, he was for many years France's top scorer and managed the national side between 1988 and 1992. He was elected President of UEFA in 2007.

After narrowly failing to reach the World Cup final in 1982, the great French side of the 1980s finally won the trophy they deserved two years later, on home soil. Star players Platini, Jean Tigana and Alain Giresse helped to secure a 2–0 victory over Spain in the European Championship final in Paris. The goals came from Platini himself (his ninth of the tournament) and Bruno Bellone.

The son of Polish immigrants, Raymond Kopaszewski, or 'Kopa' for short (left) was one of the finest players of the post-war era. He was named by Pelé as one of the 125 greatest living players in a list compiled by FIFA in 2004.

JUST FONTAINE

Striker Just Fontaine's place in football history is assured by his remarkable performance during the 1958 World Cup Finals in Sweden. His 13-goal total is still a tournament record for the most scored by a player at a single World Cup. France reached the semi-finals but were defeated 5–2 by the eventual winners Brazil.

FRANCE DREAM TEAM?	1. Fabien Barthez 2. Lilian Thuram 3. Bixente Lizarazu 4. Patrick Vieira 5. Marius Trésor 6. Marcel Desailly 7. Zinedine Zidane 8. Michel Platini 9. Just Fontaine 10. Raymond Kopa 11. Thierry Henry

ZINEDINE ZIDANE

is widely acknowledged as one of the greatest players in the history of the game. As an attacking midfielder, his range of passing, ball control and powerful shooting made him the most influential player in the French World Cup and European Championship winning teams.

Thierry Henry's pace is complemented by his ability to change position and confuse defenders.

THIERRY HENRY

Few attackers have been more feared by defenders in the last ten years than Thierry Henry. Blessed with blistering pace, exceptional skill and masterful movement both on and off the ball, Henry's grace and elegance disguises an almost clinical ability to punish opponents. From precise passing to spectacular finishing, Henry has it all.

FRANCE '98

France's finest sporting hour came on a warm evening in Paris on 12th July, 1998. Sixty years after the country had last hosted the World Cup, France made the most of home advantage. Led by captain, Didier Deschamps, and roared on by a passionate crowd at the Stade de France, France beat Brazil 3–0 to win the trophy for the first time.

FACT FILE: FRANCE
NICKNAME
Les Bleus (The Blues)

TOP GOALSCORERS
1. Thierry Henry 44 (1997–present)
2. Michel Platini 41 (1976–1987)
3. David Trézéguet 34 (1998–present)
4. Zinedine Zidane 31 (1994–2006)
5. Just Fontaine 30 (1953–1960)
 = Jean-Pierre Papin 30 (1986–1995)

MOST APPEARANCES
1. Lilian Thuram 140 (1994–present)
2. Marcel Desailly 116 (1993–2004)
3. Zinedine Zidane 108 (1994–2006)
4. Patrick Vieira 105 (1997–present)
5. Didier Deschamps 103 (1989–2000)

TROPHIES/HONOURS
FIFA WORLD CUP
1998 France 3 Brazil 0

UEFA EUROPEAN CHAMPIONSHIP
1984 France 2 Spain 0
2000 France 2 Italy 1 (aet)

OLYMPIC GOLD MEDAL
1984 France 2 Brazil 0

FIFA CONFEDERATIONS CUP
2001 France 1 Japan 0
2003 France 1 Cameroon 0

DID YOU KNOW?

Superstitious World Cup-winning defender Laurent Blanc kissed the bald head of goalkeeper Fabien Barthez before every match because he believed it brought good luck.

ITALY

The Federazione Italiana Giuoco Calcio was formed in 1898. Four stars on the logo represent each of Italy's World Cup triumphs.

> "YOU KNOW, THERE WILL ALWAYS BE A LITTLE BIT OF ITALY IN THIS TROPHY."
>
> SILVIO GAZZANIGA, MILANESE SCULPTOR OF THE CURRENT WORLD CUP

One of the world's great football nations, Italy's success is matched only by the passion of its fans. Italy are the current world champions and, with four World Cups, are the second most successful football nation after Brazil. Although built on a solid defensive style, the 'Azzurri' have nevertheless featured some of football's most exciting creative talents, from Giuseppe Meazza and Sandro Mazzola to Roberto Baggio. Containing their opponents and then hitting them with swift, skilful counter-attacks are the hallmarks of Italian play.

SPAIN '82

The 1982 World Cup final is regarded as the second best of all time, after Brazil '70. Inspired by the great Paolo Rossi and legendary goalkeeper Dino Zoff, an entertaining Italian team beat West Germany 3–1 in a match they totally dominated.

Italy's team coach Vittorio Pozzo is carried high by his squad after winning the 1934 World Cup against Czechoslovakia – the first time the Italians won the trophy. Four years later, Pozzo's team successfully defended the trophy, after winning Gold at the 1936 Olympics. Between December 1934 and 1939, Pozzo's Italy did not lose a single game.

LUIGI 'GIGI' RIVA is Italy's all-time leading goalscorer, with 35 goals in 42 matches between 1965 to 1974. Gigi was quick and intelligent, with lightning fast reactions and great ability in the air. His powerful shot earned him the nickname 'Rombo di Tuono' – or 'Sound of Thunder'. Here, Gigi is scoring Italy's opening goal against Yugoslavia in the1968 European Championships final replay.

Roberto Baggio, or 'Il Divin Codino' (The Divine Ponytail), on the way to scoring a memorable goal against Czechoslovakia in the 1990 World Cup.

| ITALY DREAM TEAM? | 1. Dino Zoff 2. Fabio Cannavaro 3. Giacinto Facchetti 4. Gaetano Scirea 5. Franco Baresi 6. Paolo Maldini 7. Roberto Baggio 8. Gianni Rivera 9. Paolo Rossi 10. Giuseppe Meazza 11. Luigi Riva |

PAOLO ROSSI

Paolo Rossi's six goals helped Italy win the 1982 World Cup. He also won the Golden Boot for top scorer and Golden Ball for best player in the tournament and was named 1982 World and European Footballer of the Year.

2006 TRIUMPH

Italy beat France to win their fourth World Cup in 2006. It was the first all-European final since Italy last won the tournament in 1982. After extra time the score was 1–1, so for only the second time ever, the final was decided on penalties. The Italians won 5–3.

Ecstatic captain Fabio Cannavaro holds up the 2006 World Cup.

Defender Paolo Maldini is a legend of Italian football. The most capped player for club, (AC Milan) and country, he has seven Serie A and five Champions League winners' medals.

FACT FILE: ITALY
NICKNAME
Azzurri (Blues)

TOP GOALSCORERS
1. Luigi Riva 35 (1965–1974)
2. Giuseppe Meazza 33 (1930–1939)
3. Silvio Piola 30 (1935–1952)
4. Roberto Baggio 27 (1988–2004)
= Alessandro Del Piero 27 (1995–present)

MOST APPEARANCES
1. Paolo Maldini 126 (1988–2002)
2. Fabio Cannavaro 116 (1997–present)
3. Dino Zoff 112 (1968–1983)
4. Giacinto Facchetti 94 (1963–1977)
5. Alessandro Del Piero 86 (1995–present)

TROPHIES/HONOURS
FIFA WORLD CUP
1934 Italy 2 Czechoslovakia 1 (aet)
1938 Italy 4 Hungary 2
1982 Italy 3 West Germany 1
2006 Italy 1 France 1 (Italy won 5–3 in a penalty shoot out)

UEFA EUROPEAN CHAMPIONSHIP
1968 Italy 1 Yugoslavia 1 (aet)
Replay: Italy 2 Yugoslavia 0

OLYMPIC GOLD MEDAL
1936 Italy 1 Norway 0 (aet)

FRANCESCO TOTTI is a current star of Italian football. Winner of the 2006–07 Golden Boot after scoring the most club goals in the whole of Europe, Totti made his national debut in 1998. He was named Man of the Match in the Euro 2000 final, which Italy lost to France, and was selected for the 23-man All-Star Team at the 2006 World Cup Finals. However, in July 2007 Totti retired from international football to concentrate on playing for his club, AS Roma.

DID YOU KNOW?

The top scorer in the 1990 World Cup was Italian player Salvatore 'Totò' Schillaci with six goals. Although Schillaci only played 16 times for his country, many Italian fans still refer to the 1990 World Cup as 'Notti Magiche di Totò Schillaci' (magical nights of Totò Schillaci).

GERMANY

"HISTORY SHOWS THAT WE CAN RAISE THE LEVEL OF OUR GAME WHEN IT MATTERS." OLIVER KAHN, GOALKEEPER AND FORMER CAPTAIN

The Deutscher Fussball-Bund (football association) was founded in 1900. It was split between 1946 and 1991 when Germany was divided into East Germany and West Germany.

Germany is arguably the most consistent footballing nation in the world. While the national side – playing as either Germany or West Germany – may not have won the World Cup as many times as Brazil or Italy, the team have reached no less than 12 major competition finals and won a total of six tournaments. Teamwork, organisation and skill are the trademarks of 'Die Nationalelf', combined with a never-say-die attitude that means no German side ever concedes defeat until the final whistle.

GREATEST MOMENTS

Perhaps Germany's finest achievement came in the 1954 World Cup Finals. The team were beaten 8–3 in one of the earlier group games by the mighty Hungary. But, amazingly, they overcame the same opponents 3–2 with a fantastic comeback in the final. This unlikely victory was known as the 'Miracle of Berne', after the Swiss city in which the final was played.

Germany's record goalscorer is Gerd Müller. Nicknamed 'Der Bomber', he scored an amazing 68 goals in just 62 international appearances.

'DER KAISER'

A brilliant leader known as 'Der Kaiser' (the Emperor), Franz Beckenbauer also had the ability to switch defence into attack via his role as sweeper. He captained the 1974 team to World Cup victory on home soil and in 1990 became only the second man to win the trophy as a player and coach when his West Germany side triumphed in Italy.

Germany's World Cup triumph of 1990 was not the greatest of games, but the narrow 1–0 win over Argentina enabled West Germany to gain revenge for their defeat by the South Americans four years earlier. Victory was secured with a late penalty scored by Andreas Brehme, pictured holding the trophy aloft.

LOTHAR MATTHÄUS

was the modern successor to Beckenbauer. A determined, outspoken man off the pitch, he was just as forthright on it, driving his side to success in the 1990 World Cup. He holds the record for German international appearances with 142 caps won over a 20-year period. Matthäus was able to play as a defender or midfielder but spent most of the later stages of his career as a sweeper.

GERMANY DREAM TEAM?   1. Sepp Maier 2. Karl-Heinz Schnellinger 3. Paul Breitner 4. Wolfgang Overath 5. Lothar Matthäus 6. Franz Beckenbauer 7. Günter Netzer 8. Fritz Walter 9. Gerd Müller 10. Helmut Rahn 11. Uwe Seeler

Jürgen Klinsmann was a successful club player across Europe and a World Cup winner in 1990. Although he was often mocked for his exaggerated dives to win free kicks, he was first and foremost a superb all-round striker. He later managed an attacking German team to the semi-finals of the 2006 World Cup.

BALLACK

Current Germany captain Michael Ballack is a dynamic midfielder with an eye for goal and a powerful header of the ball. As a young player he was nicknamed 'Little Kaiser' because of comparisons with the great Beckenbauer.

Ballack is a perfect example of the modern midfielder – athletic, skilful and a leader on the pitch.

Striker Lukas Podolski is one of the rising stars of German football. His impressive performances in the 2006 World Cup led to him being named as the FIFA Best Young Player of the tournament.

DID YOU KNOW?

In the 1974 World Cup final, eventual winners West Germany were 1–0 down before they had even touched the ball! Their Dutch opponents kept the ball for two minutes from kick off and scored a penalty.

FACT FILE: GERMANY
NICKNAME
Die Nationalelf (The National Eleven)

TOP GOALSCORERS
1. Gerd Müller 68 (1966–1974)
2. Jürgen Klinsmann 47 (1987–1998)
= Rudi Völler 47 (1982–1994)
3. Karl-Heinz Rummenigge 45 (1976–1986)
4. Uwe Seeler 43 (1954–1970)

MOST APPEARANCES
1. Lothar Matthäus 150 (1980–2000)
2. Jürgen Klinsmann 108 (1987–1998)
3. Jürgen Kohler 105 (1986–1998)
4. Franz Beckenbauer 103 (1965–1977)
5. Thomas Hässler 101 (1988–2000)

TROPHIES/HONOURS
FIFA WORLD CUP
1954 West Germany 3 Hungary 2
1974 West Germany 2 Netherlands 1
1990 West Germany 1 Argentina 0

UEFA EUROPEAN CHAMPIONSHIP
1972 West Germany 3 USSR 0
1980 West Germany 2 Belgium 1
1996 Germany 2 Czech Republic 1 (aet)

OLYMPIC GAMES
1976 East Germany 3 Poland 1

EAST GERMANY
While Germany was split into two nations between 1946 and 1991, East Germany was in the shadow of its more successful neighbour. When Germany became a single nation again, East German players such as Ulf Kirsten, Thomas Doll and Matthias Sammer played for the new, unified team. Sammer was named European Footballer of the Year in 1996.

East Germany triumphed at the 1976 Olympics in Montreal. The 3–1 victory over Poland was a great moment in East German history, with goals from Hartmut Shade, Martin Hoffman and Reinhard Häfner.

NETHERLANDS

"WE ARE THE BRAZILIANS OF EUROPE."

KEES RIJVERS, DUTCH INTERNATIONAL
1946–1960 AND MANAGER 1981–1984

The Netherlands are the greatest national team never to have won the World Cup. Despite a succession of supremely gifted players, their only major triumph has been the 1988 European Championship. Exciting, talented and inventive they undoubtedly are, but too often disagreements between the players or an inability to rise to the occasion have let the talented Oranje down.

KNVB

The Koninklijke Nederlandse Voetbalbond was formed in 1889. The lion symbol, used since 1907, is based on the emblem of the country's Royal family.

MOMENT OF GLORY

When captain Ruud Gullit received the European Championship trophy in 1988 victory was made even sweeter because it came on the home soil of their great rivals West Germany, whom they knocked out en route to the final. In the final, Gullit scored a header and Marco van Basten a volley in a convincing victory over the Soviet Union.

JOHAN CRUYFF

For many the greatest footballer of all time, Cruyff had superb technical ability. He was quick, a great passer of the ball, a fine goalscorer and could read the game expertly. He won major honours with all his clubs, Ajax, Barcelona and Feyenoord, and was European Footballer of the Year three times.

In 2003 the KNVB named Cruyff Dutch football's outstanding player of the last 50 years.

Gifted midfielder Arie Haan was a member of the 1970s Dutch team and a key exponent of the famous 'Total Football' style. During the 1978 World Cup, he scored his most famous goal — a stunning 40-yard strike against Italy in the second group stage.

SUPER STRIKER

Marco van Basten is widely regarded as one of the best strikers of all time. He scored a total of 276 goals for his clubs Ajax and AC Milan and the Dutch national team. Perhaps Van Basten's most famous goal was his spectacular volley in the Euro '88 final. He was European Footballer of the Year in 1988, 1989 and 1992, and World Player of the Year in 1992. He now manages the Netherlands.

Midfielder Clarence Seedorf has won the Champions League with three different clubs – Ajax, Real Madrid and AC Milan.

FACT FILE: NETHERLANDS

NICKNAMES
Oranje, Clockwork Orange, Orange Crush, The Orangemen

TOP GOALSCORERS
1. Patrick Kluivert 40 (1994–2004)
2. Dennis Bergkamp 37 (1990–2000)
3. Faas Wilkes 35 (1946–1961)
4. Johan Cruyff 33 (1966–1977)
= Abe Lenstra 33 (1940–1959)

MOST APPEARANCES
1. Edwin van der Sar 125 (1995–present)
2. Frank de Boer 112 (1990–2004)
3. Philip Cocu 101 (1996–2006)
4. Marc Overmars 86 (1993–2004)
= Clarence Seedorf 86 (1994–present)

TROPHIES/HONOURS
UEFA EUROPEAN CHAMPIONSHIP
1988 Netherlands 2 USSR 0

DENNIS BERGKAMP'S fine ball control and excellent first touch, combined with quick thinking and vision, made him one of the world's top players. He was nicknamed 'The Iceman' because of his calmness and he made a habit of scoring great goals, often from outside the area.

DID YOU KNOW?

In the 1970s, the Dutch invented 'Total Football'. Under this system, every player could play in every position, giving the side a fluid formation that opponents found very difficult to play against. Although this system was great to watch, it only worked if a team had 11 super-talented players and many coaches also felt that it gave the players too much responsibility on the pitch.

Ruud van Nistelrooy is one of the most reliable goalscorers in world football. He scored 28 times in 54 games for his country before announcing his retirement from international football in 2007. He has also set goalscoring records for two of the world's biggest clubs – Manchester United and Real Madrid. Fortunately for the Netherlands, van Nistelrooy reconsidered his decision to retire.

Rafael van der Vaart and Dirk Kuyt are two of the exciting young talents representing the current generation of Dutch footballers. Van der Vaart is a skilful attacking midfielder with an eye for goal, and Kuyt is a powerful, hard-working forward. While the national team has yet to find a regular way to use van der Vaart's exceptional talents, Kuyt has become a regular in the side.

NETHERLANDS DREAM TEAM? 1. Edwin van der Sar 2. Wim Suurbier 3. Ruud Krol 4. Johan Neeskens 5. Ronald Koeman 6. Wim van Hanegem 7. Johan Cruyff 8. Ruud Gullit 9. Marco van Basten 10. Dennis Bergkamp 11. Johnny Rep

SPAIN

"REPUTATIONS DO NOT WIN MATCHES AND TROPHIES, ONLY GOALS CAN DO THAT." REAL MADRID, ARGENTINA AND SPAIN LEGEND ALFREDO DI STÉFANO

Spain are the great enigma of world football. For a country that has produced so many outstanding players and with a population that has such a passion for the game, the national side has tended to underperform. Despite some of the most distinguished club sides in Europe, the Spanish national team has only the 1964 European Championship title and a couple of World Cup quarter-final placings to show for their extraordinary talents.

The Real Federación Española de Fútbol was formed in 1913. 'Real' means royal and is a title of honour given by the monarchy, reflecting the prestige football enjoys in Spain.

FAMOUS VICTORY

When Spain hosted and won the European Championship in 1964, it seemed to promise a dazzling new era for the national side. Goals from Pereda and Marcelino earned a 2–1 win over the Soviet Union and enabled the team to parade the Henri Delaunay cup amid wild celebrations at Real Madrid's Bernabéu stadium. However, just two years later Spain crashed out of the World Cup Finals at the group stage.

1960 European Footballer of the year, Luis Suárez played in the 1964 final despite injury. The inspirational midfielder set up both goals.

EMILIO BUTRAGUEÑO

Emilio Butragueño was a prolific scorer for his club Real Madrid. For the national team he scored 26 goals in 69 appearances, including four in a 5–1 thrashing of Denmark at the 1986 World Cup. He was nicknamed 'El Buitre' (the Vulture) for his deadly ability to snap up chances.

Butragueño slips past a french defender in the 1984 European Championships.

Spanish hopes for future success rest on the shoulders of young players like Cesc Fàbregas. The outstanding midfielder broke into the national team at the age of 18 in 2006, three years after he had won the Golden Shoe for top goalscorer and Golden Ball for best player at the FIFA U-17 World Championships.

SPAIN DREAM TEAM? 1. Ricardo Zamora 2. Marquitos 3. Jose Antonio Camacho 4. Luis Suárez 5. Miguel Ángel Nadal 6. Fernando Hierro 7. Amancio Amaro 8. Alfredo Di Stéfano 9. Emilio Butragueño 10. Raúl 11. Francisco Gento

SUPER STRIKER

Fernando Torres is the latest superstar of Spanish football. After a rapid rise at his boyhood favourites Atlético Madrid, he moved to Liverpool in 2007 for a transfer fee of £26 million. The striker, nicknamed 'El Niño' (the Kid), scored three goals in the 2006 World Cup Finals, including a brilliant strike in Spain's 4–0 win over Ukraine.

Torres possesses pace, balance and an abundance of skill.

Torres was the star of the 2002 U-19 European Championship, finishing as top scorer and Player of the Tournament.

FACT FILE: SPAIN

NICKNAMES
La Furia Roja (The Red Fury),
La Selección (The Selection)

TOP GOALSCORERS
1. Raúl 44 (1996–2006)
2. Fernando Hierro 29 (1989–2002)
3. Fernando Morientes 27 (1998–2007)
4. Emilio Butragueño 26 (1984–1992)
5. Alfredo Di Stéfano 23 (1957–1961)

MOST APPEARANCES
1. Andoni Zubizaretta 126 (1985–1998)
2. Raúl 102 (1996–2006)
3. Fernando Hierro 89 (1989–2002)
4. José Antonio Camacho 81 (1975–1988)
5. Iker Casillas 76 (2000–present)

TROPHIES/HONOURS

UEFA EUROPEAN CHAMPIONSHIP
1964 Spain 2 USSR 1

OLYMPIC GOLD MEDAL
1992 Poland 2 Spain 3

BERNABÉU
Named after a former Real Madrid president, the Santiago Bernabéu was built in 1947 and has a capacity of 75,000. It has hosted many prestigious matches including the 1982 World Cup final. As well as being Spain's national stadium, it is also the home of Spanish club side Real Madrid.

RAÚL

Raúl González Blanco, to give him his full name, is Spain's top scorer. By 2006 he had scored 44 goals in 102 appearances and earned a reputation as one of the best European strikers of the last 10 years. With Real Madrid his honours include three Champions League titles.

DID YOU KNOW?

Foreign footballers were banned from playing in the Spanish league from 1963 to 1973. It was felt that the high number of non-Spanish players was affecting the development of home-grown footballers and thereby having a negative impact on the national team. The ban was lifted when Barcelona signed the talented Dutchman Johan Cruyff.

EUROPEAN TEAMS

"THE DIFFERENCES BETWEEN THE BIG TEAMS AND THE SO-CALLED SMALLER TEAMS HAVE BECOME SMALLER."
OTTO REHHAGEL, COACH OF GREECE IN 2004

Football is not just the dominant sport in European nations that have already won major trophies. From Portugal in the west to Ukraine in the east, it is the most popular sport in virtually every country and home to many famous national teams and great club sides as well as millions of passionate supporters. Here is a selection of some of the most popular teams in Europe, from up-and-coming nations such as Croatia and Portugal to sleeping giants such as Russia and Poland.

GREECE

A type of football was played in Ancient Greece in 200 BCE, but Greece had to wait until 2004 for their first trophy, when they secured an unlikely but deserved victory at the European Championship.

FACT FILE

TOP GOALSCORER
Nikos Anastopoulos 29 (1977–1988)

MOST APPEARANCES
Theodoros Zagorakis 120 (1994–2007)

TROPHIES/HONOURS
UEFA EUROPEAN CHAMPIONSHIP
2004 Greece 1 Portugal 0

A solid, practical and defensive approach was the key to Greece's 2004 triumph, with the winning goal scored by Angelos Charisteas in the final against the hosts, Portugal.

SWEDEN

The story of Swedish football is one of only moderate success. The team reached the World Cup final when they played hosts in 1958, and were losing semi-finalists in 1994. On both occasions, the victors were Brazil.

FACT FILE

TOP GOALSCORER
Sven Rydell 49 (1923–1932)

MOST APPEARANCES
Thomas Ravelli 143 (1981–1997)

TROPHIES/HONOURS
OLYMPIC GOLD MEDAL
1948 Sweden 3 Yugoslavia 1

Three of Sweden's biggest recent stars, Freddie Ljungberg (centre), Henrik Larsson (left) and Zlatan Ibrahimovic (right) celebrate Ljungberg's goal in the 5–0 win against Bulgaria during their Group C Euro 2004 qualifying match.

RUSSIA

Despite a massive population, prestigious domestic clubs and a rich footballing heritage, Russia have struggled at international tournaments. As the USSR (see 'Did You Know?'), the country won the first European Championship in 1960 but so far have consistently failed to make an impression at the World Cup Finals.

Andrey Arshavin is one of Russian football's big stars. A creative and dynamic striker, who can also play in midfield, Arshavin was Russian Footballer of the Year in 2006.

FACT FILE

TOP GOALSCORER
Vladimir Beschastnykh 26 (1992–2003)

MOST APPEARANCES
Viktor Onopko 109 (1992–2004)

TROPHIES/HONOURS
(Competing as the USSR)
UEFA EUROPEAN CHAMPIONSHIP
1960 USSR 2 Yugoslavia 1 (aet)
(Competing as Russia)
none

TURKEY

Turkey are seen as an emerging force on the world football scene. The team reached the quarter-finals of the European Championship in 2000 and were World Cup semi-finalists in 2002.

Hakan Sükür has been one of Turkey's most consistent performers in the last decade. He scored one of the goals that earned Turkey an impressive third place at the 2002 World Cup Finals.

FACT FILE

TOP GOALSCORER
Hakan Sükür 51 (1992–present)

MOST APPEARANCES
Rüstü Recber 129 (1993–present)

TROPHIES/HONOURS

EUROPE DREAM TEAM? 1. Lev Yashin (USSR) 2. Eric Gerets (Belgium) 3. Robert Jarni (Croatia) 4. Dave Mackay (Scotland) 5. John Charles (Wales) 6. Josef Masopust (Czechoslovakia) 7. József Bozsik (Hungary) 8. Ladislao Kubala (Czechoslovakia/Hungary/Spain) 9. Eusébio (Portugal) 10. Ferenc Puskás (Hungary/Spain) 11. George Best (Northern Ireland)

SCOTLAND

Despite being a nation of just five million people, Scotland has enjoyed some epic international campaigns. Although the team have never won a trophy, they are one of the oldest and best supported national sides.

SCOTLAND
Founded 1873

Kenny Dalglish was one of the world's finest players during the early 1980s. A skilful and creative forward, he was known as 'King Kenny' by the Tartan Army – the name given to Scotland's passionate and devoted fans.

FACT FILE
TOP GOALSCORERS
Kenny Dalglish 30 (1971–1986)
Denis Law 30 (1958–1974)

MOST APPEARANCES
Kenny Dalglish 102 (1971–1986)

TROPHIES/HONOURS
none

POLAND

So far, Poland have not quite lived up to their promise. Their best World Cup showing was third place in the 1982 World Cup after losing 2–0 to eventual champions Italy in the semi-final.

Like many of his countrymen, the Glasgow Celtic striker Maciej Zurawski plays outside of Poland.

FACT FILE
TOP GOALSCORER
Wlodzimierz Lubanski 44 (1963–1980)

MOST APPEARANCES
Grzegorz Lato 95 (1971–1984)

TROPHIES/HONOURS
OLYMPIC GOLD MEDAL
1972 Poland 2 Hungary 1

CROATIA

Founded 1912

Of the countries that emerged from the break-up of Yugoslavia (see 'Did You Know'), Croatia have proved the most successful with third place at France '98.

Davor Šuker was a stylish and prolific striker and won the Golden Boot at the 1998 World Cup Finals.

FACT FILE
TOP GOALSCORER
Davor Šuker 45 (1990–2002)

MOST APPEARANCES
Dario Šimic 98 (1996–present)

TROPHIES/HONOURS
none

DID YOU KNOW?

Political upheavals have transformed European football in the last 20 years. The break-up of the Soviet Union, revolutions in Eastern Europe and civil war in Yugoslavia have led to the formation of several new nations and the re-emergence of old ones. The Soviet Union (USSR) was split into Russia and smaller independent countries such as Georgia, Belarus and Ukraine; Yugoslavia became Serbia, Croatia, Montenegro, Bosnia-Herezegovina, Macedonia and Slovenia and Czechoslovakia became the Czech Republic and Slovakia.

NORWAY

Norwegian football has emerged from relative international obscurity in recent years thanks to stars such as John Arne Riise and Morten Gamst Pedersen.

Manchester United legend Ole Gunnar Solskjaer is Norway's most famous player of the last decade.

FACT FILE
TOP GOALSCORER
Jørgen Juve 33 (1928–1937)

MOST APPEARANCES
Thorbjørn Svenssen 104 (1947–1962)

TROPHIES/HONOURS
none

ROMANIA

The Romania team of the 1990s were the best so far and made the quarter-finals of USA '94 and Euro 2000.

Founded 1909

Romania's 'Footballer of the Century' was Gheorghe Hagi, star of the famous '90s side.

FACT FILE
TOP GOALSCORER
Gheorghe Hagi 35 (1983–2000)

MOST APPEARANCES
Dorinel Munteanu 134 (1991–2007)

TROPHIES/HONOURS
none

HUNGARY

Modern football owes much to the great Hungarian team of the 1950s. 'The magical Magyars' pioneered a fast and skilful style with imaginative passing and movement. However, in recent times, Hungary have struggled to make an impact on the international stage.

The late Ferenc Puskás is widely regarded as one of the world's best ever players. He scored a phenomenal 84 goals in just six years for Hungary, before changing nationality and appearing for Spain.

FACT FILE
TOP GOALSCORER
Ferenc Puskás 84 (1949–1956)

MOST APPEARANCES
József Bozsik 101 (1947–1962)

TROPHIES/HONOURS
OLYMPIC GOLD MEDAL
1952 Hungary 2 Yugoslavia 0
1964 Hungary 2 Czechoslovakia 1
1968 Hungary 4 Bulgaria 1

REPUBLIC OF IRELAND

Although Gaelic games such as Gaelic football, hurling, handball and camogie are hugely popular in the Republic of Ireland, football is still the country's most popular team sport. A period of success began in the late 1980s with stars such as Niall Quinn, Ray Houghton and Roy Keane. Jack Charlton's side reached the World Cup quarter-finals in Italia '90 and the second round four years later. Recent years have seen mixed fortunes for this talented squad.

Striker Robbie Keane made his debut at just 17 and is now his country's captain as well as top goalscorer.

FACT FILE

TOP GOALSCORER
Robbie Keane 33 (1998–present)

MOST APPEARANCES
Steve Staunton 102 (1988–2002)

TROPHIES/HONOURS
none

DENMARK

Traditionally, Denmark were known for producing fine players but had never made much of an international impact as a team. That was until Euro '92, when they caused a major upset by beating West Germany 2–0 in the final in Gothenburg.

For more than a decade, Peter Schmeichel was regarded as the best goalkeeper in the world. He was a superb shot stopper and dominated his area.

Founded 1889

FACT FILE

TOP GOALSCORER
Poul 'Tist' Nielsen 52 (1910–1925)

MOST APPEARANCES
Peter Schmeichel 129 (1987–2001)

TROPHIES/HONOURS
UEFA EUROPEAN CHAMPIONSHIP
1992 Denmark 2 Germany 0
CONFEDERATIONS CUP
1995 Denmark 2 Argentina 0

UKRAINE

The modern Ukrainian team only came into existence in 1991 (see 'Did You Know?' p. 45). Featuring many players who play for or at least began their careers at the great club side Dinamo Kiev, the national team are one of the strongest in the new-look Eastern Europe.

Star striker Andriy Shevchenko was European Footballer of the Year in 2004.

FACT FILE

TOP GOALSCORER
Andriy Shevchenko 37 (1995–present)

MOST APPEARANCES
Oleksandr Shovkovskiy 84 (1994–present)

TROPHIES/HONOURS
none

PORTUGAL

With a passionate football culture and a history of gifted players and great club sides, Portugal have all the ingredients for international success. Yet for all their promise, the team have never quite realised their potential, losing the Euro 2004 final and finishing third in the 1966 World Cup.

A brilliant playmaker and goalscorer, Luis Figo was the star of the so-called 'Golden Generation' who won the World Youth Championships in 1989.

Portugal has a new superstar in Cristiano Ronaldo. Lightning quick, blessed with a blistering shot and famous for his stepovers and tricks, Ronaldo is a modern master.

FACT FILE

TOP GOALSCORER
Pauleta 47 (1997–2006)

MOST APPEARANCES
Luis Figo 127 (1991–2006)

TROPHIES/HONOURS
none

AUSTRIA

Austria could also claim to be sleeping giants of European football. They finished third in the 1954 World Cup, but have not gone beyond the second round since. 2008 will be Austria's first time in the European Championship which they will co-host with Switzerland.

All-time top scorer Toni Polster in action for his country.

FACT FILE

TOP GOALSCORER
Anton 'Toni' Polster 44 (1988–2000)

MOST APPEARANCES
Andreas Herzog 103 (1998–2002)

TROPHIES/HONOURS

CZECH REPUBLIC

The 1989 'Velvet Revolution' divided Czechoslovakia into two nations (see p.45) and the Czech Republic emerged as the stronger football team. They were runners-up in the 1996 European Championships and qualified for the 2006 World Cup in Germany.

Skilled midfielder Pavel Nedved is regarded as the best Czech footballer of his generation.

FACT FILE

TOP GOALSCORER
Jan Koller 54 (1999–present)

MOST APPEARANCES
Karel Poborský 118 (1994–2006)

TROPHIES/HONOURS
(Competing as Czechoslovakia)
UEFA EUROPEAN CHAMPIONSHIP
1976 Czechoslovakia 2 West Germany 2
Czechoslovakia won 5–3 on penalties
(Competing as Czech Republic)
none

BELGIUM

The Belgian national team's best performance was as runners-up in the 1980 European Championship, when they lost 2–1 to West Germany in the final.

Eric Gerets is one of Belgium's most famous players. A defender who won 86 caps playing for his country, Gerets also won the European Cup in 1988 with PSV Eindhoven.

FACT FILE

TOP GOALSCORERS
Paul Van Himst 30 (1960–1974)
Bernard Voorhoof 30 (1928–1940)

MOST APPEARANCES
Jan Ceulemans 96 (1977–1990)

TROPHIES/HONOURS
OLYMPIC GOLD MEDAL
1920 Belgium 2 Czechoslovakia 0

SWITZERLAND

Switzerland reached the quarter-finals of the World Cup in 1934 and 1938 but have enjoyed little success since then. They were knocked out of the 2006 Finals tournament despite not conceding a single goal.

FACT FILE

TOP GOALSCORERS
Alexander Frei 36 (2001–present)

MOST APPEARANCES
Heinz Hermann 117 (1978–1991)

TROPHIES/HONOURS
none

WALES

Founded 1876

Despite the popularity of rugby, Welsh football has enjoyed a recent boom. However, the national side continues to just miss out on major tournaments and the 1958 World Cup Finals is Wales' only qualification so far.

From John Charles to Ian Rush, Wales has produced many world class players. The best of recent years has been Ryan Giggs, Manchester United's dazzling winger.

FACT FILE

TOP GOALSCORER
Ian Rush 28 (1980–1996)

MOST APPEARANCES
Neville Southall 92 (1990–2006)

TROPHIES/HONOURS
none

SERBIA

The Serbian team was formed as one of the relics of the old Yugoslavia side that broke up in the 1990s (see p. 45). Striker Savo Milošević holds both appearance and goalscoring records for his country.

FACT FILE

TOP GOALSCORER
Savo Milošević 35 (1994–2006)

MOST APPEARANCES
Savo Milošević 101 (1994–2006)

TROPHIES/HONOURS
none

NORTHERN IRELAND

Founded 1880

With just 1.5 million people, Northern Ireland can't compete with the larger nations. However, they can claim to be British champions – they won the British Home Championships in 1984, the last time it was contested.

Striker David Healy is seen here in action against Spain, whom Northern Ireland also defeated in the Euro 2008 qualifiers.

FACT FILE

TOP GOALSCORER
David Healy 34 (2000–present)

MOST APPEARANCES
Pat Jennings 119 (1964–1986)

TROPHIES/HONOURS
none

BULGARIA

Founded 1923

Bulgaria's finest hour came in the 1994 World Cup Finals in the USA. They beat the holders Germany 2–1 in the quarter-final before losing by the same score to Italy in the semi-final.

FACT FILE

TOP GOALSCORER
Hristo Bonev 47 (1967–1979)

MOST APPEARANCES
Borislav Mikhailov 102 (1985–1999)

TROPHIES/HONOURS
none

NORTH AMERICA

"FOOTBALL IS FULL OF SURPRISES."

TRINIDAD AND TOBAGO CAPTAIN
DWIGHT YORKE

St Lucia, the Bahamas, the British Virgin Islands… this may sound like a list of dream holiday destinations but in fact they are all members of the soccer confederation that unites North and Central America and the Caribbean. As well as including some of the world's most exotic football outposts, it also represents some serious contenders for international glory, such as Mexico and the USA. Beach soccer is also popular in this region and an annual tournament is hotly contested with sides from the South American confederation.

The Confederation of North American, Central American and Caribbean Association Football (CONCACAF) came together in 1961. It produced four qualifiers in the 2006 World Cup. The best ever World Cup result for a CONCACAF member is the USA's semi-final in 1930.

GREENLAND

CANADA

UNITED STATES
OF AMERICA

MEXICO

CUBA

THE BAHAMAS

DOMINICAN REPUBLIC

BRITISH VIRGIN ISLANDS

PUERTO
RICO

ANTILLES

ST KITTS AND NEVIS

JAMAICA

HAITI

ANGUILLA

ANTIGUA AND BARBUDA

GUADELOUPE

DOMINICA

MARTINIQUE

ST LUCIA

SURINAM
FRENCH GUIANA
GUYANA
VENEZUELA
COLOMBIA
BRAZIL
PERÚ
BOLIVIA
ECUADOR
PARAGUAY
CHILE
ARGENTINA
URUGUAY
HONDURAS
GUATEMALA
EL SALVADOR
NICARAGUA
COSTA RICA
PANAMA

SOUTH AMERICA

"NOT MUCH OCCURS IN LATIN AMERICA THAT DOESN'T BEAR DIRECTLY OR INDIRECTLY ON FOOTBALL."

URUGUAYAN HISTORIAN AND AUTHOR
EDUARDO GALEANO

The nations and star names of this region read like a list of reasons to get excited about the beautiful game. Pelé, Ardiles, Maradona, Romário, Ronaldinho, Messi and a flood of attractive exports have illuminated football clubs across the globe. This stronghold of football has seen a team within its own federation win the coveted World Cup every time it has hosted the tournament.

The Confederación Sudamericana de Fútbol (South American Football Confederation) is also known as CONMEBOL or CSF. It was founded in 1916 by Argentina, Brazil, Chile and Uruguay. It has ten member nations and has produced the World Cup winners on nine occasions. CONMEBOL has four guaranteed World Cup places, plus a chance to play-off with the winners of the Oceania group.

South American football fans have blazed a flamboyant trail for the rest of the world to follow. Traditions like fiesta (street partying) and samba (music and dance), have given them a head start in knowing how to support their heroes in awesome style!

BRAZIL

"BEAUTY COMES FIRST. VICTORY IS SECONDARY. WHAT MATTERS IS JOY." SÓCRATES, BRAZIL MIDFIELDER 1979–1986

Magical, mesmeric, spellbinding – these terms aren't often lavished on football teams, except for Brazil. Universally admired for their scintillating style and breathtaking skills, Brazil are the most successful footballing nation of all time and have won the World Cup a record five times. They have also given the game arguably its greatest ever player – the legendary Pelé – and blazed a glorious trail for others to follow. For Brazil football really is 'the beautiful game'!

The Confederação Brasileira de Futebol (Brazilian Football Confederation) was founded in 1914.

Victorious captain, Cafu, collects the trophy in 2002.

Pelé's real name is Edson Arantes do Nascimento.

WORLD CUP

Brazil's World Cup triumphs include 1958, when a 17-year-old Pelé scored twice in a 5–2 win over Sweden and 1970, when victory over Italy meant they could keep the Jules Rimet trophy. Surprisingly, the 2–0 win over Germany in the 2002 final was the first ever competitive clash between these international heavyweights.

BEST EVER?

Voted FIFA Footballer of the Century in the year 2000, Pelé is the only player ever to be part of three World Cup-winning squads and he scored 77 goals in 92 appearances for his country. A sensational dribbler with an unstoppable shot, he was also an unselfish and inspired playmaker. Pelé's talent and sportsmanship made him universally loved, even by his opponents.

Many argue that Brazil's finest footballer was actually Garrincha, not Pelé. Despite a deformed spine and one leg longer than the other, he was a mesmerising dribbler. Garrincha won the World Cup in 1958 and 1962.

Zico is possibly the greatest Brazilian never to have won the World Cup. In 1982 and 1986, teams featuring Zico, Sócrates, Falcão and Junior were a joy to watch, but lost out. In the 2006 World Cup Finals Zico faced Brazil as manager of Japan.

DID YOU KNOW?

Brazil haven't always played in yellow and blue. The famous kit was designed for them by a 19-year-old fan in a competition to give the team a makeover after the nation turned against the unlucky white kit they wore in the 1950 World Cup.

BRAZIL DREAM TEAM? 1. Gílmar 2. Cafu 3. Nílton Santos 4. Didi 5. Lúcio 6. Bellini 7. Garrincha 8. Leônidas 9. Ronaldo 10. Pelé 11. Rivelino

RONALDO follows in an illustrious tradition of great Brazilian strikers. Although he has been criticised for his weight and for his poor performance in the 1998 World Cup final, his record is undeniable. He is the World Cup Finals' top scorer with 15 goals in four World Cups, and was voted the FIFA World Player of the Year in 1996, 1997 and 2002.

Kaká got his nickname as a child because he was unable to say his real name, Ricardo.

KAKÁ

Midfielder Kaká is regarded as one of the best players in the world today. His vision, range of passing and forceful shooting make him equally comfortable playing deep in midfield or pushing up into attack. He was Brazil's stand-out player in an otherwise disappointing 2006 World Cup Finals.

RONALDINHO

Ronaldinho was voted FIFA World Player of the Year in 2004 and 2005 and was part of the World Cup winning team in 2002. Famous for his close control and dribbling skills, he is also a powerful and prolific shooter, despite not being an out-and-out striker. However, it is Ronaldinho's mastery of the unexpected – his ability to pull off a pass, move, feint or shot to stun even the best of defenders – that has won him many fans around the world.

FACT FILE: BRAZIL

NICKNAMES
A Seleção (The Selected), Canarinho (Little Canary)

TOP GOALSCORERS
1. Pelé 77 (1957–1971)
2. Ronaldo 62 (1994–present)
3. Romário 55 (1987–2005)
4. Zico 52 (1971–1989)
5. Bebeto 39 (1985–1998)

MOST APPEARANCES
1. Cafu 142 (1990–2006)
2. Roberto Carlos 125 (1992–2006)
3. Cláudio Taffarel 101 (1987–1998)
4. Djalma Santos 98 (1952–1968)
5. Ronaldo 97 (1994–2006)

TROPHIES/HONOURS

FIFA WORLD CUP
1958 Brazil 5 Sweden 2
1962 Brazil 3 Czechoslovakia 1
1970 Brazil 4 Italy 1
1994 Brazil 3 Italy 2
2002 Brazil 2 Germany 0

COPA AMÉRICA
1919 Brazil 1 Uruguay 0
1922 Brazil 3 Paraguay 0
1949 Brazil 7 Paraguay 0
1989 Brazil 1 Uruguay 0
1997 Brazil 3 Bolivia 1
1999 Brazil 3 Uruguay 0
2004 Brazil 4 Argentina 2
2007 Brazil 3 Argentina 0

The Maracanã stadium in Rio de Janeiro is the biggest football arena in the world. It hosted the equivalent of a World Cup final when Brazil played Uruguay in the deciding game of the 1950 tournament, in an unusual round-robin system. Brazil lost 2–1 in front of an estimated 210,000 fans.

ARGENTINA

"IF YOU PLAY WELL AND SHOW THE ARGENTINIAN PEOPLE WHAT THEY WANT TO SEE, THEY'LL THANK YOU FOR IT ALL YOUR LIFE."

HÉCTOR ENRIQUE, PART OF ARGENTINA'S '86 TEAM

They may have lost the first ever World Cup 4–2 to Uruguay, but they've made up for it since with two World Cups, 14 Copa Américas and six victories in Pan American games. Many heroes have played a part in Argentina's dramatic history. 'El Gran Capitan', Daniel Passarella, was the first Argentine to touch the World Cup while Leopoldo Luque lit up the 1978 finals with his sensational long-range efforts on goal. Today, Juan Román Riquelme's playmaking magic gives new hope to a football-mad nation.

The first Argentinian football association was founded by Glaswegian teacher Alexander Hutton in 1891. It laid the foundations for the modern Argentine Football Association.

HISTORIC MOMENT

Argentina came of age in spectacular style when they hosted and won their first World Cup in 1978. It was a torrid tournament, full of controversy. Argentina pipped Brazil to the final on goal difference after beating Peru 6–0 in their final round two match. They then overpowered the Netherlands' 'Total Football' in the final.

Daniel Passarella triumphantly holds the World Cup aloft.

Maradona is regarded by many as the greatest player of all time.

Mario Kempes won the 1978 World Cup for Argentina with two goals in a 3–1 extra time victory over the Netherlands. He scored six goals in the Finals and was South American Player of the Year.

Maradona's talent was epitomised by the 1986 World Cup quarter-final when he took out the whole England defence with a surging, spellbinding dribble to score the 'Goal of the Century'.

MARADONA

Dazzling Diego Maradona scored 34 goals in 91 internationals. His squat, muscular frame gave him a low centre of gravity which made him almost impossible to knock off the ball. He scored five goals in the 1986 World Cup Finals and inspired his side to beat West Germany 3–2 in the final. Despite a career dogged by scandal and controversy both on and off the pitch, Maradona remains a hero in his native country.

| ARGENTINA DREAM TEAM? | 1. Ubaldo Fillol 2. Javier Zanetti 3. Silvio Marzolini 4. Omar Sívori 5. Daniel Passarella 6. Roberto Ayala 7. José Manuel Moreno 8. Ángel Labruna 9. Alfredo Di Stéfano 10. Diego Maradona 11. Mario Kempes |

STAR STRIKER

Prolific goalscorer Gabriel Batistuta hit 56 goals in 78 games for Argentina, which earned him the nickname 'Batigol'. He hit four goals in USA '94, and five in France '98 – tournaments in which his team as a whole achieved relatively little success. When Batistuta retired from the national team, Hernán Crespo took over as the main striker. Despite competition from younger players such as Messi, Tévez and Saviola, Crespo's record of more than a goal every other game speaks for itself.

NEW MARADONA?

Lionel Messi is a big game player. A visionary passer of the ball and scorer of special goals, he is on the way to fulfilling Maradona's prediction that he has a true successor at last. Messi scored two goals and created more in Argentina's impressive, but ultimately unsuccessful 2007 Copa América campaign. One of a stunning array of strikers at Barcelona, his own legend is just beginning.

DID YOU KNOW?

Messi had one of the shortest ever debuts in international football, when he was sent off after just forty seconds against Hungary. He came on in the 63rd minute and the referee believed he deliberately used an elbow against Vilmos Vanzcak.

A powerful striker with a deft touch, Carlos Tévez is Argentina's hottest new finisher. Controversially signed by Corinthians of Brazil in 2005, he braved a media storm and fan opposition to emerge as South American Player of the Year. Transferring to West Ham in 2006 then Manchester United in 2007, he seems destined for greatness.

FACT FILE: ARGENTINA
NICKNAMES
Albicelestes (White and Sky Blues),
Los Gauchos (The Cowboys)

TOP GOALSCORERS
1. Gabriel Batistuta 56 (1991–2002)
2. Hernán Crespo 36 (1995–present)
3. Diego Maradona 34 (1977–1994)
4. Luis Artime 24 (1961–1967)
5. Leopoldo Luque 22 (1975–1981)
= Daniel Passarella 22 (1976–1986)

MOST APPEARANCES
1. Javier Zanetti 118 (1994–present)
2. Roberto Ayala 115 (1994–2007)
3. Diego Simeone 106 (1988–2002)
4. Oscar Ruggeri 97 (1983–1994)
5. Diego Maradona 91 (1977–1994)

TROPHIES/HONOURS
FIFA WORLD CUP
1978 Argentina 3 Netherlands 1 (aet)
1986 Argentina 3 West Germany 2

COPA AMÉRICA
1921, 1925, 1927, 1929, 1937, 1941, 1945, 1946, 1947, 1955, 1957, 1959 (round-robin league tournaments) 1991 (round-robin, then final round of four teams in a mini league) 1993 Argentina 2 Mexico 1

CONFEDERATIONS CUP
1992 Argentina 3 Saudi Arabia 1

OLYMPIC GAMES
2004 Argentina 1 Paraguay 0

The Estadio Monumental Antonio V. Liberti is Argentina's national stadium. It is better known as El Monumental or River Plate Stadium and can hold more than 65,000 fans.

SOUTH AMERICAN TEAMS

"OUR FOOTBALL COMES FROM THE HEART, THEIRS COMES FROM THE MIND." PELÉ COMPARES THE GAME IN SOUTH AMERICA AND EUROPE

South America has so much more to offer than just Brazil and Argentina. From historically illustrious teams such as Uruguay, to optimistic minnows such as Venezuela, this diverse continent captures everything that is fascinating about the world game. South America often produces a dark horse to illuminate a World Cup.

Recoba is famous for his dribbling, technique, and strong, accurate left-foot shot.

FACT FILE

TOP GOALSCORER
Héctor Scarone 31 (1917–1930)

MOST APPEARANCES
Rodolfo Rodriguez 78 (1976–1986)

TROPHIES/HONOURS

FIFA WORLD CUP
1930 Uruguay 4 Argentina 2
1950 Uruguay topped a four team final group

COPA AMÉRICA
1916, 1917, 1920, 1923, 1924, 1926, 1935, 1942, 1956, 1959, 1967, 1959, 1967 (round-robin league tournaments)
1983 Uruguay 3 Brazil 1 (agg)
1987 Uruguay 1 Chile 0
1995 Uruguay 1 Brazil 1 (Uruguay won 5–3 in a penalty shoot-out.

OLYMPIC GAMES
1924 Uruguay 3 Switzerland 0
1928 Uruguay 2 Argentina 1 (replay)

URUGUAY

The Asociación Uruguaya de Fútbol was founded in 1900 and was one of the founder members of CONMEBOL. Although they are one of the few nations to have won the World Cup more than once, Uruguay have been through a lengthy lean spell in recent years which has unfortunately coincided with the upsurge of their local rivals Argentina. In 2006, Uruguay didn't even qualify for the World Cup Finals – they missed out after losing a nail-biting play-off to Australia.

Victory in the first ever World Cup is not Uruguay fans' fondest memory – securing the trophy in 1950 at the expense of hosts Brazil was an even sweeter triumph.

ÁLVARO RECOBA, has scored 11 goals in 69 internationals. He managed to upstage Brazilian striker Ronaldo on their shared debut for Inter Milan. The Uruguayan scored two late goals, one a 35-metre rocket.

PARAGUAY

Founded 1906

Chilavert celebrates scoring Paraguay's third goal in a 5–1 win over Bolivia in 2001.

Although overshadowed by more glamorous neighbours, Paraguay have come close to causing major World Cup upsets. Making round two in 1998, they were only squeezed out by a 'golden goal' in the 114th minute by ultimate winners, France. In 2002 it was a round two exit again, this time 1–0 to eventual finalists, Germany.

Inspired, impulsive and often controversial, José Luis Chilavert combined daring goalkeeping with a talent for scoring free-kicks and penalties. He scored eight goals in international matches and an amazing 62 throughout his career.

FACT FILE

TOP GOALSCORER
José Cardozo 25 (1991–2006)

MOST APPEARANCES
Carlos Gamarra 110 (1993–2006)

TROPHIES/HONOURS

COPA AMÉRICA
1953 and 1979 (round-robin league tournaments)

SOUTH AMERICA DREAM TEAM?
1. José Luis Chilavert (Paraguay) 2. Víctor Rodríguez Andrade (Uruguay) 3. José Nasazzi (Uruguay) 4.Obdulio Varela (Uruguay) 5. Héctor Chumpitaz (Peru) 6. Elías Figueroa (Chile) 7. Carlos Valderrama (Colombia) 8. Juan Alberto Schiaffino (Uruguay) 9. Alberto Spencer (Ecuador/Uruguay) 10. Teófilo Cubillas (Peru) 11. Leonel Sánchez (Chile)

COLOMBIA

A 1–0 victory over Mexico in the 2001 Copa América is the only major trophy for this under-achieving side. Their only World Cup appearance of recent years was in France '98, where they managed just one win, 1–0 against Tunisia. Tragedy struck at the 1994 World Cup Finals, when defender Andrés Escobar scored an own-goal in a 2–1 defeat to the USA. He was shot dead a short time later.

VALDERRAMA was a gifted playmaker with a style all his own, and not just because of his hairstyle! In 111 internationals his unhurried style and classy touch made the toughest game look like a stroll in the park. His Colombia team impressed at Italy '90 and were the only side to avoid defeat against eventual winners Germany.

Valderrama was instantly recognisable thanks to his hairstyle.

FACT FILE

TOP GOALSCORER
Adolfo Valencia 31 (1992–1998)

MOST APPEARANCES
Carlos Valderrama 111 (1983–1998)

TROPHIES/HONOURS
COPA AMÉRICA
2001 Colombia 1 Mexico 0

Fiery striker Faustino Asprilla notched up an impressive 20 goals in 57 caps. Among his memorable displays was Colombia's legendary 5–0 thrashing of Argentina in 1993. Red cards, rows and great stories for the press were never far away when 'Tino' was involved.

VENEZUELA

Venezuela are the only side in the South American confederation never to have qualified for a World Cup Finals. However, inspired by top players such as Juan Arango, they hope to lose their pushover status en route to the 2010 Finals.

FACT FILE

TOP GOALSCORER
Ruberth Morán 15 (1996–2007)

MOST APPEARANCES
José Manuel Rey 93 (1999–present)

TROPHIES/ HONOURS
none

BOLIVIA

Bolivia participated in the first World Cup in 1930 and again in 1950, but in recent years they have had little impact on the tournament, apart from a trip to the Finals in the USA in 1994.

FACT FILE

TOP GOALSCORER
Victor Agustín Ugarte 16 (1947–1963)

MOST APPEARANCES
Marco Antonio Sandy 93 (1993–2003)
= Luis Héctor Cristaldo 93 (1989–2005)

TROPHIES/HONOURS
COPA AMÉRICA
1963 (round-robin tournament)

ECUADOR

Traditionally regarded as South American lightweights, Ecuador impressed at the 2006 World Cup Finals, beating Poland and Costa Rica before losing to England in the second round.

FACT FILE

TOP GOALSCORER
Agustín Delgado 31 (1994–present)

MOST APPEARANCES
Iván Hurtado 146 (1993–present)

TROPHIES/ HONOURS
none

PERU

Between 1970 and 1982 Peru's flowing football was admired across the globe. Teófilo Cubillas scored 5 goals in 2 World Cups, but a 1970 quarter-final was their best result and they have not graced the Finals for 24 years.

FACT FILE

TOP GOALSCORER
Teófilo Cubillas 26 (1968–1982)

MOST APPEARANCES
Roberto Palacios 122 (1992–present)

TROPHIES/HONOURS
COPA AMÉRICA
1939 (round-robin league tournament)
1975 Peru 3 Colombia 1 (agg)

Héctor Chumpitaz played in two World Cup Finals and helped his side lift the Copa América in 1975.

CHILE

Established in 1895, the Federación de Fútbol de Chile was also one of the founder members of CONMEBOL. As host of the 1962 World Cup Finals, Chile recorded a best-ever third place. In 1998, Marcelo Salas' goals brightened their World Cup. He scored twice in a 2–2 draw with Italy as well as in their 4–1 defeat to Brazil in the second round.

Matías Fernández was voted South American Footballer of the Year in 2006. This attacking midfielder is also a free kick specialist.

FACT FILE

TOP GOALSCORER
Marcelo Salas 37 (1994–present)

MOST APPEARANCES
Leonel Sánchez 84 (1955–1968)

TROPHIES/HONOURS

USA

> "TEN YEARS AGO COUNTRIES LAUGHED AT US AND WE DIDN'T GET RESPECT BUT IT IS COMPLETELY DIFFERENT NOW. YOU CAN JUST SENSE THAT IT IS A BIG GAME TO PLAY US."
>
> FORMER US CAPTAIN CLAUDIO REYNA

Once known for bringing razzmatazz, cheerleaders and big screen replays to the game they like to call 'soccer', the USA can now boast a robust national team. Eyebrows were raised when the US was allocated the 1994 World Cup, but qualification for every World Cup since has silenced critics. They may call a clean sheet a 'shut out' but their fresh blood and new ideas have invigorated the world game.

The United States Soccer Federation was formed in 1913 and it was affiliated to FIFA in the same year. It was actually called the US Football Federation until 1945 when it was changed to 'soccer'.

Bart McGhee (left) and Bert Patenaude (right)

HISTORY MAKERS

The USA exceeded expectations at the 1930 World Cup and reached the semi-finals. American Bart McGhee scored the first ever goal in a World Cup Finals in a 3–0 win against Belgium and his team mate Bert Patenaude is generally credited with scoring the first ever World Cup hat-trick against Paraguay.

RECENT SUCCESS

In 2007 the USA overcame the rest of North and Central America to triumph in the CONCACAF Gold Cup. Also the host country, the USA beat Mexico 2–1 in the final.

USA DREAM TEAM?	1. Kasey Keller 2. Eddie Pope 3. Paul Caligiuri 4. Tab Ramos 5. Marcelo Balboa 6. Walter Bahr 7. Claudio Reyna 8. John Harkes 9. Joe Gaetjens 10. Landon Donovan 11. Brian McBride

SHUT OUT KINGS

The USA have a fine crop of world class goalkeepers. Brad Friedel (top, 82 caps) was nicknamed 'The Human Wall' for his performances in the 2002 World Cup, while Kasey Keller (middle, 102 caps) famously kept a clean sheet against Brazil in the USA's shock 1–0 victory in 1998. Tim Howard (bottom, 29 caps) has won an FA Cup medal with Manchester United in 2004 and currently plays for Everton.

TEAM LEADER

So far, USA captain Landon Donovan has scored 35 goals in 99 appearances. He was US Soccer's Male Athlete of the Year in 2003 and 2004, and was honoured with a place in the MLS All-Time Best Team. He plays his club football for LA Galaxy, alongside David Beckham.

Since Claudio Reyna's retirement, Donovan has been the USA's first choice No.10.

The first American ever to be named in a World Cup All-Tournament team (2002), Claudio Reyna (112 caps) appeared in four USA World Cup squads from 1994 to 2006. He preceded Donovan as USA captain, and his leadership skills and battling midfield style earned him the nickname 'Captain America'. Reyna currently plays for Red Bull New York in the MLS.

Centre forward Eric Wynalda (106 caps) has scored 34 goals for the USA. He was the first US-born player to play in the German Bundesliga, for Saarbrucken (1992–1994). In 1996 he scored the first ever goal in the MLS, for San Jose Clash.

DID YOU KNOW?

In the 1950 World Cup the USA beat England 1–0 in one of the greatest upsets of all time, thanks to keeper Frank Borghi and goalscorer Joe Gaetjens.

In 1984 the national side, then known as Team America, played in the North American Soccer League. It was believed that regular competition would improve the side but they finished bottom of the league.

FREDDY ADU

18-year-old Ghana-born Fredua Koranteng Adu looks destined to be a big star for the USA. He already holds the unique record of a hat-trick in both the U-17 and U-20 World Cups, and has now signed for Portuguese side Benfica.

CONCACAF TEAMS

"WHOEVER INVENTED FOOTBALL SHOULD BE WORSHIPPED AS A GOD."

FORMER MEXICO COACH AND STRIKER HUGO SANCHEZ

The CONCACAF has 40 members and is dominated by Mexico and the USA. The federation also includes three South American nations – Guyana, Surinam and French Guiana. Since 1991 CONCACAF's showpiece tournament has been the Gold Cup. With seven Gold Cup wins Mexico are the most successful national team but the USA are catching up fast. The USA hosted the tournament in 2007 and won it for the third time.

Rafa Márquez is Mexican football's modern superstar.

MEXICO

Founded 1927

Since the 1990s, Mexico have established themselves as a regional and world football power. They combine a direct, physical approach with individual brilliance. Striker Hugo Sánchez is widely regarded as the greatest Mexican player of all time and was the national coach until April 2008.

Goalkeeper Antonio Carbajal made his World Cup Finals debut as a 21-year-old in 1950, and 16 years later became the first player to appear in five consecutive Finals tournaments. He was respected for his safe hands and his leadership, but in all his 11 games at the Finals he ended up on the winning side only once.

CUBA

With baseball as the national sport, Cuba has never been a major football power. However, the national team have shown greater promise in recent times, reaching the last four of the CONCACAF Gold Cup in 2003 and only narrowly missing out on qualification for the 2006 World Cup Finals in Germany.

FACT FILE

TOP GOALSCORER
Information unknown

MOST APPEARANCES
Information unknown

TROPHIES/HONOURS
none

Rafael Márquez is Mexico's captain. He plays as a defender or midfielder and made his international debut at 17 years old. He became the first Mexican to win a UEFA Champions League medal when his club, Barcelona, won the title in 2006.

FACT FILE

TOP GOALSCORER
Jared Borgetti 43 (1997–present)

MOST APPEARANCES
Claudio Suárez 178 (1992–2006)

TROPHIES/HONOURS
CONCACAF CHAMPIONSHIP AND GOLD CUP
1965, 1971, 1977 (round-robin team tournaments)
1977 (top World Cup qualifying team awarded trophy)
1993 Mexico 4 USA 0
1996 Mexico 2 Brazil 0
1998 Mexico 1 USA 0
2003 Mexico 1 Brazil 0

CONFEDERATIONS CUP
1999 Mexico 4 Brazil 3

CONCACAF DREAM TEAM? 1. Antonio Carbajal (Mexico) 2. Claudio Suárez (Mexico) 3. Róger Flores (Mexico) 4. Mauricio Solís (Costa Rica) 5. Rafael Márquez (Mexico) 6. Gilberto Yearwood (Honduras) 7. Luis Garcia (Mexico) 8. Dwight Yorke (Trinidad & Tobago) 9. Hugo Sánchez (Mexico) 10. Cuauhtemoc Blanco (Mexico) 11. Emmanuel Sanon (Haiti)

COSTA RICA

Founded 1921

First successful in the early 1960s, Costa Rica suffered a slump in the 1970s and 1980s. The national side have re-emerged as a force in the 1990s and 2000s and qualified for three World Cups. Costa Rica are currently ranked 56th in the world which makes them Central America's most successful team.

With 45 goals in 72 international matches, Paolo Wanchope is one of Costa Rica's most prolific strikers. He has played club football in England, Spain, Japan and the USA.

FACT FILE

TOP GOALSCORER
Rolando Fonseca 47 (1992–present)
MOST APPEARANCES
Luis Marín 123 (1993–present)

TROPHIES/HONOURS
CONCACAF CHAMPIONSHIP AND GOLD CUP
1963, 1969 (round-robin team tournaments)
1989 (top World Cup qualifying team awarded trophy)

TRINIDAD AND TOBAGO

Nicknamed the 'Soca Warriors', Trinidad and Tobago are the Caribbean's most successful national team. However, a row over bonus payments following Trinidad and Tobago's first ever World Cup in 2006 means that many of the team's stars no longer play for their country.

One-time T&T captain Dwight Yorke played in Manchester United's famous 1999 treble-winning side.

FACT FILE

TOP GOALSCORER
Stern John 67 (1995–present)
MOST APPEARANCES
Angus Eve 118 (1994–present)

TROPHIES/HONOURS
none

JAMAICA

Known as the 'Reggae Boyz', Jamaica caught the world's attention when they made it to the 1998 World Cup Finals, their first visit to the tournament. However, the team have struggled recently and are now ranked 94th in the world.

FACT FILE

TOP GOALSCORER
Theodore Whitmore 24 (1993–2005)
MOST APPEARANCES
Durrant Brown 107 (unknown)

TROPHIES/HONOURS
none

Midfielder Theodore Whitmore is Jamaica's all-time top scorer, and was his country's Footballer of the Year in 1998.

HAITI

A golden age in the late 1960s and 1970s saw Haiti reach the World Cup Finals in 1974. However, political and social problems led to a decline in fortune for the national football team. Now ranked 83rd by FIFA, and playing home games in Miami, USA, the future looks brighter.

FACT FILE

TOP GOALSCORER
Golman Pierre 23 (1996–2003)

MOST APPEARANCES
Pierre-Richard Bruny 75 (1998–present)

TROPHIES/HONOURS
none

HONDURAS

Hondurans are passionate about football and in 1970 the result of a match led to a war against El Salvador. So far, Honduras have appeared only once in the World Cup Finals, in 1982. However, thanks to stars such as David Suazo, the team could be considered a rising power.

FACT FILE

TOP GOALSCORERS
Carlos Pavón 47 (1993–present)

MOST APPEARANCES
Amado Guevara 107 (1994–present)

TROPHIES/HONOURS
none

CANADA

Victory in the 2000 CONCACAF Gold Cup was seen to be Canada's big breakthrough, but failure to qualify for the 2006 World Cup was a major setback.

Founded 1912

Canada striker Tomasz Radzinski has played at the top level in England and Belgium.

FACT FILE

TOP GOALSCORERS
John Catliff 19 (unknown)
Dale Mitchell 19 (1980–1993)
MOST APPEARANCES
Randy Samuel 82 (1982–1997)

TROPHIES/HONOURS
CONCACAF CHAMPIONSHIP AND GOLD CUP
1985 (top World Cup qualifying team awarded trophy)
2000 Canada 2 Colombia 0

AFRICA

> "WHEREVER YOU GO THERE [AFRICA], THEY'RE ALL PLAYING FOOTBALL ALL THE TIME. EVERYWHERE"
>
> CARLOS BILARDO, FORMER LIBYA AND ARGENTINA COACH

CAPE VERD ISLAN

When the Brazilian legend Pelé said that an African nation would win the World Cup by the year 2000, his prediction was a little premature. However, his remarks helped to bring African football to the world's attention. During the last decade, the footballing world has had to sit up and take notice of Africa. Skilful and entertaining teams such as Ghana, Senegal and Egypt have emerged, as well as talented individuals such as Côte d'Ivoire's Didier Drogba and Cameroon's Samuel Eto'o. In this diverse continent, football has a power beyond politics or religion to unite divided nations and bring a shared sense of identity.

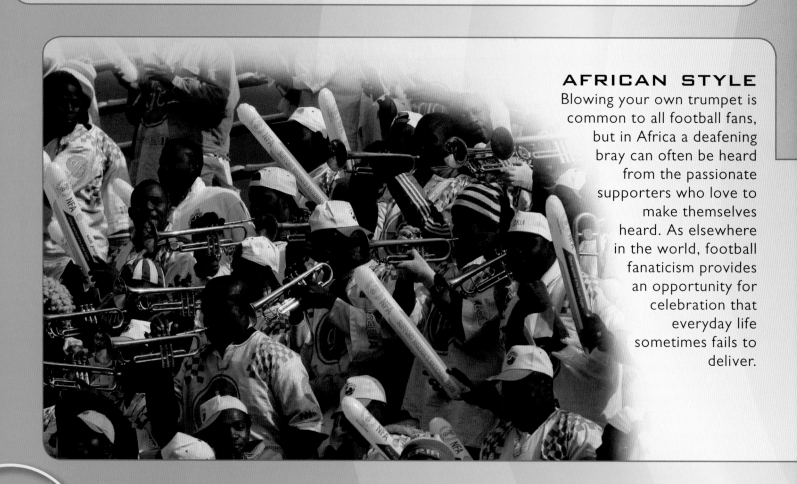

AFRICAN STYLE

Blowing your own trumpet is common to all football fans, but in Africa a deafening bray can often be heard from the passionate supporters who love to make themselves heard. As elsewhere in the world, football fanaticism provides an opportunity for celebration that everyday life sometimes fails to deliver.

MOROCCO

TUNISIA

ALGERIA

LIBYA

EGYPT

ESTERN
AHARA

MAURITANIA

ERITREA

MALI

NIGER

CHAD

SUDAN

SENEGAL

DJIBOUTI

THE
AMBIA

BURKINA
FASO

GUINEA

NIGERIA

ETHIOPIA

GUINEA-
ISSAU

CÔTE
D'IVOIRE

CENTRAL AFRICAN
REPUBLIC

SOMALIA

IERRA
EONE

BENIN

UGANDA

KENYA

LIBERIA

TOGO

GHANA

CAMEROON

DEMOCRATIC
REPUBLIC
OF THE
CONGO

EQUATORIAL
GUINEA

GABON

SÃO TOMÉ
& PRINCIPE

RWANDA

BURUNDI

TANZANIA

REPUBLIC OF
THE CONGO

MALAWI

ANGOLA

COMOROS

ZAMBIA

MADAGASCAR

ZIMBABWE

MOZAMBIQUE

NAMIBIA

BOTSWANA

SWAZILAND

SOUTH
AFRICA

LESOTHO

DID YOU KNOW?

The first African country to win a FIFA world tournament was Nigeria when the youth team beat West Germany 2–0 in the final of the 1985 World Under-17 Championships.

The first president of Ghana, Dr Kwame Nkrumah, was a significant force in realising the potential of African football in promoting both African independence and national unity.

SOUTH AFRICA

> **"2010 IS ON EVERYONE'S LIPS AND THE PEOPLE OF SOUTH AFRICA ARE LOOKING FORWARD TO GIVING THE WORLD A WARM AFRICAN WELCOME."**
>
> MOLEFI OLIPHANT, PRESIDENT OF THE SOUTH AFRICAN FA

South Africa are proudly pioneering a new era of African football after spending three decades in sporting exile. In 1962 they were expelled by FIFA for refusing to field a mixed-race team and were only allowed back when the apartheid (racial segregation) regime ended in 1992. South Africa celebrated by beating Cameroon 1–0 in their comeback match, thanks to a late penalty by Theophilus 'Doctor' Khumalo. Now the 'Bafana Bafana' prepare to welcome the World Cup to Africa for the first time.

The South African Football Association was founded in 1991, after a long struggle to rid sport in South Africa of all its past racial division.

SUCCESS!

For many South Africans, it was enough simply to host the African Cup of Nations in 1996, but to win was unbelievable, especially for the 80,000 home fans. A year later Phil Masinga's winning goal against Congo saw South Africa qualify for their first World Cup.

Super sub Mark Williams secured a place in South African sporting history with the only two goals in the 1996 African Cup of Nations final. Although he travelled widely as a player, his career was overshadowed by that 1996 tournament, where he scored five goals in total – one more than strike partner John 'Shoes' Moshoeu.

Aaron Mokoena in action against Ghana in 2006.

YOUNG STAR

Aaron Mokoena is the youngest player ever to play for South Africa. He won his first cap in 1999 against Botswana at the age of 18 years and 56 days. This versatile player, known as 'The Axe', can play in defence or midfield and is currently captain of his national team.

SHAUN BARTLETT

One of South Africa's all-time top scorers is a striker with a tendency to score spectacular goals. Shaun Bartlett's long-range volley for Charlton Athletic was voted England's goal of the season in 2001, and he scored two fiercely-struck goals in the 1998 World Cup.

SOUTH AFRICA DREAM TEAM?	
1. Andre Arendse 2. Aaron Mokoena 3. Neil Tovey 4. Jomo Sono 5. Lucas Radebe 6. Mark Fish 7. 'Doctor' Khumalo 8. Patrick Ntsoelengoe 9. Steve Mokone 10. Benni McCarthy 11. Kaizer Motaung	

FACT FILE: SOUTH AFRICA

NICKNAME
Bafana Bafana (The Boys)

TOP GOALSCORERS
1. Benni McCarthy 30 (1997–present)
2. Shaun Bartlett 28 (1995–2005)
3. Phil Masinga 19 (1992–2001)
4. Siyabonga Nomvethe 15 (1999–present)
5. Donald Wilson 11 (1947)

MOST APPEARANCES
1. Shaun Bartlett 74 (1995–2005)
2. John Moshoeu 73 (1993–2004)
3. Lucas Radebe 70 (1992–2003)
= Benni McCarthy 70 (1997–present)
5. Andre Arendse 67 (1995–2004)

TROPHIES/HONOURS
AFRICAN NATIONS CUP
1996 South Africa 2 Tunisia 0

Orlando Pirates and Leeds United supporters admired central defender Lucas Radebe for his inspiring leadership and strength. He captained South Africa's World Cup teams in 1998 and 2002. Since retiring from the game he has become an anti-racism campaigner, FIFA Fair Play Award winner and children's charity worker.

Benni McCarthy in action in the African Cup of Nations qualifying in 2006.

BENNI MCCARTHY

Although South Africa's star striker has enjoyed impressive spells with Ajax Cape Town, Ajax Amsterdam, Celta Vigo and Porto, his international career has been disrupted by disputes with coaches. Despite quitting the team three times, McCarthy is still a folk hero in his native country.

SOCCER CITY
The FNB Stadium, built in Johannesburg in 1987 to house 80,000 spectactors, is being demolished for the World Cup Finals. In its place will be the all-new Soccer City Stadium. Its design inspired by traditional African pottery, the new stadium will allow up to 104,000 people to watch the 2010 World Cup final.

2010
The World Cup Finals are on their way to Africa at last! Just one FIFA delegate's vote denied South Africa the chance to host the 2006 tournament, but now the pressure is on to bring the ambitious plans for 2010 to life. Of the ten venues, five will be entirely new ones with more seats promised per match than at any World Cup since 1994.

CÔTE D'IVOIRE

> "WHEN WE PLAY, ALL OF IVORY COAST IS HAPPY."
>
> MIDFIELDER YAYA TOURÉ

Côte d'Ivoire's (also known as Ivory Coast) first visit to the World Cup Finals in 2006 earned 'the Elephants' many admirers, even if their entertaining football was not quite enough to reach the second round.

Since 2006, the Côte d'Ivoire national team have continued to emerge as a new force in world football, and more and more top-class Ivoirian talents are playing for the world's most prestigious clubs.

The FIF (Fédération Ivoirienne de Football) was founded in 1960.

FACT FILE: CÔTE D'IVOIRE

NICKNAME
Les Éléphants (The Elephants)

TOP GOALSCORERS
1. Didier Drogba 33 (2002–present)
2. Information not available
3. Information not available
4. Information not available
5. Information not available

MOST APPEARANCES
1. Didier Zokora 73 (2000–present)
2. Didier Drogba 52 (2002–present)
3. Cyrille Domoraud 51 (1995–present)
= Bonaventure Kalou 51 (1998–present)
5. Kolo Touré 45 (2000–present)

TROPHIES/HONOURS
AFRICAN CUP OF NATIONS
1992 Côte d'Ivoire 0 Ghana 0
(Côte d'Ivoire won 11–10 in a penalty shoot-out)

Drogba was the top scorer in the English Premier League in 2006–2007 with 20 goals for Chelsea.

DROGBA

Didier Drogba is one of the most prolific strikers in the world today. His pace and power terrify defenders, while his finishing is as graceful as it is clinical. Drogba also uses his status as a sporting hero in his work as a UN Goodwill Ambassador.

Feyenoord forward Bonaventure Kalou scored a decisive penalty to give Côte d'Ivoire a much-deserved victory in the 2006 World Cup Finals. Despite the 3–2 win over Serbia, the promising Africans were edged out by Argentina and the Netherlands in a difficult group.

TOP TALENT

Kolo Touré (right) and his younger brother Yaya are products of the Côte d'Ivoire's flourishing youth academies. Kolo is a versatile defender, while Yaya is a surging midfielder. Watch out for youngest brother Ibrahim, an up-and-coming striker.

DID YOU KNOW?

Laurent Pokou held the record as top African Cup of Nations goalscorer for 38 years. He scored six at the 1968 tournament and then eight more two years later, including five in a single match. Pokou's record was broken in 2008 by Cameroon's Samuel Eto'o.

CÔTE D'IVOIRE DREAM TEAM? 1. Alain Gouaméné 2. Emmanuel Eboué 3. Dominique Sam Abou 4. Didier Zokora 5. Kolo Touré 6. Cyrille Domoraud 7. Bonaventure Kalou 8. Yaya Touré 9. Laurent Pokou 10. Didier Drogba 11. Youssouf Falikou Fofana

GHANA

"FOOTBALL IS NOT SIMPLY THE MOST POPULAR SPORT IN GHANA, IT'S LIKE A RELIGION."

OTTO PFISTER, COACH OF GHANA'S U-17 WORLD CUP WINNERS IN 1991

The Ghana Football association was founded in 1957.

Over the years, Ghana has acquired a reputation for developing dynamic young teams. They won the Under-17s World Cup in 1991 and 1995 and a bronze medal at the 1992 Olympic Games. Like their neighbours and rivals, Côte d'Ivoire, Ghana made their World Cup Finals debut in 2006 but only Egypt have won the African Cup of Nations more times than Ghana's 'Black Stars'.

FACT FILE: GHANA

NICKNAME
The Black Stars

TOP GOALSCORERS
1. Abédi 'Pelé' Ayew 33 (1981–1998)
2. Information not available
3. Information not available
4. Information not available
5. Information not available

MOST APPEARANCES
1. Abédi 'Pelé' Ayew 73 (1981–1998)
2. Information not available
3. Information not available
4. Information not available
5. Information not available

TROPHIES/HONOURS
AFRICAN CUP OF NATIONS
1963 Ghana 3 Sudan 0
1965 Ghana 3 Tunisia 2 (aet)
1978 Ghana 2 Uganda 0
1982 Ghana 1 Libya 1 (Ghana won 7–6 in a penalty shoot-out)

Muntari scored the first goal in Ghana's 2–0 victory over the Czech Republic in the 2006 World Cup Finals.

YOUNG STAR

Midfielder Sulley Muntari is already a firm favourite with Ghana fans thanks to his dazzling dribbling skills and combative playing style. Despite an often fiery temperament, Muntari is a vital part of the Ghana team.

Michael Essien (right) and captain Stephen Appiah were the midfield motors as Ghana – the youngest squad at the 2006 World Cup – became the only African side in the second round. The versatile Essien has long been seen as a future African Footballer of the Year – a prize won by flamboyant Ghana midfielders Ibrahim Sunday in 1971 and Karim Abdul Razak in 1978.

DID YOU KNOW?

The world's first black professional footballer, Arthur Wharton, was born in what is now Accra, Ghana. He played for various teams in the English leagues from 1885 to 1902.

Three-times African Footballer of the Year Abédi 'Pelé' Ayew (left) is arguably one of the greatest ever African footballers and surely worthy of his illustrious nickname. He is Ghana's most capped player as well as the top scorer and he was one of the first African footballers to enjoy success in Europe, in particular with French side Olympique Marseille.

GHANA DREAM TEAM? 1. Robert Mensah 2. Ofei Ansah 3. Kwasi Appiah 4. Michael Essien 5. Samuel Kuffour 6. Charles Addo Odametey 7. Baba Yara 8. Karim Abdul Razak 9. Opoku 'Bayie' Afriyie 10. Abédi 'Pelé' Ayew 11. Mohammed 'Polo' Ahmed

FACT FILE: CAMEROON

NICKNAME
The Indomitable Lions

TOP GOALSCORERS
1. Patrick Mboma 33 (1995-2004)
2. Samuel Eto'o 28 (1996–present)
= Roger Milla 28 (1978–1994)
4. Information not available
5. Information not available)

MOST APPEARANCES
1. Rigobert Song 118 (1993–present)
2. Roger Milla 102 (1978–1994)
3. Lauren 80 (1998–present)
4. Geremi 67 (1996–present)
5. Marc-Vivien Foé 64 (1993–2003)

TROPHIES/HONOURS
AFRICAN CUP OF NATIONS
1984 Cameroon 3 Nigeria 1
1988 Cameroon 1 Nigeria 0
2000 Cameroon 2 Nigeria 2 (aet)
(Cameroon won 4–3 on penalties)
2002 Cameroon 0 Senegal 0 (aet)
(Cameroon won 3–2 on penalties)

OLYMPIC GOLD MEDAL
2000 Cameroon 2 Spain 2
(Cameroon won 5–3
on penalties)

Fédération Camerounaise de Football was founded in 1959.

CAMEROON

"IT'S THANKS TO FOOTBALL THAT A SMALL COUNTRY COULD BECOME GREAT."

CAMEROON LEGEND ROGER MILLA

Cameroon captivated the world when they opened Italia '90 by defeating reigning champions Argentina. They went on to reach the quarter-finals – becoming the first African side ever to do so. Although Cameroon surprisingly missed out on the 2006 World Cup Finals a young side, inspired by the great Samuel Eto'o, are bouncing back confidently.

STAR STRIKER
Samuel Eto'o has never looked back since making his international debut at the age of 15. The lightning-quick striker has averaged almost a goal per game for his country, and picked up an unprecedented hat-trick of African Footballer of the Year prizes in 2003, 2004 and 2005.

Eto'o is a skilled playmaker and strong in defence.

Rigobert Song (above) became the youngest player to be red-carded in a World Cup in 1994, aged 17. He was sent off again four years later but the rugged defender recovered to become Cameroon's most-capped and most reliable player.

Roger Milla (left) came out of semi-retirement to become the hero of the 1990 World Cup Finals. At the age of 38, the veteran Cameroon striker scored four times in Italia '90, celebrating each goal in his unique style. Four years later, at USA '94, Milla became the World Cup's oldest scorer with a goal against Russia.

While Samuel Eto'o has created headlines with big-money moves to Real Madrid and Barcelona, it is actually fellow forward Patrick Mboma who is Cameroon's all-time top scorer. Mboma was also the leading scorer in the 2000 and 2002 African Cup of Nations campaigns and African Footballer of the Year in 2000.

CAMEROON DREAM TEAM? 1. Thomas Nkono 2. Rigobert Song 3. Lauren 4. Marc-Vivien Foé 5. Stephen Tataw 6. Emmanuel Kundé 7. Geremi 8. Théophile Abega 9. Patrick Mboma 10. Roger Milla 11. Samuel Eto'o

NIGERIA

"WE ARE STILL THE TEAM TO BEAT IN AFRICA. EVERY GAME FOR US IS LIKE A FINAL."

FORMER NIGERIA CAPTAIN JAY-JAY OKOCHA

The Nigeria Football Association was founded in 1945.

When the 'Super Eagles' are soaring, their blend of exuberant passing and awesome power inspires dreams of a first African World Cup winner. They certainly have the potential: Nigeria's 'Golden Eaglets' won the U-17 World Championships in 1985, 1993 and 2007. The senior team won Olympic gold in 1996 but so far have not gone beyond the second round of the World Cup Finals.

NWANKWO KANU

As a teenager, striker Nwankwo Kanu (right) was part of Nigeria's 1993 U-17 World Championship winning team. Three years later he added an Olympic gold medal and now, over a decade later, Kanu is Nigeria's captain.

Like long-time captain Augustine 'Jay-Jay' Okocha, Obafemi Martins (above) not only scores and sets up breathtaking goals, he celebrates them with acrobatic style. Two-times Young African Footballer of the Year Martins is spearheading a Nigerian revival alongside powerful midfield prodigy Mikel Jon Obi.

Nwankwo Kanu has won more major medals than any other African footballer.

FACT FILE: NIGERIA

NICKNAME
Super Eagles

TOP GOALSCORERS
1. Rashidi Yekini 37 (1984–1998)
2. Segun Odegbami 24 (1976–1981)
3. Sunday Oyarekhua 17 (1971–1975)
4. Samson Siasia 16 (1989–1998)
= Yakuba Aiyegbeni 16 (2000–present)

MOST APPEARANCES
1. Muda Lawal 86 (1975–1985)
2. 'Jay-Jay' Okocha 74 (1993–2006)
3. Nwankwo Kanu 70 (1994–present)
4. Peter Rufai 68 (1981–1998)
5. Finidi George 66 (1991–2002)

TROPHIES/HONOURS
AFRICAN CUP OF NATIONS
1980 Nigeria 3 Algeria 0
1994 Nigeria 2 Zambia 1

OLYMPIC GOLD MEDAL
1996 Nigeria 3 Argentina 2

All-time top scorer, Rashidi Yekini (left) scored Nigeria's first ever World Cup Finals' goal in USA '94, in a 3–0 win over Bulgaria. Strikers Yekini and Daniel Amokachi, plus wingers Tijani Babandiga and Finidi George, inspired Nigeria to the second round of the tournament.

Nigeria clinched their first major trophy in the year they first hosted the African Cup of Nations, beating Algeria 3–0 in 1980 before 80,000 fans in Lagos. Captain and future coach Christian Chukwu lifted the trophy after two goals from Segun Odegbami and one from Muda Lawal. Further success came 14 years later in Tunisia, when Nigeria beat Zambia in the final and Yekini won the Golden Boot.

NIGERIA DREAM TEAM? 1. Peter Rufai 2. Christian Chukwu 3. Taribo West 4. Augustine 'Jay-Jay' Okocha 5. Stephen Keshi 6. Uche Okechukwu 7. Finidi George 8. Segun Odegbami 9. Rashidi Yekini 10. Nwankwo Kanu 11. Emmanuel Amuneke

AFRICAN TEAMS

"AFRICAN FOOTBALL IS DEVELOPING AND GETTING BETTER ALL THE TIME."

FORMER GHANA COACH FREDERICK OSAM-DUODU

The 2006 World Cup demonstrated African football's increasing strength and depth as surprise packages, including Angola and Togo, made their debuts. More widely recognised heavyweights such as Nigeria, Cameroon and South Africa did not even qualify. So, with the likes of Mali also emerging fast, competition for Africa's five remaining places in 2010 looks set to be more exhilarating than ever.

SENEGAL

Senegalese football seemed to burst from nowhere in 2002 when they reached their first African Cup of Nations final and then beat holders France 1–0 in the opening game of the World Cup Finals. The 'Lions of Teranga' made it as far as the quarter-finals in that tournament.

Two-time African Footballer of the Year El Hadji Diouf has led Senegal's rise from outsiders to contenders.

FACT FILE
TOP GOALSCORERS
Mamadou Diallo 21 (1994–2000)
= Henri Camara 21 (1999–present)

MOST APPEARANCES
Henri Camara 52 (1999–present)

TROPHIES/HONOURS
none

TUNISIA

Tunisia made history in 1978 when they became the first African country to win a match at a World Cup Finals. They came from behind to beat Mexico 3–1 in the tournament hosted by Argentina. They took 20 years to return to the Finals, but were the only Africans there in both 2002 and 2006. Their first African Cup of Nations triumph came in 2004.

Brazil-born striker Francileudo Santos scored four times for Tunisia at the 2004 African Cup of Nations, including this opener in the final against Morocco.

FACT FILE
TOP GOALSCORER
Francileudo Dos Santos 22 (2004–present)

MOST APPEARANCES
Sadok Sassi 'Attouga' 110 (1964–1978)

TROPHIES/HONOURS
AFRICAN CUP OF NATIONS
2004 Tunisia 2 Morocco 1

ALGERIA

Despite a shock 2–1 win over West Germany in the 1982 World Cup Finals, Algeria were denied the chance of being the first African team to make it to the second round thanks to Germany's win over Austria in the final group game. Algeria returned to the Finals in 1986, but have not qualified since then.

West German defender Paul Breitner tries to control the ball under pressure from Algerian midfielder Mustapha Dahleb during the 1982 World Cup Finals.

FACT FILE
TOP GOALSCORER
Rabah Madjer 40 (1978–1992)

MOST APPEARANCES
Mahieddine Meftah 107 (unknown)

TROPHIES/HONOURS
AFRICAN CUP OF NATIONS
1990 Algeria 1 Nigeria 0

GUINEA

Guinea still await a World Cup debut, despite some success in Europe for players including Titi Camara at Marseille and Liverpool and Bobo Baldé at Toulouse and Celtic. It remains to be seen when Guinea will emerge from the shadows of its more famous neighbours Mali, Senegal and Côte d'Ivoire.

FACT FILE
TOP GOALSCORERS
Information not available

MOST APPEARANCES
Information not available

TROPHIES/HONOURS

EGYPT

Predictably nicknamed 'The Pharaohs', Egypt have reigned supreme a record six times in the African Cup of Nations and given African football some of its most revered names – from 1928 Olympics semi-finals star Mukhtar Al-Tetsh to Hossam Hassan in the modern era.

FACT FILE

TOP GOALSCORERS
Hossam Hassan 80 (1985–2006)

MOST APPEARANCES
Hossam Hassan 170 (1985–2006)

TROPHIES/HONOURS
AFRICAN CUP OF NATIONS
1957 Egypt 4 Ethiopia 0
1959 Egypt 2 Sudan 1
1986 Egypt 0 Cameroon 0 (Egypt won 5–4 in a penalty shoot-out)
1998 Egypt 2 South Africa 0
2006 Egypt 0 Côte d'Ivoire 0 (Egypt won 4–2 in a penalty shoot-out)
2008 Egypt 1 Cameroon 0

Hosts Egypt became the first country to win the African Cup of Nations five times when they beat Côte d'Ivoire on penalties in front of an ecstatic Cairo crowd in February 2006.

MOROCCO

In 1986 Morocco became the first African team to top a World Cup first round group. They finished ahead of England, Poland and Portugal to qualify for the second round. They lost 1–0 to eventual tournament runners-up West Germany.

FACT FILE

TOP GOALSCORERS
Salaheddine Bassir 43 (unknown–2005)

MOST APPEARANCES
Noureddine Naybet 115 (1990–2006)

TROPHIES/HONOURS
AFRICAN CUP OF NATIONS
1976 (round-robin league tournament)

ANGOLA

Angola made their World Cup Finals debut in 2006 and earned creditable draws with Mexico and Iran, but lost 1–0 to former colonial rulers Portugal and did not progress beyond the group stage.

FACT FILE

TOP GOALSCORERS
Fabrice 'Akwá' Maieco 36 (1995–present)

MOST APPEARANCES
Fabrice 'Akwá' Maieco 80 (1995–present)

TROPHIES/HONOURS
none

MALI

Mali played their first World Cup qualifier in 2000 and look like a force for the future thanks to stars such as Fredi Kanouté and Mahamadou Diarra.

FACT FILE

TOP GOALSCORERS
Information not available

MOST APPEARANCES
Information not available

TROPHIES/HONOURS
none

TOGO

Togo's first World Cup Finals in 2006 involved three defeats and a threatened strike by the players. However, just reaching the Finals tournament was a positive sign for the tiny West African nation.

FACT FILE

TOP GOALSCORERS
Emmanuel Adebayor 16 (2000–present)

MOST APPEARANCES
Jean-Paul Abolo 67 (1992–present)

TROPHIES/HONOURS
none

LIBERIA

Although they have never reached the World Cup Finals, George Weah put Liberian football on the world map. He also coached and funded Liberia, or 'The Lone Stars'.

Founded 1936

Striker George Weah is the only African so far to become FIFA World Player of the Year (in 1995). In 2005 Weah, unsuccessfully, ran for president in Liberia.

FACT FILE

TOP GOALSCORERS
James Debbah 42 (1988–2004)

MOST APPEARANCES
Joe Nagbe 96 (1985–2001)

TROPHIES/HONOURS
none

DEMOCRATIC REPUBLIC OF CONGO

DR Congo's golden age was 1974. Under their former name, Zaire, they won their second African Cup of Nations and made their only World Cup Finals appearance so far.

FACT FILE

TOP GOALSCORERS
Lomana LuaLua 17 (2002–present)

MOST APPEARANCES
Information not available

TROPHIES/HONOURS
AFRICAN CUP OF NATIONS
1968 Congo-Kinshasa (now DR Congo) 1 Ghana 0
1974 Zaire (now DR Congo) 2 Zambia 0

AFRICA DREAM TEAM? 1. Badou Zaki (Morocco) 2. Hatem Trabelsi (Tunisia) 3. Pierre Kalala (DR Congo) 4. Lakhdar Belloumi (Algeria) 5. Ibrahim Youssef (Egypt) 6. Noureddine Naybet (Morocco) 7. Mahmoud El-Khatib (Egypt) 8. Kalusha Bwalya (Zambia) 9. George Weah (Liberia) 10. Hossam Hassan (Egypt) 11. Salif Keita (Mali)

MONGOLIA

DEMOCRATIC
PEOPLES
REPUBLIC OF
KOREA

UZBEKISTAN

KYRGYZSTAN

TURKMENISTAN

TAJIKISTAN

CHINA

SYRIA
LEBANON
JORDAN

IRAQ

IRAN

AFGHANISTAN

REPUBLIC
OF KOREA

KUWAIT

PAKISTAN

BHUTAN

QATAR

NEPAL

SAUDIA
ARABIA

UNITED
ARAB
EMIRATES

INDIA

BANGLADESH

LAOS

OMAN

BURMA

VIETNAM

YEMEN

THAILAND

CAMBODIA

BRUNEI

SRI LANKA

MALAYSIA

SINGAPORE

ASIA

"THE FUTURE IS ASIA"

AFC MOTTO

INDONESIA

When co-hosts the Republic of Korea (also known as South Korea) lined up to play Germany in the semi-final of the 2002 World Cup Finals it was the first time an Asian side had reached that stage of the tournament. Although Korea lost the match 1–0, they proved that Asian teams were serious international contenders. Making a bigger impact on the world stage is a prime objective for this region, and a major plan is under way to revitalise the domestic leagues in ambitious countries such as China, Japan, Iran and of course, the Republic of Korea.

Founded in 1954, the AFC (Asian Football Confederation) is divided into four sub groups: East Asia, containing the Rebublic of Korea, Democratic People's Republic of Korea, China and Japan; West Asia, covering the Middle East; Central and South Asia, including India and Pakistan; and the ASEAN representing Southeast Asia and, since 2006, Australia.

OCEANIA

"WE HAVE SHOWN THAT THE SOUTH PACIFIC CAN PRODUCE EXCEPTIONAL FOOTBALL TALENT."
OFC PRESIDENT REYNALD REMARII

Formed in 1966, by Australia, New Zealand and Fiji, the OFC (Oceania Football Confederation) is the smallest and also the weakest of the world's football confederations. Of its current eleven members, only one has ever qualified for the World Cup Finals – New Zealand, who failed to get past the group stage in 1982.

Beautiful tropical paradises are not generally noted for their footballing success, but places like the Solomon Islands, Tahiti and Fiji provide stunning locations for the beautiful game to thrive in. Since the departure of Australia in 2006, many of the Oceania federation national teams hover dangerously close to the bottom of FIFA's rankings. However, even in this success-starved region, the game of football can boast many passionate followers.

DID YOU KNOW?

Kuwait set a new international record when they beat Bhutan 20–0 in February 2000. However, they only held onto the record for 14 months as in 2001 Australia beat Tonga 22–0 and then thrashed American Samoa 31–0 in the same year.

JAPAN • PHILIPPINES • NORTHERN MARIANA ISLANDS • REPUBLIC OF THE MARSHALL ISLANDS • GUAM • FEDERATED STATES OF MICRONESIA • PALAU • NAURU • PAPUA NEW GUINEA • KIRIBATI • INDONESIA • SOLOMON ISLANDS • TUVALU • SAMOA • AMERICAN SAMOA • COOK ISLANDS • FIJI • NIUE • VANUATU • TONGA • TAHITI • NEW CALEDONIA • AUSTRALIA • NEW ZEALAND

SUPER-POLITE FANS

This eye-catching South Korean is a member of a fan group known as the Red Devils and dresses accordingly. However, despite their devilish tastes in fancy dress, South Korean supporters are universally admired for their politeness and respect for opposing fans.

THE MIDDLE EAST

Middle East football has known mixed fortunes over the years. However, in this often turbulent region, football is widely welcomed as a force for peace, unity and hope. Iraq's 2007 Asian Cup victory was a major boost not only for the war-torn country but also for the Middle East region as a whole.

IRAN

Iranian football entered a golden age in 1968 with three consecutive Asian Cups, gold at the 1974 Asian Games and a draw with Scotland at the 1978 World Cup Finals. Modern day heroes Mehdi Mahdavikia and Ali Karimi hope to emulate that success.

Striker Ali Daei (above) has scored more international goals than any man on earth – 109 in 149 games since his international debut in 1993. He was appointed national coach in 2008.

ISRAEL

Israel were runners-up in the first two AFC Asian Cups in 1956 and 1960 and eventually won the tournament in 1964. All-time top scorer Mordechai Spiegler skippered the side at their first World Cup Finals in 1970. While Israel haven't yet returned to the Finals, they ran France and Switzerland close in the 2006 qualifiers. Israel left the AFC in 1994 to join UEFA and Israeli club sides also participate in European competitions.

Founded 1928

FACT FILE

TOP GOALSCORER
Mordechai Spiegler 32 (1963–1977)

MOST APPEARANCES
Arik Benado 95 (1998–present)

TROPHIES/HONOURS
AFC ASIAN CUP
1964 (round-robin league tournament)

When Iran faced the USA at the 1998 World Cup Finals, the two teams symbolically exchanged flowers before kick-off. Iran won 2–1 thanks to goals from Hamid Reza Estili and Mehdi Mahdavikia.

FACT FILE

TOP GOALSCORER
Ali Daei 109 (1993–2006)

MOST APPEARANCES
Ali Daei 149 (1993–2006)

TROPHIES/ HONOURS
AFC ASIAN CUP
1968 (round-robin league tournament)
1972 Iran 2 Korea Republic 2 (aet)
1976 Iran 1 Kuwait 0

SAUDI ARABIA

Saudi Arabia have won the Asian Cup three times. They first visited the World Cup Finals in 1994, reaching the second round and have qualified for every Finals since.

Founded 1959

FACT FILE

TOP GOALSCORER
Majed Abdullah 67 (1977–1994)

MOST APPEARANCES
Mohammed Al-Deayea 181 (1990–2006)

TROPHIES/HONOURS

AFC ASIAN CUP
1984 Saudi Arabia 2 China 1
1988 Saudi Arabia 0 Korea Republic 0 (Saudi Arabia won 4–3 in a penalty shoot-out)
1996 Saudi Arabia 0 United Arab Emirates 0 (Saudi Arabia won 4–2 in a penalty shoot-out)

Saeed Al-Owairan's surging 70-yard solo effort against Belgium in 1998 was one of the World Cup's greatest-ever goals.

IRAQ

Iraqi players, officials and fans were happy just to reach the 2007 AFC Asian Cup, after years of repression under the Ba'ath regime. But in one of football's biggest upsets, they beat Saudi Arabia 1–0 in the final. Perhaps it should not have been a complete surprise – Iraq were also semi-finalists at the 2004 Olympic Games in Athens.

Iraq captain Younis Mahmoud scored the winning goal in the 2007 Asian Cup final. Goalkeepr Noor Sabri also put in a match-winning performance.

FACT FILE

TOP GOALSCORER
Hussein Saeed 63 (1976–1990)

MOST APPEARANCES
Hussein Saeed 126 (1976–1990)

TROPHIES/HONOURS
AFC ASIAN CUP
2007 Iraq 1 Saudi Arabia 0

MIDDLE EAST DREAM TEAM? 1. Mohammed Al-Deayea (Saudi Arabia) 2. Mehdi Mahdavikia (Iran) 3. Bassim Abbas (Iraq) 4. Avi Nimni (Israel) 5. Rahman Rezaei (Iran) 6. Tal Ben-Haim (Israel) 7. Ali Karimi (Iran) 8. Saeed Al-Owairan (Saudi Arabia) 9. Ali Daei (Iran) 10. Majed Abdullah (Saudi Arabia) 11. Mordechai Spiegler (Israel)

UNITED ARAB EMIRATES

Although nearly 85 per cent of the United Arab Emirates' population are foreign citizens, the national team still managed to reach the 1990 World Cup Finals. However, Brazilan coach Mario Zagallo was sacked just before the tournament and the UAE lost all three games. The UAE also lost the 1996 Asian Cup final to Saudi Arabia in a penalty shoot-out.

FACT FILE

TOP GOALSCORER
Adnan Al-Talyani 53 (1983–1997)

MOST APPEARANCES
Adnan Al-Talyani 164 (1983–1997)

TROPHIES/HONOURS
none

Adnan Al-Talyani is UAE's most prolific scorer and most capped player. In fact only three men in the world have won more international caps than the UAE striker.

LEBANON

Lebanon became members of FIFA as early as 1935 but have had little to cheer about since then, apart from a successful hosting of the 2000 AFC Asian Cup Finals.

FACT FILE

TOP GOALSCORER
Roda Antar 23 (2000–present)

MOST APPEARANCES
Roda Antar 48 (2000–present)

TROPHIES/HONOURS
none

PALESTINE

FIFA recognised Palestine as an independent football association in 1998. A troubled home land means that the team play in Qatar and train in Egypt.

FACT FILE

TOP GOALSCORER
Fahed Attal 12 (unknown)

MOST APPEARANCES
Information not available

TROPHIES/HONOURS
none

QATAR'S

long-awaited emergence seemed to be underway when striker Khalfan Ibrahim was named the 2006 Asian Footballer of the Year. In the same year Qatar triumphed in both the Asian Games and the Arab world's Gulf Cup.

FACT FILE

TOP GOALSCORER
Information not available

MOST APPEARANCES
Information not available

TROPHIES/HONOURS
none

KUWAIT

won the Asian Cup in 1980 and also created one of the World Cup's most bizarre moments in 1982, when the team stormed off the field until a French 'goal' was disallowed for offside.

FACT FILE

TOP GOALSCORER
Bashar Abdullah 75 (1996–present)

MOST APPEARANCES
Bashar Abdullah 134 (1996–present)

TROPHIES/HONOURS
AFC ASIAN CUP 1980
Kuwait 3 Korea Republic 0

BAHRAIN

were FIFA's most improved side in 2004, after rising 95 places to 44th in the rankings in four years. They also achieved their best-ever fourth in that year's Asian Cup.

FACT FILE

TOP GOALSCORER
A'ala Hubail 30 (2003–present)

MOST APPEARANCES
Abdulrazzaq Mohamed 102 (unknown)

TROPHIES/HONOURS
none

SYRIA

Syria's finest hour came when they won the 1994 AFC Youth Championship by beating Japan 2–1 in the final.

FACT FILE

TOP GOALSCORER
Information not available

MOST APPEARANCES
Information not available

TROPHIES/HONOURS
none

JORDAN

Jordan achieved their highest FIFA ranking of 37 in 2004, after qualifying for their first ever Asian Cup and then reaching the quarter-finals.

FACT FILE

TOP GOALSCORER
Information not available

MOST APPEARANCES
Information not available

TROPHIES/HONOURS
none

OMAN

Although Oman are still yet to reach the World Cup Finals or get through the Asian Cup's first round, they are ranked in FIFA's top 100 teams.

FACT FILE

TOP GOALSCORER
Amad Al-Hosni (unknown)

MOST APPEARANCES
Information not available

TROPHIES/HONOURS
none

YEMEN

South Yemen played in the 1976 Asian Cup, where they lost heavily to Iran, before the creation of a united Yemen side in 1990.

FACT FILE

TOP GOALSCORER
Information not available

MOST APPEARANCES
Information not available

TROPHIES/HONOURS

REPUBLIC OF KOREA

"KOREAN PEOPLE LOVE THE NATIONAL TEAM AND THEIR SUPPORT... IS INCREDIBLE."

AFSHIN GHOTBI, ASSISTANT COACH AT THE 2002 AND 2006 WORLD CUPS

FACT FILE: REPUBLIC OF KOREA

NICKNAMES
Taeguk Warriors, Tigers, Red Devils

TOP GOALSCORERS
1. Cha Bum-Kun 55 (1972–1986)
2. Hwang-Sun-Hong 50 (1988–2002)
3. Choi Soon-Ho 30 (1980–1991)
= Kim Do-Hoon 30 (1994–2003)
5. Choi Yong-Soo 27 1995–2003)

MOST APPEARANCES
1. Hong Myung-Bo 135 (1990–2002)
2. Yoo-Sang-Chul 122 (1994–2004)
3. Cha Bum-Kun 121 (1972–1986
4. Lee Woon-Jae 109 (1994–2007)
5. Hwang Sun-Hong 103 (1988–2002)

TROPHIES/HONOURS
AFC ASIAN CUP
1956 Republic of Korea 4 Taiwan 1 (agg)
1960 Republic of Korea 1 China 0

The Republic of Korea experienced unexpected glory in 2002 when they co-hosted the World Cup Finals. Thanks to manager Guus Hiddink's astute leadership, some exciting young players and passionate fans, the team reached the semi finals. Life since then has been a bit of an anti-climax but South Korean football continues to draw well-earned respect worldwide.

KFA
The Korea Football Association was founded in 1928.

Park Ji-Sung was a hero when his volley beat Portugal in the 2002 World Cup.

CHA BUM-KUN
Cha Bum-Kun was nicknamed 'Cha Boom', and any goalkeeper who tried to stop one of his shots knew why. The striker's move to Germany in 1977 paved the way for other Asian footballers to move to Europe, but few could emulate Cha's ability and his achievements. Many young Germans grew up idolising him, including Michael Ballack, Jürgen Klinsmann and Oliver Kahn.

PARK JI-SUNG
Manchester United's Park Ji-Sung played under manager Guus Hiddink for both South Korea and PSV Eindhoven. In fact it was Hiddink who made the wise decision to switch Park from a defensive midfield role to the wing.

DID YOU KNOW?
In the 1977 Park's Cup, Korea were losing 4–1 to Malaysia before Cha Bum-Kun scored an amazing seven-minute hat-trick to level the score.

Ahn Jung-Hwan paid a high price for the greatest moment of his footballing career – the golden goal that knocked Italy out of the 2002 World Cup in the second round. His Italian employers Perugia fired the striker, saying he had "ruined Italian soccer".

As a classy centre-back and rallying captain, Hong Myung-Bo provided a firm foundation for the 2002 World Cup team. He was voted the tournament's third best player before retiring with a record 135 caps.

REPUBLIC OF KOREA DREAM TEAM? 1. Lee Woon-Jae 2. Choi Jin-Cheul 3. Lee Young-Pyo 4. Song Chong-Gug 5. Hong Myung-Bo 6. Kim Tae-Young 7. Park Ji-Sung 8. Kim Nam-Il 9. Cha Bum-Kun 10. Kim Joo-Sung 11. Seol Ki-Hyeon

JAPAN

"OUR FANS ARE AMONG THE BEST IN THE WORLD." TAKESHI OKADA, JAPAN MANAGER AT THE '98 WORLD CUP

The Japan Football Association was formed in 1921. Its symbol is a mythical three-legged raven.

After decades living in the shadow of sports such as baseball, table-tennis and martial arts, Japanese football came of age when the new professional J-League was launched in 1993. A successful co-hosting of the World Cup followed in 2002. This, combined with AFC Asian Cup triumphs in 2000 and 2004, has elevated football to the second most popular sport in Japan.

KAZU

After leaving for Brazil aged 15 and playing for Pelé's old team Santos, Kazuyoshi Miura (left) returned to Japan in 1990. Known as 'Kazu', the super striker won the first two J-League Championships with Verdy Kawasaki before becoming 1993 Asian Footballer of the Year and then joining Genoa in Italy. Kazu famously performed a unique dance when he scored a great goal.

Shunsuke Nakamura (right) is a midfield playmaker and free-kick specialist who has played for both Reggina in Italy and Celtic in Scotland. Although he did not feature in Japan's 2002 World Cup squad, he later returned to the team. He was Japan's star performer in their 2004 Asian Cup victory and scored Japan's opening goal against Australia in the 2006 World Cup.

Takahara previously played for Japanese club Júbilo Iwata.

Central midfielder Hidetoshi Nakata (left) was a key part of Japan's football boom. Although Junichi Inamoto scored more goals and Kazuyuki Toda had even brighter dyed hair, it was Nakata who captured the hearts of the Japanese people. His 2001 Serie A title with AS Roma was celebrated across Japan, but his decision to retire after the 2006 World Cup at the age of 29 was a major shock.

FACT FILE: JAPAN

NICKNAMES
Nihon Daihyo (Japanese Representatives), Blues, Blue Samurai

TOP GOALSCORERS
1. Kunishige Kamamoto 55 (1964–1977)
=. Kazuyoshi Miura 55 (1990–2000)
3. Takuya Takagi 28 (1992–1997)
4. Hiromi Hara 24 (1978–1988)
5. Naohiro Takahara 23 (2000–present)

MOST APPEARANCES
1. Masami Ihara 122 (1988–1999)
2. Yoshikatsu Kawaguchi 114 (1997–present)
3. Kazuyoshi Miura 89 (1990–2000)
4. Alessandro Dos Santos 82 (2002–present)
5. Hidetoshi Nakata 77 (1997–present)

TROPHIES/HONOURS
AFC ASIAN CUP
1992 Japan 1 Saudi Arabia 0
2000 Japan 1 Saudi Arabia 0
2004 Japan 3 China 1

TAKAHARA

Japan and Eintracht Frankfurt striker Naohiro Takahara was joint top scorer at the 2007 Asian Cup. In 2001 he became the first Japanese player in the Argentine first division when he was loaned to Boca Juniors.

DID YOU KNOW?

Kunishige Kamamoto's seven goals made him the top scorer at the 1968 Summer Olympics in Mexico City, where Japan won the bronze medal. Kamamoto is Japan's all-time top scorer and has now swapped football for politics.

JAPAN DREAM TEAM? 1. Yoshikatsu Kawaguchi 2. Akira Kaji 3. Koji Nakata 4. Hidetoshi Nakata 5. Tsuneyasu Miyamoto 6. Masami Ihara 7. Junichi Inamoto 8. Shunsuke Nakamura 9. Kunishige Kamamoto 10. Kazuyoshi Miura 11. Yasuhiko Okudera

CHINA

"FOOTBALL IS VERY MUCH IN THE HEARTS OF THE CHINESE PEOPLE."

ARIE HAAN, CHINA MANAGER 2002–2004

The Chinese Football Association was originally founded in 1924, but it was replaced by a new body in 1949 after the country became the People's Republic of China.

In 2004 Dong Fangzhuo moved from Dalian Shide to Manchester United, but the young striker and winger had to wait three years for his United debut.

Over the years, China has struggled to make a significant impact on the world of football. However, recent years have brought encouraging signs such as qualifying for their first World Cup in 2002 – although they lost all three games without scoring. A professional domestic league is also gaining ground and football is rapidly becoming a popular sport amongst a population of 1.3 billion.

HAO HAIDONG

Talented striker Hao Haidong (far left) scored a record 41 goals in 115 appearances for his country. His status as China's greatest football figure is challenged only by fellow forward Lee Wei Tong, captain of the country's 1936 Olympic team and later a vice-president of FIFA.

China have twice finished AFC Asian Cup runners-up, but perhaps the country's finest achievement was to hold then world champions Brazil to a 0–0 draw in 2002. Ronaldo, Ronaldinho and Rivaldo could find no way past inspired goalkeeper Liu Yunfei, while Sun Jihai came agonisingly close to a glorious winner.

FACT FILE: CHINA

NICKNAMES
Team China, Guozu (National Foot), Guojia Dui (National Team)

TOP GOALSCORERS
1. Hao Haidong 41 (1992–2004)
2. Liu Haiguang 36 (1983–1990)
3. Ma Lin 33 (1984–1990)
4. Li Hui 28 (1983–1988)
5. Su Maozhen 26 (1992–2002)

MOST APPEARANCES
1. Li Ming 141 (1992–2004)
2. Jia Xiuquan 136 (1983–1992)
3. Fan Zhiyi 132 (1992–2002)
4. Xie Yuxin 120 (1987–1996)
5. Li Fusheng 119 (1976–1984)

TROPHIES/HONOURS
none

ZHENG ZHI

He calls himself the best Chinese player of his generation, and Zheng Zhi's confidence is matched by his versatility. Although he is best known as a goalscoring midfielder and occasional forward, he began his international career as a defender.

Zheng Zhi's work rate makes him an ideal captain.

DID YOU KNOW?

In China an estimated TV audience of 250 million people watched their team lose 3–1 to Japan in the 2004 Asian Cup final, a Chinese record for a sporting event.

CHINA DREAM TEAM? 1. Ou Chuliang 2. Zheng Zhi 3. Sun Jihai 4. Li Ming 5. Fan Zhiyi 6. Jia Xiuquan 7. Li Tie 8. Shao Jia Yi 9. Hao Haidong 10. Lee Wei Tong 11. Yang Chen

AUSTRALIA

"THE FUTURE IS ALWAYS BRIGHT FOR AUSTRALIAN FOOTBALL"

HARRY KEWELL

The Australian Soccer Association was founded in 1961 and is now called Football Federation Australia.

Like the USA, Australia is not yet as dominant in football as it is in other sports. The team failed to score in their first World Cup in 1974, but after a long wait they returned in 2006 and only an injury-time penalty for Italy denied them a place in the quarter-finals. After years of record wins in Oceania, Australia left to join the more competitive AFC in 2006.

As a 17-year-old, Harry Kewell left the Australian Academy of Sport to join England's Leeds United. A nimble and dangerous striker and Australia's youngest international, Kewell moved to Liverpool in 2003 where he has most often played on the left wing. Although Kewell's career has been hampered by injury in recent years, his reputation as perhaps the most talented Australian footballer of all time remains.

Tim Cahill scored Australia's first World Cup Finals goal in a dramatic 3–1 win over Japan. The tough-tackling midfielder also has a welcome knack of scoring regularly.

FACT FILE: AUSTRALIA
NICKNAME
Socceroos

TOP GOALSCORERS
1. Damian Mori 29 (1992–2002)
2. John Aloisi 27 (1997–present)
3. John Kosmina 25 (1977–1988)
= Attila Abonyi 25 (1967–1977)
5. Archie Thompson 21 (2001–present)
= David Zdrilic 21 (1997–present)

MOST APPEARANCES
1. Alex Tobin 87 (1988–1998)
2. Paul Wade 84 (1986–1996)
3. Tony Vidmar 76 (1991–2006)
4. Peter Wilson 64 (1970–1977)
5. Brett Emerton 62 (1998–present)

TROPHIES/HONOURS
OFC NATIONS CUP
1980 Australia 4 Tahiti 2
1996 Australia 11 Tahiti 0 (agg)
2000 Australia 2 New Zealand 0
2004 Australia 11 Solomon Islands 1 (agg)

Australia captain Mark Viduka hugs coach Guus Hiddink during his nation's impressive 2006 World Cup Finals. Often criticised for his physique, Viduka is a deft finisher and even the strongest defenders struggle to battle him off the ball.

The Australian team before their second round match against Italy in the 2006 World Cup Finals.

SOCCEROOS

Australia lost World Cup play-offs to Argentina in 1993, Iran in 1997 and Uruguay in 2001. When they finally beat Uruguay in 2005 to qualify for the 2006 World Cup Finals, their long-suffering fans were ecstatic.

DID YOU KNOW?

Australia claimed a world record for the highest score in an international when they beat American Samoa 31–0 in April 2001. Striker Archie Thompson scored a record 13 goals but was not picked for the Socceroos' next game.

AUSTRALIA DREAM TEAM?   1. Mark Bosnich 2. Joe Marston 3. Tony Vidmar 4. Ned Zelic 5. Peter Wilson 6. Craig Moore 7. Mark Bresciano 8. Johnny Warren 9. Frank Farina 10. Mark Viduka 11. Harry Kewell

ASIA AND OCEANIA

"THIS IS A FOOTBALL CONTINENT. I CAN'T THINK OF ONE COUNTRY IN ASIA THAT IS NOT INTERESTED IN FOOTBALL."
PETER VELAPPAN, AFC GENERAL SECRETARY UNTIL 2007

Football has a long-standing tradition in many parts of Asia, In fact early 20th century Philippines striker Paulino Alcántara still holds the scoring record for Spanish club Barcelona with 357 goals in as many games. Staging the 2007 Asian Cup in four countries – Indonesia, Malaysia, Thailand and Vietnam – showed just how important football is across the whole continent. In Oceania, New Zealand are the likeliest candidates for international glory.

THAILAND

Thailand have been South-East Asian Games football champions 12 times but they are still striving for their big international breakthrough, despite the firepower of strikers Piyapong Piew-on and Kiatisuk Senamuang.

Kiatisuk 'Zico' Senamuang is nicknamed after the legendary Brazilian footballer and manager as a tribute to his lethal finishing and South American-style flamboyance. He worked as a policeman before becoming a professional footballer and has played in Malaysia, Singapore and Vietnam.

FACT FILE
TOP GOALSCORER
Piyapong Piew-on 103 (1981–1997)
MOST APPEARANCES
Kiatisuk Senamuang 130 (1993–present)

TROPHIES/HONOURS
none

After beating Cambodia in 1972, Thailand waited 35 years for their next win in an Asian Cup Finals match. Victory came in front of their home fans in Bangkok, as Oman had no answer to Pipat Thonkanya's two goals in the 2007 group match.

NEW ZEALAND

NEW ZEALAND FOOTBALL
Founded 1891

Australia's transfer to the AFC leaves New Zealand as Oceania's dominant team and has boosted their chances of representing the region at a World Cup Finals, as they did in 1982. The 'All Whites' may lack the prestige of the country's cricket and rugby teams, but players such as Blackburn Rovers defender Ryan Nelsen hope to change that.

FACT FILE
TOP GOALSCORER
Vaughan Coveny 30 (1992–present)
MOST APPEARANCES
Steve Sumner 105 (1976–1988)

TROPHIES/HONOURS
OFC NATIONS CUP
1973 (round-robin league tournament)
1998 New Zealand 1 Australia 0
2002 New Zealand 1 Australia 0

New Zealand football owes much to the 1957 emigration of England international Ken Armstrong (left). The ex-Chelsea midfielder helped the game gain popularity while also playing for several clubs. He made 13 appearances for his adopted country.

ASIA DREAM TEAM? 1. R Arumugam (Malaysia) 2. Ryan Nelsen (New Zealand) 3. Adrian Elrick (New Zealand) 4. Steve Sumner (New Zealand) 5. Ku Kam Fai (Hong Kong) 6. Soh Chin Aun (Malaysia) 7. Pak Doo-Ik (Korea DPR) 8. Mirjalol Kasymov (Uzbekistan) 9. Paulino Alcántara (Philippines) 10. Mokhtar Dahari (Malaysia) 11. Wynton Rufer (New Zealand)

DPR KOREA

North Korea had an astounding 1966 World Cup Finals. Their all-out attacking style knocked out Italy and they raced into a 3–0 lead against Portugal, only to lose 5–3. However, international obscurity has followed since then.

FACT FILE

TOP GOALSCORER
Information not available

MOST APPEARANCES
Information not available

TROPHIES/HONOURS
none

Pak Doo-Ik's goal beat Italy in the 1966 World Cup Finals.

HONG KONG

Although Hong Kong has been reunified with China since 1997, it has a separate national team. Playing as Hong Kong China, the team's biggest win was 15–0 against Guam in 2005.

FACT FILE

TOP GOALSCORER
Information not available

MOST APPEARANCES
Information not available

TROPHIES/HONOURS
none

VIETNAM

Reaching the quarter-finals of their first Asian Cup in 2007 was a boost for co-hosts Vietnam. A unified Vietnam team – combining South and North – only began playing together in 1991 and hopes are high for future success.

FACT FILE

TOP GOALSCORER
Lê Huynh Dúc 30 (1995–2002)

MOST APPEARANCES
Lê Huynh Dúc 63 (1995–2002)

TROPHIES/HONOURS
none

MALAYSIA

Malaysian football had its heyday in the 1970s and early 1980s, with Mokhtar Dahari dynamic up front and R Arumugam often unbeatable in goal. They beat the USA 3–0 at the 1972 Olympics, but have struggled internationally since then.

FACT FILE

TOP GOALSCORER
Mokhtar Dahari 125 (1972–1985)

MOST APPEARANCES
R Arumugam 196 (1973–1986)

TROPHIES/HONOURS
none

UZBEKISTAN

is Asia's strongest ex-Soviet state and the team were quarter-finalists in the 2004 and 2007 Asian Cups. Star striker Maksim Shatskikh has proved a worthy successor to Andriy Shevchenko at Ukraine's Dinamo Kiev.

FACT FILE

TOP GOALSCORER
Mirjalol Kasymov 29 (unknown–2006)

MOST APPEARANCES
Mirjalol Kasymov 65 (unknown–2006)

TROPHIES/HONOURS
none

INDONESIA

As Dutch East Indies, Indonesia were the World Cup Finals' first Asian competitors, losing 6–0 to Hungary in 1938. With a five million playing population, Indonesia has the potential to be 'the Brazil of Asia'.

Founded 1930

FACT FILE

TOP GOALSCORER
Kurniawan Dwi Yulianto 33 (1995–2006)

MOST APPEARANCES
Kurniawan Dwi Yulianto 60 (1995–2006)

TROPHIES/HONOURS
none

PAKISTAN

Football fever is strong in Pakistan, despite the sport being overshadowed by cricket. Gradual progress is aided by the likes of ex-Premiership defender Zesh Rehman and captain and playmaker Muhammad Essa (right).

FACT FILE

TOP GOALSCORER
Muhammad Essa 20 (2000–present)

MOST APPEARANCES
Jaffar Khan 59 (2001–2007)

TROPHIES/HONOURS
none

Muhammad Essa is a free-kick specialist as well as a talented and creative passer of the ball.

INDIA

Football was brought to India by British army officers in the mid-19th century and the Durand Cup, established in 1888, is the third-oldest football competition in the world. The World Cup remains a distant prospect for India. Although they qualified in 1950, the team later withdrew after refusing to wear football boots.

Founded 1937

Despite his short stature, Baichung Bhutia is a giant of Indian football – his country's captain, top scorer and ambassador abroad.

FACT FILE

TOP GOALSCORER
Baichung Bhutia 20 (1997–present)

MOST APPEARANCES
Information not available

TROPHIES/HONOURS

German football fans watch a penalty shoot-out in their quarter-final match against Argentina in the 2006 World Cup Finals. Germany won the shoot-out 4–2.

FAMOUS COMPETITIONS

"IF YOU DON'T WANT SUCCESS IT'S NOT WORTH PLAYING – WINNING TROPHIES IS THE MAIN THING."

ENGLAND AND LIVERPOOL
MIDFIELDER STEVEN GERRARD

From the FIFA World Cup to the African Cup of Nations, each international competition has its own special magic. Agonising months, even years, of nail-biting qualifying matches played in far-flung stadia all seem worth it when you realise your team are in with a shot at the big prize. That's the best thing about cup football – it gives lesser-known teams a chance to step up and show the world who they are and allows the big teams to dazzle and delight a worldwide audience. Unfortunately, there can only ever be one winner. Until next time, of course.

FIFA WORLD CUP™

"FIRST AND FOREMOST, THE WORLD CUP SHOULD BE A FESTIVAL OF FOOTBALL."
FRANZ BECKENBAUER

The World Cup is seen by many as the greatest sporting event on Earth. Held every four years, it brings together the top international teams after three years of qualifying matches. The last final, in Germany in 2006, was watched by a global audience of 715 million. In the 18 tournaments played, only seven nations have ever won the title: Argentina, Brazil, England, France, Germany, Italy and Uruguay.

THE CUP

The current FIFA World Cup trophy was first awarded in 1974. It replaced the Jules Rimet trophy which Brazil were allowed to keep after their third tournament win in 1970. The bottom of the trophy bears the name and year of every winner since West Germany in 1974. The trophy will need to be replaced in 2038 because there will be no more space!

Designed by Italian Silvio Gazzaniga, the trophy is 36cm (14 in) high, weighs just over 6kg (13 lb), and is made of 18-carat gold.

FACT FILE:
FIFA WORLD CUP™ FINALS

TOP GOALSCORERS
1. Ronaldo (Brazil) 15 (1994–2006)
2. Gerd Müller (West Germany) 14 (1966–74)
3. Just Fontaine (France) 13 (1958)
4. Pelé (Brazil) 12 (1958–70)
5. Jürgen Klinsmann (Germany) 11 (1990–98)
= Sándor Kocsis (Hungary) 11 (1954)

FASTEST GOALS
1. Hakan Sükür (Turkey) v South Korea 2002 – 11 seconds
2. Václav Mašek (Czechoslovakia) v Mexico 1962 – 15 seconds
3. Pak Seung-Zin (North Korea) v Portugal 1966 – 23 seconds
4. Ernst Lehner (Germany) v Austria 1934 – 24 seconds
5. Bryan Robson (England) v France 1982 – 27 seconds

Ronaldo beat Gerd Müller's record with a goal against Ghana in the 2006 Finals. Former Brazil captain Cafu also holds the record for most appearances in the World Cup final with three, and Brazil are the only team to be present at every World Cup Finals.

JULES RIMET was president of FIFA for an incredible 33 years – from 1921 to 1954 – and was instrumental in making football the world game. It was thanks to this Frenchman that the first Finals were held in 1930. In 1946 the original trophy was renamed the Jules Rimet Trophy in his honour.

The trophy was stolen in 1983 and has never been recovered. It is thought to have been melted down by the thieves.

GREATEST GOALS

The World Cup Finals have been blessed with many amazing goals, from 17-year-old Pelé's stunning volley against Sweden in 1958 to Netherlands' Arie Haan's long range strike against West Germany in 1978. Here are two of the very best of all time:

In one glorious minute of the 1986 quarter-final, Argentina's Diego Maradona dribbled 50 metres (55 yards), passing four England players, to score the goal voted FIFA's Greatest World Cup Goal in a 2002 poll.

Carlos Alberto's goal in the 1970 final epitomises Brazil's extraordinary skill. Nine players dribbled and passed the ball the length of the pitch before defender Alberto charged into space and powered home Pelé's pass from the edge of the area.

CONTROVERSY

Since the very beginning, World Cup Finals have never been short of talking points both on and off the pitch. From arguments over the choice of hosts to controversial goals, disputed decisions and violent tackles, the World Cup has seen it all.

In the 1966 final, a close-range shot from England's Geoff Hurst hit the bar, bounced down and back into play. The linesman ruled that it was a goal and England went on to win the match. However, many people argue that the whole of the ball did not cross the line – meaning it wasn't a goal.

Italy versus Chile in the 1962 Finals was one of the dirtiest matches ever as players fought and police had to break up mass brawls. It became known as the 'Battle of Santiago'.

In 1986, Maradona claimed his first goal against England was due "a little to the head of Maradona, a little to the hand of God". Other people just say it was handball!

This is the actual size of the World Cup trophy.

WORLD CUP WINNERS **Brazil:** 5 times – 1958, 1962, 1970, 1994, 2002 **Italy:** 4 times – 1934, 1938, 1982, 2006 **Germany:** 3 times –1954, 1974, 1990 **Argentina:** twice – 1978, 1986 **Uruguay:** twice –1930, 1950 **England:** once – 1966 **France:** once –1998

FIFA WORLD CUP™ FINALS

1930 URUGUAY

FINAL:
Uruguay 4 Argentina 2

THIRD PLACE:
Not awarded

GOLDEN BOOT:
Guillermo Stábile 8 (Argentina)

GOLDEN BALL: Guillermo Stábile (Argentina)

ALL STAR TEAM
1. Enrique Ballesteros (Uruguay) 2. José Nasazzi (Uruguay) 3. Milutin Ivkovic (Yugoslavia) 4. Luis Monti (Argentina) 5. Álvaro Gestido (Uruguay) 6. José Andrade (Uruguay) 7. Pedro Cea (Uruguay) 8. Héctor Castro (Uruguay) 9. Héctor Scarone (Uruguay)10. Guilliermo Stábile (Uruguay) 11. Bert Patenaude (USA)

1934 ITALY

FINAL:
Italy 2 Czechoslovakia 1 (aet)

THIRD PLACE:
Germany

GOLDEN BOOT:
Oldrich Nejedlý 5 (Czechoslovakia)

GOLDEN BALL: Giuseppe Meazza (Italy)

ALL STAR TEAM
1. Ricardo Zamora (Spain) 2. Jacinto Quincoces (Spain) 3. Eraldo Monzeglio (Italy) 4. Luiz Monti (Italy) 5. Attilio Ferraris (Italy) 6. Leonardo Cilaurren (Spain) 7. Giussepe Meazza (Italy) 8. Raimundo Orsi (Italy) 9. Enrique Guaita (Italy) 10. Matthias Sindelar (Austria) 11. Oldrich Nejedlý (Czechoslovakia)

1938 FRANCE

FINAL:
Italy 4 Hungary 2

THIRD PLACE:
Brazil

GOLDEN BOOT:
Leônidas da Silva 7 (Brazil)

GOLDEN BALL: Leônidas da Silva (Brazil)

ALL STAR TEAM
1. František Plánicka (Czechoslovakia) 2. Pietro Rava (Italy) 3. Alfredo Foni (Italy) 4.Domingos da Guia (Brazil) 5. Michele Andreolo (Italy) 6. Ugo Locatelli (Italy) 7. Silvio Piola (Italy) 8. Gino Colaussi (Italy) 9. György Sárosi (Hungary) 10. Gyula Zsengellér (Hungaryl) 11. Leônidas da Silva (Brazil)

1950 BRAZIL

FINAL:
Uruguay 2 Brazil 1

THIRD PLACE:
Sweden

GOLDEN BOOT:
Ademir 9 (Brazil)

GOLDEN BALL: Zizinho (Brazil)

ALL STAR TEAM
1. Roque Máspoli (Uruguay) 2. Erik Nilsson (Sweden) 3. José Parra (Spain) 4. Schubert Gambetta (Uruguay) 5. Obdulio Varela (Uruguay) 6. Walter Bahr (USA) 7. Alcides Ghiggia (Uruguay) 8. Zizinho (Brazil) 9.Ademir (Brazil) 10. Jair (Brazil) 11. Schiaffino (Uruguay)

1954 SWITZERLAND

FINAL:
West Germany 3 Hungary 2

THIRD PLACE:
Austria

GOLDEN BOOT:
Sándor Kocsis 11 (Hungary)

GOLDEN BALL: Sándor Kocsis (Hungary)

ALL STAR TEAM
1. Gyula Grosics (Hungary) 2. Ernst Ocwirk (Austria) 3. József Bozsik (Hungary) 4. José Santamaria (Uruguay) 5. Fritz Walter (West Germany) 6. Bauer (Brazil) 7. Helmut Rahn (West Germany) 8. Nándor Hidegkuti (Hungary) 9. Ferenc Puskás (Hungary) 10. Sándor Kocsis (Hungary) 11. Zoltán Czibor (Hungary)

1958 SWEDEN

FINAL:
Brazil 5 Sweden 2

THIRD PLACE:
France

GOLDEN BOOT:
Just Fontaine 13 (France)

GOLDEN BALL: Raymond Kopa (France)

ALL STAR TEAM
1. Lev Yashin (USSR) 2. Djalma Santos (Brazil) 3. Bellini (Brazil) 4. Nílton Santos (Brazil) 5. Danny Blanchflower (Northern Ireland) 6. Didi (Brazil) 7. Pelé (Brazil) 8. Garrincha (Brazil) 9. Just Fontaine (France) 10. Raymond Kopa (France) 11. Gunnar Gren (Sweden)

1962 CHILE

FINAL
Brazil 3 Czechoslovakia 1

THIRD PLACE:
Germany

GOLDEN BOOT:
Garrincha 4 (Brazil), Vavá 4 (Brazil), Leonel Sánchez 4 (Chile), Dražan Jerkovic 4 (Yugoslavia), Valentin Ivanov 4 (USSR), Flórián Albert 4 (Hungary)

GOLDEN BALL: Garrincha (Brazil)

ALL STAR TEAM
1. Antonio Carbajal (Mexico) 2. Djalma Santos (Brazil) 3. Cesare Maldini (Italy) 4. Valeriy Voronin (USSR) 5. Karl-Heinz Schnellinger (West Germany) 6. Zagallo (Brazil) 7. Zito (Brazil) 8. Josef Masopust (Czechoslovakia) 9. Vavá (Brazil) 10. Garrincha (Brazil) 11. Leonel Sánchez (Brazil)

1966 ENGLAND

FINAL:
England 4 West Germany 2

THIRD PLACE:
Portugal

GOLDEN BOOT:
Eusébio 9 (Portugal)

GOLDEN BALL: Bobby Charlton (England)

ALL STAR TEAM
1. Gordon Banks (England) 2. George Cohen (England) 3. Bobby Moore (England) 4. Valeriy Voronin (USSR) 5. Silvio Marzolini (Argentina) 6. Franz Beckenbauer (West Germany) 7. Mário Coluna (Portugal) 8. Bobby Charlton (England) 9. Flórián Albert (Hungary) 10. Uwe Seeler (West Germany) 11. Eusébio (Portugal)

1970 MEXICO

FINAL:
Brazil 4 Italy 1

THIRD PLACE:
West Germany

GOLDEN BOOT:
Gerd Müller 10 (West Germany)

GOLDEN BALL: Pelé (Brazil)

ALL STAR TEAM
1. Ladislao Mazurkiewicz (Uruguay) 2. Carlos Alberto Torres (Brazil) 3. Piazza (Brazil) 4. Franz Beckenbauer (West Germany) 5. Giacinto Facchetti (Italy) 6. Gérson (Brazil) 7. Gianni Rivera (Italy) 8. Bobby Charlton (England) 9. Pelé (Brazil) 10. Gerd Müller (West Germany) 11. Jairzinho (Brazil)

1974 WEST GERMANY

FINAL:
West Germany 2 Netherlands 1

THIRD PLACE:
Poland

GOLDEN BOOT:
Grzegorz Lato 7 (Poland)

GOLDEN BALL: Johan Cruyff (Netherlands)

ALL STAR TEAM
1. Jan Tomaszewski (Poland) 2. Berti Vogts (West Germany) 3. Wim Suurbier (Netherlands) 4. Franz Beckenbauer (West Germany) 5. Marinho Chagas (Brazil) 6. Wolfgang Overath (West Germany) 7. Kazimierz Deyna (Poland) 8. Johan Neeskens (Netherlands) 9. Rob Rensenbrink (Netherlands) 10. Johan Cruyff (Netherlands) 11. Grzegorz Lato (Poland)

1978 ARGENTINA

FINAL:
Argentina 3 Netherlands 1

THIRD PLACE:
Brazil

GOLDEN BOOT:
Mario Kempes 6 (Argentina)

GOLDEN BALL: Mario Kempes (Argentina)

ALL STAR TEAM
1. Ubaldo Fillol (Argentina) 2. Berti Vogts (West Germany) 3. Ruud Krol (Netherlands) 4. Daniel Passarella (Argentina) 5. Alberto Tarantini (Argentina) 6. Dirceu (Brazil) 7. Franco Causio (Italy) 8. Rob Rensenbrink (Netherlands) 9. Teófilo Cubillas (Peru) 10.Daniel Bertoni (Argentina) 11. Mario Kempes (Argentina)

1982 SPAIN

FINAL:
Italy 3 West Germany 1

THIRD PLACE:
Poland

GOLDEN BOOT:
Paolo Rossi 6 (Italy)

GOLDEN BALL: Paolo Rossi (Italy)

ALL STAR TEAM
1. Dino Zoff (Italy) 2. Claudio Gentile (Italy) 3. Luizinho (Brazil) 4. Fulvio Collovati (Italy) 5. Júnior (Brazil) 6. Zbigniew Boniek (Poland) 7. Falcão (Brazil) 8. Michel Platini (France) 9. Zico (Brazil) 10. Paolo Rossi (Italy) 11. Karl-Heinz Rummenigge (Brazil)

1986 MEXICO

FINAL:
Argentina 3 West Germany 2

THIRD PLACE:
France

GOLDEN BOOT:
Gary Lineker 6 (England)

GOLDEN BALL: Diego Maradona (Argentina)

ALL STAR TEAM
1. Harald Schumacher (West Germany) 2. Josimar (Brazil) 3. Manuel Amoros (France) 4. Maxime Bossis (France) 5. Jan Ceulemans (Belgium) 6. Felix Magath (West Germany) 7. Michel Platini (France) 8. Diego Maradona (Argentina) 9. Preben Elkjær-Larsen (Denmark) 10. Emilio Butragueño (Spain) 11. Gary Lineker (England)

1990 ITALY

FINAL:
West Germany 1 Argentina 0

THIRD PLACE:
Italy

GOLDEN BOOT:
Salvatore Schillaci 6 (Italy)

GOLDEN BALL: Salvatore Schillaci (Italy)

ALL STAR TEAM
1. Sergio Goycochea (Argentina) 2. Andreas Brehme (West Germany) 3. Paolo Maldini (Italy) 4. Franco Baresi (Italy) 5. Diego Maradona (Argentina) 6. Lothar Matthäus (West Germany) 7. Roberto Donadoni (Italy) 8. Paul Gascoigne (England) 9. Salvatore Schillaci (Italy) 10. Roger Milla (Cameroon) 11. Tomáš Skuhravý (Czechoslovakia)

1994 USA

FINAL:
Brazil 0 Italy 0 (aet)
Brazil won 3–2 on penalties

THIRD PLACE:
Sweden

GOLDEN BOOT:
Hristo Stoichkov 6 (Bulgaria), Oleg Salenko 6 (Russia)

GOLDEN BALL: Romário (Brazil)

ALL STAR TEAM
1. Michel Preud'homme (Belgium) 2. Jorginho (Brazil) 3. Márcio Santos (Brazil) 4. Paulo Maldini (Italy) 5. Dunga (Brazil) 6. Krasimir Balakov (Bulgaria) 7. Gheorghe Hagi (Romania) 8. Thomas Brolin (Sweden) 9. Romário (Brazil) 10. Hristo Stoichkov (Bulgaria) 11. Roberto Baggio (Italy)

1998 FRANCE

FINAL:
France 3 Brazil 0

THIRD PLACE:
Croatia

GOLDEN BOOT:
Davor Šuker 6 (Croatia)

GOLDEN BALL: Ronaldo (Brazil)

STAR PLAYERS

Goalkeepers: Fabien Barthez (France), José Luis Chilavert (Paraguay) **Defenders:** Roberto Carlos da Silva (Brazil), Marcel Desailly (France), Lilian Thuram (France), Frank de Boer (Netherlands), Carlos Gamarra (Paraguay) **Midfielders:** Dunga (Brazil), Rivaldo (Brazil), Michael Laudrup (Denmark), Zinedine Zidane (France), Edgar Davids (Netherlands) **Forwards:** Ronaldo (Brazil), Davor Šuker (Croatia) Brian Laudrup (Denmark), Dennis Bergkamp (Netherlands)

2002 SOUTH KOREA & JAPAN

FINAL:
Brazil 2 Germany 0

THIRD PLACE:
Turkey

GOLDEN BOOT:
Ronaldo 8 (Brazil)

GOLDEN BALL: Oliver Kahn (Germany)

STAR PLAYERS

Goalkeepers: Oliver Kahn (Germany), Rüstü Reçber (Turkey) **Defenders:** Roberto Carlos (Brazil), Sol Campbell (England), Fernando Hierro (Spain), Hong Myung-Bo (South Korea), Alpay Özalan (Turkey) **Midfielders:** Rivaldo (Brazil), Ronaldinho (Brazil), Michael Ballack (Germany), Yoo Sang-Chul (South Korea) **Forwards:** Ronaldo (Brazil), Miroslav Klose (Germany), El Hadji Diouf (Senegal), Hasan Sas (Turkey)

2006 GERMANY

FINAL:
Italy 1 France 1 (aet)
Italy won 5–3 on penalties

THIRD PLACE:
Germany

GOLDEN BOOT:
Miroslav Klose 5 (Germany)

GOLDEN BALL: Zinedine Zidane (France)

STAR PLAYERS

Goalkeepers: Gianluigi Buffon (Italy), Jens Lehmann (Germany), Ricardo (Portugal) **Defenders:** Roberto Ayala (Argentina), John Terry (England), Lilian Thuram (France), Philipp Lahm (Germany), Fabio Cannavaro (Italy), Gianluca Zambrotta (Italy), Ricardo Carvalho (Portugal) **Midfielders:** Zé Roberto (Brazil), Patrick Vieira (France), Zinedine Zidane (France), Michael Ballack (Germany), Andrea Pirlo (Italy), Gennaro Gattuso (Italy), Luis Figo (Portugal), Cristiano Ronaldo (Portugal), **Forwards:** Hernán Crespo (Argentina), Thierry Henry (France), Miroslav Klose (Germany), Francesco Totti (Italy), Luca Toni (Italy)

UEFA EUROPEAN CHAMPIONSHIP

"FOOTBALL UNITES AND TRANSCENDS EUROPE."

UEFA PRESIDENT AND EUROPEAN CHAMPIONSHIP-
WINNING FRANCE MIDFIELDER MICHEL PLATINI

The UEFA European Championship ranks second only to the World Cup for prestige and popularity in international football. More than 50 countries enter the qualifying stages, while the major nations of the continent vie for supremacy. Held every four years, the tournament began in 1960 with a four-team competition, but has grown to become a month-long contest involving 16 teams.

AN IDEA
Henri Delaunay, former secretary of the French FA, first suggested the idea of a European Championship in 1927 but the first tournament did not take place until 1960.

2008
The European Championship trophy was named in Henri Delaunay's honour. A new trophy has been created for the 2008 tournament in Austria and Switzerland with a sturdier base and more space for the winners' names. However, the trophy looks very similar to the old one and will retain Delaunay's name.

Jürgen Klinsmann celebrates scoring a goal against Russia during Euro '96 in England.

FIRST CHAMPIONSHIPS
The USSR defeated Yugoslavia 2–1 in the first European Championship final in Paris. Led by the legendary goalkeeper Lev Yashin, the Soviets needed extra time to complete their victory, with the winning goal scored by Viktor Ponedelnik.

GERMAN SKILL
Germany are the most successful team in the European Championship. As West Germany and the reunified side, they have won the tournament three times and been runners-up twice. The last triumph in 1996 came when the Germans beat the much fancied hosts England in a thrilling semi-final, before a 2–1 extra-time victory over the Czech Republic in the final.

DID YOU KNOW?
Oliver Bierhoff's 94th minute winner for Germany in the 1996 final was the first time a major international tournament was decided by a 'golden goal'. The rule stated that in extra time, the match would end immediately if one team scored a goal. This way of deciding the outcome of a match became known as a 'golden goal'.

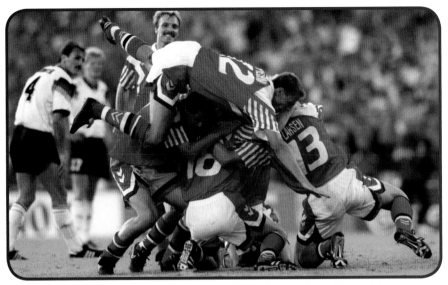

One of the most famous tournaments was in 1992 when outsiders Denmark beat favourites Germany 2–0 in Gothenburg's Ullevi stadium, thanks to goals from John Jensen and Kim Vilfort. The Danes were only at the finals because of the late withdrawal of Yugoslavia, who had to pull out of the competition due to civil war.

FACT FILE: UEFA EUROPEAN CHAMPIONSHIP

(see p.128 for complete list of winners)

TOP GOALSCORERS
1. Michel Platini (France) 9
2. Alan Shearer (England) 7
3. Patrick Kluivert (Netherlands) 6
4. Milan Baroš (Czech Republic) 5
= Thierry Henry (France) 5
= Zinedine Zidane (France) 5
= Jürgen Klinsmann (Germany) 5
= Marco Van Basten (Netherlands) 5
= Nuno Gomes (Portugal) 5
= Savo Miloševic (Serbia) 5

MOST SUCCESSFUL TEAMS
1. Germany (3 wins)
2. France (2 wins)
3. USSR (1 win)
= Czechoslovakia (1 win)
= Italy (1 win)
= Spain (1 win)
= Netherlands (1 win)
= Denmark (1 win)
= Greece (1 win)

Before Euro 2004 Greece had never won a game at an international tournament!

GOAL KING

Michel Platini holds the record for the most goals scored by one player in a European Championship. He scored nine on the way to France's triumph in 1984, including the opener in the 2–0 defeat of Spain in the final. This total also makes him the Championship's all-time top scorer.

SURPRISE WIN

When Greece took to the field for the opening group game in Euro 2004 against the hosts Portugal, no one would have predicted that three weeks later both sides would be contesting the final. Greece won that game 2–1 and the final 1–0, thanks to a goal from Angelos Charisteas.

AFRICAN CUP OF NATIONS

FACT FILE: AFRICAN CUP OF NATIONS
(See p.128 for complete list of winners)

TOP GOALSCORERS
1. Samuel Eto'o (Cameroon) 16
2. Laurent Pokou (Côte d'Ivoire) 14
3. Rashidi Yekini (Nigeria) 13
4. Hassan El-Shazly (Egypt) 12
= Michael Essien (Ghana) 12

MOST SUCCESSFUL TEAMS
1. Egypt (5 wins)
2. Ghana (4 wins)
= Cameroon (4 wins)
3. Congo DR (2 wins)
= Nigeria (2 wins)

"A WARNING TO YOU EUROPEANS: ONE DAY WE'LL BEAT YOU TO BECOME WORLD CHAMPIONS!"

CONFEDERATION OF AFRICAN FOOTBALL PRESIDENT ISSA HAYATOU

Just three teams (Egypt, Sudan and Ethiopia) took part in the first CAF African Cup of Nations in Sudan in 1957. However, it is now a prestigious biennial event with 16 teams participating in the 2008 tournament in Ghana. The competition is usually held in January, but with many African players playing in European leagues, pressure is growing to move it to the summer.

CAMEROON

Although much of the world first discovered the delights of Cameroon's football at the 1990 World Cup Finals, the seeds of the team's success were sown in the early 1980s. The 'Indomitable Lions' made three consecutive finals that decade and won two of them, most notably beating Nigeria 3–1 in the 1984 final. Cameroon also captured the first two titles of the 21st century thanks to their calmness in penalty shoot-outs. Their third victory in 2000 earned them the right to keep the trophy.

The current ACN trophy (left) is the third. Ghana were allowed to keep the original Abdelaziz Abdallah Salem Trophy after their third triumph in 1978, and the African Unity Cup was kept by Cameroon in 2000.

DID YOU KNOW?

No player has scored more goals in one African Cup of Nations than Ndaya Mulamba's nine for Zaire (now DPR Congo) in 1974.

EGYPT

The 'Pharaohs' won the first two ACN titles – Raafat Ateya scored the first-ever ACN goal in 1957 and Al-Diba hit all four goals in that year's final. Egypt have won the title six times, including a penalty shoot-out victory over Côte D'Ivoire in 2006.

Mohamed Aboutreika scored Egypt's decisive penalty in the 2006 final.

GHANA

Ghana's 'Black Stars' put African football on the map by winning the 1963 and 1965 tournaments in irresistible style. A third win in 1978 entitled them to keep the trophy, but there have been lengthy, impatient waits between victories since then. Abédi 'Pelé' Ayew announced himself as a 17-year-old wonder in Ghana's fourth success in 1982. However, he was suspended for the epic 11–10 shoot-out defeat to Côte d'Ivoire ten years later.

AFC ASIAN CUP

"THIS IS NOT JUST ABOUT FOOTBALL... THIS HAS BROUGHT GREAT HAPPINESS TO A WHOLE COUNTRY."

JORVAN VIEIRA, BRAZILIAN COACH OF
2007 AFC ASIAN CUP WINNERS IRAQ

The AFC Asian Cup was first held in 1956 in Hong Kong and won by the Republic of Korea. The competition was then held every four years until 2007 when the AFC brought the tournament forward a year to avoid clashing with the Olympics and the European Championship. For the first time, the competition was co-hosted by four nations (Indonesia, Malaysia, Vietnam and Thailand) – and AFC new boys Australia made their debut.

FACT FILE: AFC ASIAN CUP
(See p.128 for complete list of winners)

TOP GOALSCORERS
1. Ali Daei (Iran) 14
2. Lee Dong-Gook (Republic of Korea) 10
3. Naohiro Takahara (Japan) 9
4. Jassem Al Houwaidi (Kuwait) 8
5. Choi Soon-Ho (Republic of Korea) 7
= Behtash Fariba (Iran) 7
= Hossein Kalani (Iran) 7

MOST SUCCESSFUL TEAMS
1. Saudi Arabia (3 wins)
= Iran (3 wins)
= Japan (3 wins)
2. Republic of Korea (2 wins)
3. Israel (1 win)
= Kuwait (1 win)
= Iraq (1 win)

IRAN
Iran won every game in the 1968, 1972 and 1976 tournaments to take three consecutive trophies. However, in recent years they have struggled to rediscover this form despite the goalscoring efforts of Javad Nekounam (right, centre) in 2007.

SAUDI ARABIA
Saudi Arabia won the tournament in 1984 and 1988. They were runners-up to Japan in 1992, but reclaimed the trophy in 1996 (above) when Mohammed Al-Deayea was the penalty-saving hero.

JAPAN
In 2004 Shunsuke Nakamura's man-of-the-match display helped Japan to their third win since 1992. Japan beat China 3–1 in the final and captain Tsuneyasu Miyamoto proudly lifted the trophy (right).

Younis Mahmoud lifts the Asian Cup after Iraq's 2007 victory in Jakarta, Indonesia.

IRAQ
Australia were the favourites in 2007, but outsiders Iraq, led by captain and crucial goalscorer Younis Mahmoud, were the surprise winners. Iraq's coach, Jorvan Vieira, had been in charge for just two months.

DID YOU KNOW?
Iran's Ali Daei is the all-time Asian Cup top scorer, netting 14 goals at the 1996, 2000 and 2004 tournaments.

COPA AMÉRICA

"THE COPA AMÉRICA IS MORE DIFFICULT THAN THE WORLD CUP BECAUSE OF THE RIVALRY THAT EXISTS IN SOUTH AMERICA." DUNGA, WHO WON THE COPA WITH BRAZIL AS A PLAYER AND AS COACH

The Copa América is the oldest – and most fiercely contested – international tournament. It was introduced in 1916, to mark a century of Argentina's independence from Spain. The format, name and frequency of the competition have varied greatly over the years but it is now established as a 12-team tournament held every four years, with hosting rights rotated between the ten CONMEBOL countries.

Two or three CONCACAF guest nations are invited to the Copa América tournament. In 2001 guests Honduras (left) stunned Brazil 2–0 in the 2001 quarter-final. Mexico also finished runners-up in that year.

Victory in 2007 meant that Brazil retained the trophy they had also won in 2004.

Joint record-holders Uruguay won the first ever Copa América in 1916 and have won it 13 times since then. Enzo Francescoli (above, pictured in 1995) was the architect of their 1983, 1987 and 1995 victories.

ARGENTINA
Victory in 1993 brought Argentina their 14th Copa América, and their last international trophy to date. Oscar Ruggeri (right) captained the side and two goals from Gabriel Batistuta proved too much for guests Mexico in the final. Argentina were runners up to Brazil in 2004 and 2007 and are still chasing a 15th Copa América to take them ahead of Uruguay.

BRAZIL
In 2007, the result seemed a foregone conclusion. Brazilian stars such as Kaká and Ronaldinho were absent while Riquelme and Messi lit up a majestic Argentina side. However, Brazil outmuscled their old rivals 3–0 in the final to win the Copa for the eighth time.

Robinho's six goals made him the tournament's top scorer.

DID YOU KNOW?
Argentina striker Martín Palermo missed three penalties during Colombia's 3–0 win in the 1999 Copa América – an international record.

CONCACAF GOLD CUP

"THE GOLD CUP IS STILL THE MOST IMPORTANT EVENT FOR US." BOB BRADLEY, US COACH SINCE 2006.

CONCACAF's showpiece has had a varied history and throughout the 1980s it was chiefly used to decide World Cup places. In 1990 it was rebranded as the CONCACAF Gold Cup and since then the tournament has enjoyed greater prestige. Although the competition is dominated by Mexico and the USA, the 2007 event brought encouraging displays from Canada, Honduras and Guadeloupe.

FACT FILE: CONCACAF GOLD CUP
(See p.128 for complete list of winners)

TOP GOALSCORERS
1. Zaguinho (Mexico) 13
2. Landon Donovan (USA) 12
3. Carlos Pavón (Honduras) 9
= Eric Wynalda (USA) 9
4. Paulo Wanchope (Costa Rica) 8
= Walter Centeno (Costa Rica) 8
= Brian McBride (USA) 8

MOST SUCCESSFUL TEAMS
1. Mexico (7 wins)
2. USA (4 wins)
3. Costa Rica (3 wins)
4. Canada (2 wins)

MEXICO
In 1993, striker Zaguinho inspired Mexico to a famous victory. Zaguinho (right, real name Luis Roberto Alves) hit 12 goals and the USA were thrashed 4–0 in the final. Mexico have won the tournament three times since 1993, giving them a record seven wins.

CANADA 2000
Jason de Vos and Carlo Corazzin got the goals to conquer Colombia in the final, but Canada's victory in 2000 owed much to goalkeeper Craig Forrest (above right).

USA
In 2007, new coach Bob Bradley helped the USA to continue their good form against rivals Mexico by winning the final 2–1. The USA first entered the tournament in 1989, but lost to Costa Rica in the final. Nevertheless, this secured the USA a place at the 1990 World Cup Finals.

Guests from other federations were invited to the Gold Cup between 1996 to 2005. Brazil were runners-up twice and the Republic of Korea reached the semi-finals in 2002.

The USA retained the trophy against Mexico thanks to goals from Landon Donovan and Benny Feilhaber.

DID YOU KNOW?

In 2003, USA striker Landon Donovan scored four of his team's goals in their 5–0 victory over Cuba in the quarter-final.

In 2007, USA goalkeeper Kasey Keller appeared in his sixth CONCACAF Gold Cup – a tournament record.

WOMEN'S COMPETITIONS

"WOMEN'S SOCCER HAS GONE THROUGH AN UNBELIEVABLE DEVELOPMENT IN RECENT YEARS AND THAT WILL CONTINUE, I AM SURE."

NADINE ANGERER, GERMANY'S 2007 WORLD CUP-WINNING GOALKEEPER

The female game's flagship competition, the Women's World Cup was only staged for the first time in 1991 but is already attracting strong challenges from five continents. The 2007 contest enjoyed a higher profile than ever before as Brazil's path to the final upset the usual USA/European dominance. Interest in the women's game is growing and with 26 million female players around the world, the sky is the limit for women's football.

In 2007 Birgit Prinz proudly holds the World Cup trophy as Germany retain the title they won in 2003.

THE WORLD CUP

China welcomed the world in 2007, four years after an outbreak of the SARS disease forced the World Cup Finals to be relocated to the USA. Shanghai's Hongkou Stadium staged the spectacular opening ceremony and the tournament enjoyed unprecedented levels of support.

2007 FINAL

Germany were worthy champions in 2007 and did not concede a goal in the entire tournament. They started their campaign with an 11–0 thrashing of Argentina. Striker and team captain Birgit Prinz scored a hat-trick in that match and she also scored in the final. Brazil were beaten 2–0 in the final, during which German goalkeeper Nadine Angerer saved a penalty.

OLYMPICS

Women's football debuted at the Olympic Games in 1996. The USA have won gold twice, but in 2000 Norway made them settle for the silver medal (above).

AFC WOMEN'S ASIAN CUP

The AFC Women's Asian Cup is one of the longest-running international women's competitions. It was introduced in 1975 and first won by New Zealand. China have largely dominated the competition since then – they have triumphed eight times, including a 2006 win over hosts Australia on penalties (celebrated right).

EUROPEAN CHAMPIONSHIP

Germany won the first UEFA Women's Championship in 1991, beating Norway 3–1 in the final. The same sides played out the same scoreline in England in 2005 (celebrated above, by Germany's Inka Grings, Conny Pohlers and Britta Carlson). Amazingly, Norway's narrow victory over Italy in 1993 is the only time Germany have failed to take the title.

OTHER WOMEN'S COMPETITIONS

Beginning in 1991, the first four Sudamericano Femenino contests were won by Brazil. However, Argentina finally turned the tables on Brazil in 2006, despite a talented team which included the legendary Marta. Argentina beat their old rivals 2–0 in the final, thanks to goals from Eva Nadia González and María Belén Potassa.

At the other end of the world, in the Oceania region, the OFC Women's Championship has been shared between New Zealand and Australia, with three wins apiece. Chinese Taipei are following on close behind with two trophies, in 1986 and 1989. New Zealand won the tournament in 2007, scoring 21 goals in three games.

CONCACAF WOMEN'S GOLD CUP

The USA have enjoyed a secure grip on the CONCACAF Women's Gold Cup, winning six out of seven contests. 1998 champions Canada were beaten in the 2006 final by a last-minute penalty from Kristine Lilly (pictured right, player on far left).

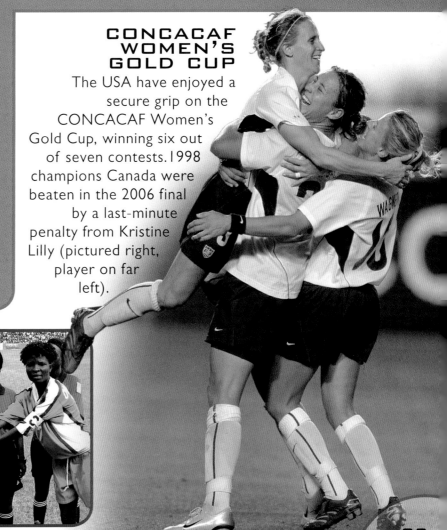

CAF WOMEN'S CHAMPIONSHIP

Nigeria and Ghana have contested three CAF Women's Championship finals and all of them have been won by Nigeria. In fact, Nigeria have won all seven CAF tournaments. In the 2006 final (pictured right) Nigeria beat Ghana 1–0, thanks to Perpetua Nkwocha's early goal. Success in the CAF Championships meant that both countries qualified for the 2007 Women's World Cup.

Players from rival English teams Chelsea and Manchester United sportingly shake hands before a Premier League match.

CLUB FOOTBALL

Supporting your favourite club can be tough. When results are bad, the weather is foul and your local rivals have inflicted yet another painful defeat, you might wonder why you ever chose them in the first place. But somehow you just can't stop yourself from caring — once you've given your heart to a team, that's it. For life. After all, there's always next season...

UEFA CHAMPIONS LEAGUE

"THE CHAMPIONS LEAGUE IS THE COMPETITION EVERYONE WANTS TO BE IN."
STEVEN GERRARD, LIVERPOOL'S TROPHY-WINNING CAPTAIN IN 2005.

The Champions League is possibly the most prestigious club competition in the world. Originally called the European Cup, it changed its name in 1992 and adopted a league-and-knockout format. The spectacular season-long competition features the best club sides from Europe and many of the world's finest players, and generates huge television and sponsorship deals.

AJAX
The great Ajax side of Johan Cruyff, Johnny Rep, Arie Haan and co. reigned supreme during the early 1970s, winning three European Cups in a row thanks to victories over Panathinaikos (1971), Inter (1972) and Juventus (1973). Opponents had no answer to Ajax's philosophy of 'Total Football' (see p.41).

BAYERN MUNICH
Bayern Munich also achieved three consecutive triumphs, between 1974 and 1976. Great players such as Franz Beckenbauer, Uli Hoeness (right), Georg Schwarzenbeck, Sepp Maier, Paul Breitner and Gerd Müller were key to the team's success. Bayern secured their fourth trophy in 2001.

Captain Paolo Maldini lifts the trophy after Milan's 2–1 defeat of Liverpool in 2007.

AC MILAN
Italy's most successful European Cup/Champions League club are AC Milan with seven victories, most recently in 2007. Arguably Milan's finest win was the 4–0 humiliation of Barcelona in 1994. The team, managed by Fabio Capello, produced a performance viewed by some as the best ever by a club team.

FAMOUS COMEBACK
Losing 3–0 to AC Milan at half time during the 2005 final in Istanbul, four-times winners Liverpool looked doomed. But the English team launched an unforgettable comeback, inspired by skipper Steven Gerrard (right, scoring Liverpool's first goal). Unbelievably, Liverpool drew level with Milan and then earned their fifth trophy thanks to a nail-biting 3–2 win in the penalty shoot out. However, two years later Milan had their revenge and defeated Liverpool 2–1 in a much more straightforward final.

REAL MADRID
Real Madrid are the most successful team in Europe's top competition with nine wins. They won the first five European Cups (1956–1960), lifted the trophy again in 1966, and have brought the Champions League title back to Spain on a further three occasions (1998, 2000 and 2002). Here Manuel Sanchís and his teammates celebrate the club's 2000 victory (right).

UEFA CUP

"WINNING THE UEFA CUP WAS THE HIGHLIGHT OF MY CAREER." HAKAN SÜKÜR, WINNER WITH GALATASARAY IN 2000

Europe's second most important club competition began in 1955 as the Inter-Cities Fairs Cup. It was renamed the UEFA Cup in 1971, and teams qualified on the basis of domestic league position. In 1999 the competition was merged with the UEFA Cup Winners' Cup to include winners of domestic cup competitions. Nowadays, losing sides from the qualifying rounds of the Champions League are also eligible for the UEFA Cup.

FAMOUS VICTORY

Porto's Deco (right) and Nuno Valente (left) hold the UEFA Cup aloft after their side won a wonderfully exciting 2003 final 3–2 against Celtic in Seville. Porto triumphed after scoring a 'silver goal' (see p.149) in extra time. A year later they went one better and won the Champions League.

(See p.131 for complete list of winners)

FACT FILE: UEFA CUP

TOP GOALSCORERS
1. Information not available
2. Information not available
3. Information not available
4. Information not available
5. Information not available

MOST SUCCESSFUL TEAMS
3 WINS
Internazionale (Italy)
Juventus (Italy)
Liverpool (England)
2 WINS
Borussia Mönchengladbach (Germany)
Feyenoord (Netherlands)
IFK Gothenburg (Sweden)
Parma (Italy)
Real Madrid (Spain)
Sevilla (Spain)
Tottenham Hotspur (England)

Frédéric Kanouté of Seville celebrates with teammates in 2007.

SEVILLA

Sevilla's 3–1 win on penalties over their countrymen Espanyol in the 2007 UEFA Cup final meant the Spanish side became the first club to retain the trophy since Real Madrid in 1986. Sevilla had thrashed Middlesbrough 4–0 in 2006.

Italian giants Juventus have won the trophy a record three times. Their first triumph was in 1977 against Athletic Bilbao and victory in 1990 (celebrated left) came when they defeated fellow Italians Fiorentina 3–1 on aggregate. Juventus last won the trophy in 1993.

CUP WINNERS' CUP

Italian team Lazio have held the European Cup Winners' Cup for more than nine years. However, this is because the Roman side got to keep the trophy after winning the last competition in 1999. The ECWC had run for 38 seasons, but came to an end when it was absorbed into the UEFA Cup. Lazio beat Mallorca 2–1, thanks to goals from Christian Vieri (right, centre) and Pavel Nedved (far right).

COPA LIBERTADORES

"WHEN I ARRIVED AT RIVER [PLATE] MY DREAM WAS TO WIN THE COPA LIBERTADORES."

ARGENTINA STRIKER HERNÁN CRESPO, WHO WON THE TROPHY WITH RIVER PLATE IN 1996

The Copa Libertadores was introduced in 1960 as South America's challenge to the European Cup (now Champions League), and this exciting annual contest certainly seems to guarantee more goals per game than its European counterpart. The format is similar to the Champions League, with the top teams from each country competing for the trophy. It began with just nine clubs, but now 38 clubs compete for the Copa.

TOP SCORER

Ecuador's Alberto Spencer was the Libertadores' most lethal striker, with 54 goals in 77 games between 1960 and 1972. He earned three winners' medals with Peñarol of Uruguay.

BOCA JUNIORS

Argentina's Boca Juniors have dominated the Copa in the 21st century. In 2007 Juan Román Riquelme (on loan from Spain's Villareal) inspired a 5–0 two-leg triumph over Brazil's Grêmio, netting three goals himself.

INDEPENDIENTE

Argentinian teams have dominated the competition at times, especially Independiente. Their 4–1 play-off victory over Peñarol in 1965 (left) was the second of seven wins, the last of which came in 1984.

A 2004 rule change permitted clubs from the same country to contest the final. This resulted in two all-Brazil showdowns in a row. In 2005 São Paulo beat Atlético Paranaense 5–1 over two legs (pictured above) but the following year they could only only finish runners-up after losing 4–3 on aggregate to fellow Brazilians Internacional.

CONCACAF CHAMPIONS' CUP

"CONCACAF HAS BECOME BETTER AND BETTER EACH AND EVERY YEAR, AT ALL LEVELS."

CHIVAS USA SPORTING DIRECTOR THOMAS RONGEN

The CONCACAF Champions' Cup was first introduced in 1962, but the USA did not participate until 1997, when CONCACAF granted the recently-formed MLS (Major League Soccer) two places in the tournament. The cup is contested by the leading club sides in the region, and has so far been dominated by clubs from Mexico. From 2009 onwards, CONCACAF hope to expand the Champions' Cup to bring a European-style Champions League competition to North and Central America.

LA GALAXY
In 2000, Los Angeles Galaxy became only the second US side to take the trophy, beating Honduran side Olimpia 3–2 in the final. Defender Ezra Hendrickson was the surprise two-goal hero in California, with Cobi Jones (left) also scoring. DC United had been the first North American winners in 1998, only a year after US teams first entered the competition.

MEXICO
Mexican teams Club América and Cruz Azul have both won the competition a record five times. Mexican star striker Cuauhtémoc Blanco (right) and defender Duilio Davino (left) helped Club América to ther last victory in 2006.

Colombian keeper Miguel Calero has lifted the trophy twice with Pachuca, in 2002 and 2007.

PACHUCA
In 2007 Mexican side CF Pachuca beat compatriots Chivas de Guadalajara 7–6 in a penalty shoot-out. Pachuca goalkeeper and captain Miguel 'El Condor' Calero (left) did not make a save in the shoot-out – instead, Chivas forward Alberto Medina hit the post.

NECAXA
Ecuadorian midfielder Álex Aguinaga (second left) was opening scorer and player of the tournament when Mexico's Necaxa won their first CONCACAF Champions' Cup in 1999. Necaxa beat LD Alajuelense of Costa Rica 2–1 in the final, three years after they had finished runners-up to Cruz Azul in a mini-league final system.

DEPORTIVO SAPRISSA
Costa Rica's Saprissa recorded their third CONCACAF victory as Rónald Gómez and Christian Bolaños helped defeat UNAM Pumas of Mexico 3–2 in a two leg final. Saprissa are nicknamed 'El Monstruo Morado' (The Purple Monster) because of their purple kit, which is said to be the result of their original red shirts and blue shorts mixing in the wash in 1937.

ENGLISH CLUBS

"THANK YOU FOR LETTING ME PLAY IN YOUR BEAUTIFUL FOOTBALL."
FRENCHMAN ERIC CANTONA, FORMER MANCHESTER UNITED STRIKER

England is often seen as the home of football. It has the oldest football association (1863), the oldest professional league (1888) and what borders on a national obsession with the game. English football is famous for its fast and physical style, and the arrival of foreign players has helped raise the standard of technical skill. In 1992 the top 20 clubs formed the Premier League which brought major changes to the English game. Factors such as new stadiums, bigger crowds and rich foreign owners have brought huge financial success, particularly for the biggest clubs such as Manchester United and Arsenal. Every team is desperate to remain in the Premier League, but each season three clubs are promoted from the division below and three are relegated.

There are 92 senior clubs in the English Football League. The Premier League is the top division and is made up of 20 teams.

ARSENAL
EMIRATES STADIUM, LONDON

Arsenal are by far London's most successful club, with 13 league titles and ten FA Cups. The modern team have been transformed under Frenchman Arsene Wenger (left centre), with young stars like Cesc Fàbregas (left, centre) producing entertaining and free-flowing football.

CHELSEA
STAMFORD BRIDGE, LONDON

Billionaire Roman Abramovich has helped Chelsea to become one of England's most successful sides. Since he bought the club in 2003 they have won the league twice (2005 and 2006), the League Cup twice (2005 and 2007) and the FA Cup once in 2007, with Didier Drogba (above) scoring the winning goal.

TOTTENHAM HOTSPUR
WHITE HART LANE, LONDON

Spurs have struggled in recent years but they are famous for being the only 'non-league' side to win the FA Cup (1901), the first British side to win a European trophy (1963), and the first to win the 'Double' (the league title and the FA Cup) in the 20th century (1961, right).

FAMOUS CLUBS

Portsmouth FC

Fulham

Bolton Wanderers

Middlesborough

Arsenal

Nottingham Forest

PRESTON NORTH END

DEEPDALE, PRESTON, LANCASHIRE

Preston North End were the first winners of the Football League in 1889 and by winning the FA Cup the same year became the only club to secure the prestigious 'Double' for more than 70 years.

NEWCASTLE UNITED

ST. JAMES' PARK, NEWCASTLE

Newcastle United have been one of England's top clubs since the early 1900s, winning four league titles and six FA Cups. Nicknamed the Magpies because of their famous black and white kit, United have not won a major trophy since the 1969 Inter Cities Fairs Cup, despite coming close.

EVERTON

GOODISON PARK, LIVERPOOL

With nine league titles and five FA Cup wins, Everton are one of England's most successful clubs of all time and fierce local rivals of Liverpool. Despite a lack of recent glory, Goodison Park is still one of the best grounds in England for atmosphere.

LIVERPOOL

ANFIELD, LIVERPOOL

'The Mighty Reds' are England's most successful club side, with 18 league titles, five European Cups and 17 other major trophies. The 1984 team (above) almost won every competition they played in. They won the European Cup, the League title and the League Cup, but lost in the fourth round of the FA Cup.

The Premier League has been won by just four clubs – Man Utd, Chelsea, Arsenal and Blackburn.

MANCHESTER UNITED

OLD TRAFFORD, MANCHESTER

With millions of fans across the globe, Man Utd are one of the world's biggest clubs. Current boss Sir Alex Ferguson is the most successful British manager of all time, with 21 major trophies won by his team, which includes home-grown stars Ryan Giggs (left) and Gary Neville (right).

Everton

Newcastle United

Chelsea

Blackpool

Wolverhampton Wanderers

FRENCH CLUBS

"FOOTBALL IS A FANTASTIC AND INTELLIGENT GAME WHICH TEACHES US HOW TO LIVE TOGETHER."
MICHEL PLATINI

The French league (Le Championnat) has produced legends such as Just Fontaine, Michel Platini and Zinedine Zidane. Attacking flair and technical ability are features of the French game, and coaches such as Aimé Jacquet, Gérard Houllier and Guy Roux have built strong youth development systems. However, despite their undeniable talent, French teams have underachieved in European competitions.

The French League began in 1932, and is split into two divisions, Ligues 1 and 2, each with 20 teams.

OLYMPIQUE LYONNAIS

STADE GERLAND, LYON

Lyon are the most successful French club of modern times, winning all seven Ligue 1 titles between 2002 and 2007 – a French record. Despite domestic success 'Les Gones' have never got past the quarter-final of any European competition.

Lyon's Brazilian free-kick master Juninho Pernambucano in action for Lyon against Bordeaux in the 2007 French Cup final.

FC SOCHAUX

STADE AUGUSTE BONAL, MONTBÉLIARD

FC Sochaux were France's first professional club. Formed in 1928, they enjoyed early success and won the league in 1935 and 1938. After years of underachievement, a young, talented team have re-emerged, winning the French Cup in 2007 (above).

LEAGUE TROPHY
The Ligue 1 trophy was first contested in 1932–1933, when it was won by Olympique Lillois (now Lille). St Étienne, with 10 titles, are the most successful club.

FAMOUS CLUBS

SM Caen

Le Mans UC72

RC Lens

AS Monaco

AS Nancy-Lorraine

OGC Nice

OLYMPIQUE MARSEILLE

STADE VÉLODROME, MARSEILLE

France's best-supported club, Marseille have won eight league titles, a record ten French Cups, and in 1993 became the only ever French Champions League winners. A corruption scandal saw OM relegated in 1994 but they have bounced back in recent years. Legendary players include Jean-Pierre Papin (left) and Didier Deschamps.

FC NANTES ATLANTIQUE

LA BEAUJOIRE-LOUIS FONTENEAU, NANTES

Now languishing in Ligue 2, Nantes have won eight league titles since 1965. The Canaries are famed for their one-touch football, and for a youth system that produced players of the quality of Desailly and Deschamps.

FC GIRONDINS DE BORDEAUX

STADE CHABAN DELMAS, BORDEAUX

Some of the biggest names in modern French football have played for the five-times champions Bordeaux, including Alain Giresse, Christophe Dugarry, Eric Cantona, Jean Tigana and Zinedine Zidane. After a slump in the early 1990s, Bordeaux are slowly re-establishing their place near the top of Ligue 1.

AS MONACO

STADE LOUIS II, MONACO

The club from the tiny country of Monaco is one of the most successful teams in French football. They have won seven French titles and reached the final of the UEFA Champions League in 2004.

AS ST ÉTIENNE

STADE GEOFFROY-GUICHARD, ST ÉTIENNE

'Les Verts' (the Greens) dominated French football in the 1960s and 70s thanks to great players such as Michel Platini (right), but did not achieve the same success in Europe.

PARIS ST-GERMAIN

PARC DES PRINCES, PARIS

Formed in 1970 by the merger of two Paris clubs, Paris FC and Stade Saint-Germain, PSG rapidly established a reputation as a cup team, winning the French Cup seven times. The club has featured such stars as David Ginola (above), Youri Djorkaeff and George Weah.

 Paris St-Germain
 FC Girondins de Bordeaux
 Toulouse FC
 FC Lorient
 RC Strasbourg

ITALIAN CLUBS

*"FOOTBALL IS A PHENOMENON IN ITALY. IT'S ALL
THEY TALK ABOUT. IT'S CRAZY!"* DAVID TRÉZÉGUET, FRANCE AND
JUVENTUS STRIKER

Italian league football is split into four divisions with a total of 78 clubs.

Italian football, or 'calcio', has few rivals when it comes to passion, intensity and success. Big clubs like AC Milan, Internazionale, Roma and Juventus play in famous stadiums, field many of the world's finest players, and enjoy fanatical support. Italian teams are famed for an organised, defensive style combined with exciting individual flair. In the 1980s and 1990s Serie A could claim to be the best division in the world as foreign stars such as Maradona, van Basten, Papin and Gullit, plus home-grown talents such as Franco Baresi, Roberto Mancini and Gianluca Vialli lit up the Italian game. Recent corruption scandals and crowd trouble have tarnished the reputation of Italian football, but Italian clubs still rank among the greats.

GENOA
STADIO LUIGI FERRARIS, GENOA
Recent years may have been a struggle for the modern Genoa side, but the club can lay claim to being the first of Italy's great teams, winning nine league titles or 'scudetti' between 1898 and 1924.

AS ROMA
STADIO OLIMPICA, ROME
Proudly wearing their city's ancient wolf symbol on their shirts, the 'Giallorossi' (the Yellow-Reds) have won a total of three titles and nine Italian Cups. Their 2007 cup win is celebrated above.

AC MILAN
SAN SIRO, MILAN
Mighty AC Milan have won the European Cup no less than seven times and the scudetto (league) on 17 occasions. Pictured above is the club's legendary defender Paolo Maldini, still playing at the age of 39.

FAMOUS CLUBS

- AC MILAN
- AFC FIORENTINA
- AS LIVORNO CALCIO
- AS ROMA
- ATALANTA BC

- BOLOGNA FC 1909
- CAGLIARI CALCIO
- EMPOLI FC
- FC MESSINA PELORO
- GENOA

TORINO

STADIO OLIMPICO DE TORINO, TURIN

Torino were the finest Italian side of the 1940s. They won four consecutive league titles 1946–49, before tragedy struck in the Mount Superga disaster of 1949, when a plane carrying the team crashed near Turin, killing 18 players.

JUVENTUS

STADIO OLIMPICO DE TORINO, TURIN

Italy's most popular club are followed by supporters from Sicily to the Alps. Nicknamed 'La Vecchia Signora' (the Old Lady) the club have won two European Cups and 27 scudetti, and have a history of producing brilliant players like Alessandro del Piero (left).

LAZIO

STADIO OLIMPICO, ROME

Lazio have won two league titles (1974 and 2000), four Italian cups, and one European Cup Winners' Cup (1999). They share their ground with fierce local rivals Roma.

Inter players celebrate winning the 2007 Serie A title.

INTERNAZIONALE

SAN SIRO, MILAN

Internazionale were founded when some members split away from AC Milan in 1908. Pioneering the defensive style known as 'catenaccio' (meaning doorbolt), Internazionale were dominant during the 1960s, winning the European Cup twice. They are also known as Inter or Inter Milan.

- HELLAS VERONA FC
- JUVENTUS
- INTERNAZIONALE
- LAZIO
- NAPOLI

- PARMA FC
- TORINO
- UC SAMPDORIA
- UDINESE
- US CITTA DI PALERMO

GERMAN CLUBS

"THERE ARE NO RIGHT OR WRONG, OR FAIR RESULTS. THERE'S JUST THE FINAL SCORE."
OTTO REHHAGEL

The modern Bundesliga formed in 1963, for teams in what was then West Germany. After the country's unification in 1991, the East and West German leagues were merged, but the top tier is still dominated by clubs from the former West Germany. Football is hugely popular in Germany, and German club sides attract some of the largest crowds in the world. Germany's two professional divisions, the Bundesliga and the 2. Bundesliga, each have 18 teams.

Three teams are relegated from the Bundesliga and three promoted each season.

HAMBURGER SV
HSH NORDBANK ARENA

The only club never to have been relegated from the top division, Hamburg have won seven national titles, and were European Champions in 1983.

BAYERN MUNICH
ALLIANZ ARENA, MUNICH

Not only Germany's most successful club, with 21 national championships and four European Cups to their name, Bayern Munich are also the world's third biggest, after Real Madrid and Barcelona of Spain. In 2006–2007 Bayern finished a disappointing fourth in the Bundesliga but spent millions on new players and re-established their dominance by winning the following year's title.

Matthias Sammer played for Borussia Dortmund from 1993 to 1998 and later managed the club.

BORUSSIA DORTMUND
WESTFALENSTADION, DORTMUND

After initial success in the 1950s and 1960s, Dortmund re-emerged as a major club in the 1990s. Winners of six German titles and the Champions League in 1997, their average home attendance of 80,000 is the highest in Europe.

Bayern hope striker Miroslav Klose will fire them back to the top of the Bundesliga.

FAMOUS CLUBS

Eintracht Frankfurt

Hertha BSC Berlin

Werder Bremen

Bayer Leverkusen

FC Bayern Munich

Hannover 96

Hamburger SV

SCHALKE 04
VELTINS-ARENA, GELSENKIRCHEN

Founded in 1904, Schalke won the league six times between 1934 and 1942 and were a significant force in German football. Apart from their seventh league win in 1958 (their last to date) major success eluded Schalke for most of the second half of the 20th Century. However, victory in the 1997 UEFA Cup final – their first in Europe – signalled the start of Schalke's revival. So far in the 21st century, Schalke have been Bundesliga runners-up three times and have won the German Cup twice.

VFB STUTTGART
GOTTLIEB-DAIMLER-STADION, STUTTGART

2007 league champions Stuttgart have won a total of five national titles, but are yet to enjoy sustained European success. The club have one of the most successful youth development programmes in Germany and have also featured world class names such as Jürgen Klinsmann, Denmark's Jon Dahl Tomasson and Brazil's Giovane Élber.

WERDER BREMEN
WESERSTADION, BREMEN

Four-times German champions Werder Bremen established themselves as a footballing power under coach Otto Rehhagel in the 1980s. Now regular Champions League competitors, they have a reputation for attractive football. Werder hope that German internationals such as Per Mertesacker, Torsten Frings (above left) and Clemens Fritz. will give them the edge over their long-time rivals, Bayern Munich.

BAYER LEVERKUSEN
BAYARENA, LEVERKUSEN

Bayer emerged as a force in the late 1980s, but so far have won only one German Cup and a UEFA Cup. Former players include Rudi Völler and Michael Ballack and the club is known for its family-friendly image.

FC NÜRNBERG
EASYCREDIT-STADION, NUREMBERG

In the 1920's, nine-times champions Nürnberg were Germany's most popular and successful team. Since then, they have endured lean times – a German Cup win in 2007 (left) was followed by relagation the following season.

- BORUSSIA DORTMUND
- DSC ARMINIA BIELEFELD
- ENERGIE COTTBUS
- FC DYNAMO DRESDEN
- FC HANSA ROSTOCK
- FC NÜRNBERG
- KARLSRUHER FC
- MSV DUISBURG
- SCHALKE 04
- VFB STUTTGART
- VFL BOCHUM
- VFL WOLFSBURG

DUTCH CLUBS

"FOOTBALL IS SIMPLE. BUT THE HARDEST THING IS TO PLAY FOOTBALL IN A SIMPLE WAY." JOHAN CRUYFF

The Netherlands' top Dutch league, the Eredivisie, has 18 clubs; the second tier, the Eerste Divisie, has 20.

Dutch football is dominated by three clubs, Ajax, PSV Eindhoven and Feyenoord. Since 1965 only one team outside this big three has taken the league title, although in recent years smaller teams such as AZ Alkmaar, FC Twente and SC Herenveen have shown themselves to be an increasing threat. The Dutch game is traditionally played in an open, attacking style, which brought Dutch sides their greatest success in Europe in the 1970s. But the country's small size means its clubs can't compete financially with the big leagues of Spain, Italy, Germany and England, and top players now rarely spend more than two or three seasons in the Netherlands before transferring abroad.

Ajax players (right) celebrate after their thrilling penalty shoot-out victory over AZ Alkmaar in the 2007 KNVB Cup final in Rotterdam.

PSV EINDHOVEN

PHILIPS STADION, EINDHOVEN

PSV were the 2007 (above) and 2008 League champions, and in 1988 became one of only three Dutch teams to win the European Cup (now the Champions League). Dutch champions 21 times, PSV have featured famous players such as the van de Kerkhof brothers, Ruud van Nistelrooy, Philip Cocu and Ronaldo.

Ronald Koeman (above) played for PSV between 1986 and 1989 and managed the club in the 2006–2007 season.

AJAX

AMSTERDAM ARENA, AMSTERDAM

Ajax have won a record 29 titles and four European Cups. The great Ajax team of the 1966–73 era pioneered the concept of 'Total Football' under coach Rinus Michels. The number 14 shirt has been retired in honour of the club's most famous player, the great Johan Cruyff.

FAMOUS CLUBS

FC Twente

Go Ahead Eagles

Vitesse

N.E.C

Ajax

ADO Den Haag

Klaas-Jan Huntelaar has scored 97 goals since joining Ajax in 2006.

Huntelaar can use both feet, and is strong in the air — a classic striker.

SPARTA ROTTERDAM

HET KASTEEL, ROTTERDAM

The Netherlands' oldest club was formed in 1888 and, inspired by England's Sunderland FC, adopted a red and white striped kit in 1889. League champions six times before 1960, Sparta have recently regained their place in the top division after a three year absence.

WILLEM II

WILLEM II STADION, TILBURG

Named after a 19th century Dutch king, Willem II have not been league champions since 1955 but are now establishing a presence in European competition for the first time. Famous former players include Marc Overmars, Jaap Stam and Finland's Sami Hyypiä.

AZ ALKMAAR

DSB STADION, ALKMAAR

Founded in 1967, AZ is the only side outside the big three (Ajax, PSV and Feyenoord) to win the League since 1964. They won it in 1981 but were relegated from the Eredivisie in 1988. Since their return in 1998 they have undergone a remarkable revival, finishing third in the league in 2004–5 and runners-up in the KNVB cup in 2007.

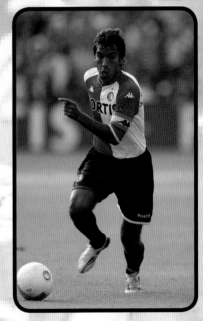

FEYENOORD

FEYENOORD STADION, ROTTERDAM

League champions 14 times and European Cup winners once, Feyenoord hope to repeat past triumphs under captain Giovanni van Bronckhorst (right).

Sparta Rotterdam

Willem II

AZ Alkmaar

FC Groningen

VVV-Venlo

SPANISH CLUBS

"FOOTBALL IS AN EXCUSE TO MAKE US HAPPY"

JORGE VALDANO, FORMER REAL ZARAGOZA AND REAL MADRID STRIKER

Spain's La Liga is one of the world's top three leagues, alongside those in England and Italy, and it has a reputation for thrilling, attacking football. First contested in 1928, it has only ever been won by nine clubs. For years the big two – Real Madrid (31 titles) and Barcelona (18 titles) – dominated, but recently the league has become more competitive with teams such as Sevilla FC, Real Sociedad and Valencia CF challenging for the title.

Spain's top professional division is La Liga, with 20 teams. The next level is the Segunda División, with 22 teams.

FC BARCELONA

CAMP NOU, BARCELONA

Founded in 1899, winners of 18 Spanish titles, 31 Spanish cups and two European Cups, and never relegated, Barcelona are one of the biggest clubs in the world. With a reputation for flamboyant, entertaining football, Barça have nearly 2,000 supporter clubs worldwide and are an integral part of the Catalan region of Spain. Their motto is 'Més que un club' (More than a club).

Barcelona's Camp Nou, or 'new field' (left) is Europe's biggest stadium, holding 98,772 spectators who fill the ground to watch superstar players such as Samuel Eto'o, Lionel Messi and Thierry Henry.

Barcelona's Ronaldinho takes a penalty during a 2007 La Liga match against Athletic Bilbao at the Camp Nou Stadium.

REAL SOCIEDAD

ANOETA, SAN SEBASTIÁN

Twice league champions in the early 1980s, Real Sociedad have fluctuated between the top two divisions for most of their history and currently play in the second flight.

FAMOUS CLUBS

Real Zaragoza

Recreativo de Huelva

Racing Santander

CA Osasuna

Murcia

Real Madrid

ATHLETIC BILBAO

SAN MAMÉS, BILBAO

Eight-times champions Bilbao are one of only three Spanish sides never to be relegated from La Liga, and they have won the Spanish Cup more times than any other club except Barcelona. Bilbao have a long-standing policy known as 'cantera', where they only sign players from the Basque region. In recent years, they have drifted in mid-table, putting the cantera policy under pressure.

SEVILLA FC

RAMÓN SÁNCHEZ PIZJUÁN, SEVILLE

Champions only once (in 1946), Sevilla returned to La Liga in 2000. They won the Spanish Cup (left) in 2007 and back-to-back UEFA Cups in 2006 and 2007 with a skilful, high-tempo game.

VALENCIA CF

ESTADIO MESTELLA, VALENCIA

Champions in the 1940s, 1970s and twice since 2000, Valencia attract passionate support bettered only by the big two. Their current success has been based on a defensive style at odds with Spanish league tradition, but the emergence of lethal striker David Villa (right) has injected a touch of flair.

ATLÉTICO MADRID

VICENTE CALDERÓN, MADRID

In the 1960s and 1970s, only Atlético challenged the dominance of city neighbours Real. (Above, Atlético as champions in 1973.) They remain Spain's third most successful club, although they have struggled in recent years.

REAL MADRID

SANTIAGO BERNABÉU, MADRID

True giants of world football, Real have won a record nine European Cups and 31 La Liga titles, including a dramatic last day victory in 2007. Over the years, legends such as Alfredo di Stéfano, Ferenc Puskás, Emilio Butragueño, David Beckham and Ronaldo have worn the famous white shirt and they are the richest club in the world. Spain star Raúl (far right) has also made more than 480 appearances for Madrid.

Real Valladolid

Levante UD

- DEPORTIVO LA CORUNA
- GETAFE CF
- RC CELTA DE VIGO
- RCD ESPANYOL
- REAL BETIS
- VILLAREAL CF

EUROPEAN CLUBS

"LET FOOTBALL REMAIN THE GAME THAT HAS BEEN THE DREAM OF GENERATIONS, THAT FILLS CHILDREN WITH WONDER, AND UNITES EUROPEANS." MICHEL PLATINI

Although European club competition, particularly the Champions League, is dominated by the big sides from the major nations, the rest of Europe nevertheless provides some famous clubs. Portugal, Scotland, Greece and Turkey, for example, all boast a fiercely contested domestic league system, with passionate rivalries between clubs that enjoy huge support. Other countries such as Ukraine and Sweden have also produced club sides that have fared well in European competition.

RANGERS

IBROX, GLASGOW, SCOTLAND

Rangers are one half of the 'Old Firm' – the name given to Scotland's two biggest clubs, who have enjoyed a long and often bitter local rivalry. Rangers have won a phenomenal 51 Scottish league titles, 31 Scottish Cups, and won the European Cup Winners' Cup in 1972.

USA international DaMarcus Beasley is a current Rangers' star.

DINAMO KIEV

LOBANOVSKY DINAMO STADIUM, KIEV, UKRAINE

Since Ukraine became an independent country in 1991, Dinamo Kiev have dominated domestic football and won the first nine league titles.

Vladislav Vashchuk (front, left) and Valentin Belkevich (front, right) celebrate winning the 2007 Ukrainian Cup.

CELTIC

CELTIC PARK, GLASGOW, SCOTLAND

The other half of Glasgow's 'Old Firm' Celtic have won 42 league titles and 34 Scottish Cups. They were the first British side to win the European Cup, when the 'Lisbon Lions' defeated Italian side Internazionale 2–1 in Portugal in 1967.

FENERBAHÇE

SÜCRÜ SARACOGLU, STADYUMU, ISTANBUL, TURKEY

Fenerbahçe are one of Turkey's biggest clubs, and the best supported. Based in the Asian east of Istanbul, the club have won the league title 17 times and been runners-up 15 times.

A new recruit in 2006 was Brazilian former Real Madrid star, Roberto Carlos.

FAMOUS CLUBS

FC Steaua Bucaresti (Romania)

SK Slavia Prague (Czech Republic)

Standard Liège (Belgium)

Anderlecht (Belgium)

Dinamo Kiev (Ukraine)

FC Basel 1893 (Switzerland)

SPORTING LISBON

ESTÁDIO JOSÉ ALVALADE, LISBON, PORTUGAL

Sporting are one of the most successful clubs in Portugal with 18 league titles and enjoy a strong rivalry with their Lisbon neighbours, Benfica. In 2003 the club moved to its impressive new home, the 52,000 capacity Estádio José Alvalade.

ANDERLECHT

CONSTANT VANDEN STOCK STADIUM, BRUSSELS, BELGIUM

Anderlecht are the biggest club side in Belgium by some margin, with 29 domestic titles and three victories in European competition – twice in the Cup Winners' Cup (1976 and 1978) and once in the UEFA Cup (1983).

BENFICA

ESTÁDIO DA LUZ, LISBON, PORTUGAL

Benfica are the most successful club in Portugal with a total of 31 league titles and 24 Portuguese Cups. They have also won the UEFA Champions League twice (1961 and 1962, when it was known as the European Cup) and are Portugal's best-supported team with an estimated 14 million fans around the world.

Striker Nuno Gomes has had two spells at Benfica, from 1997 to 2000 and from 2002 to the present time.

OLYMPIACOS

GEORGIOS KARAISKÁKIS STADIUM, ATHENS, GREECE

Olympiacos are the best supported and most successful of the three major Athens sides. The team have won the Greek national championship a record 36 times.

Raúl Bravo celebrates Olympiacos' 3–1 victory over Werder Bremen in the Champions League in 2007.

IFK GOTHENBURG

ULLEVI STADIUM, GOTHENBURG, SWEDEN

IFK Gothenburg are one of the biggest clubs in Sweden, and they are certainly the most successful, with 18 league titles. They are also the only Swedish side ever to lift a trophy in European competition, with two UEFA Cup triumphs in 1982 and 1987.

CSKA MOSCOW

DINAMO STADIUM, MOSCOW, RUSSIA

Formerly the team of the Soviet Red Army, CSKA have enjoyed a revival in recent years, winning the Russian league title in 2003, 2005 and 2006. They also won the UEFA Cup in 2005, becoming the first Russian side to win a major European competition.

SPARTA PRAGUE

AXA ARENA, PRAGUE, CZECH REPUBLIC

Sparta were a successful team in the old Czechoslavakian league. They have also dominated the new Czech Republic premier league since its formation in 1993, with ten victories in 14 seasons.

Sparta Prague players celebrate winning the Czech league in 2007.

Panathinaikos FC (Greece)

Galatasaray (Turkey)

- AEK ATHENS (GREECE)
- CSKA SOFIA (BULGARIA)
- FC PORTO (PORTUGAL)
- PARTIZAN BELGRADE (SERBIA)
- SHAKHTAR DONETSK (UKRAINE)
- STANDARD LIEGE (BELGIUM)

SOUTH AMERICA

"FOOTBALL IS PASSION, MULTITUDE, THE JOY OF LIVING."

FORMER ARGENTINA FOOTBALLER AND PLAYERS' UNION
GENERAL SECRETARY JORGE DOMINGUEZ

Although lack of financial muscle means many top stars leave for Europe, there is no doubting the flair and excitement of the region's game or the passion of South American football fans. The top sides from each country (38 altogether) qualify for the annual Copa Libertadores (see p.98) to decide the South American champions and, predictably, teams from Argentina and Brazil have dominated the competition.

COLO COLO

ESTADIO MONUMENTAL DAVID ARELLANO, SANTIAGO, CHILE

Chilean champions Colo Colo have won more national cups (26) than any other team, and are the only Chilean team ever to win the Copa Libertadores (in 1991).

Alexis Sánchez celebrates scoring a hat-trick for Colo Colo against Venezuela's Caracas during their Libertadores Cup match in March 2007. Sánchez is nicknamed 'El Niño Maravilla' (the Wonder Kid).

CLUB NACIONAL DE FOOTBALL

PARQUE CENTRAL, MONTEVIDEO, URUGUAY

Uruguayan giants Nacional have won 41 domestic titles and are three-times world club champions. The first World Cup Finals match was played at their stadium in 1930.

Forward Andrés Márquez of Nacional (right) competes for the ball with Elvis González (left) of Colombia's Cúcuta Deportivo.

CLUB BOLÍVAR

ESTADIO LIBERTADOR SIMON BOLÍVAR, LA PAZ, BOLIVIA

Named after the country's founder, Simon Bolívar, the La Paz team have won 15 titles, making them the most successful team in the professional league era (1977 onwards).

SÃO PAULO

MORUMBI, SAO PAULO, BRAZIL

A record of five league titles (one more than Corinthians), 21 state championships and three World Club crowns make São Paolo Brazil's most successful club. Their stadium holds 80,000 spectators.

São Paulo's Aloísio celebrates a goal against Boca Juniors in September 2007.

FAMOUS CLUBS

- BARCELONA SPORTING CLUB (ECUADOR)
- BOTAFOGO (BRAZIL)
- CA PENAROL (URUGUAY)
- CIENCIANO DEL CUZCO (PERU)
- ESTUDIANTES (ARGENTINA)
- FLAMENGO (BRAZIL)
- GREMIO (BRAZIL)
- INDEPENDIENTE (ARGENTINA)
- INTERNACIONAL (BRAZIL)

BOCA JUNIORS

ESTADIO ALBERTO J. ARMANDO, BUENOS AIRES, ARGENTINA

True giants of the world game, Boca Juniors hold a world record 17 international titles, alongside AC Milan. The legendary Diego Maradona is a fan and they enjoy a fierce local rivalry with River Plate.

Boca Juniors celebrate winning the Copa Libertadores in 2007.

ATLÉTICO NACIONAL

ATANASIO GIRARDOT, MEDELLIN, COLOMBIA

The first Columbian winners of the Copa Libertadores (in 1989), Nacional have won ten league titles, the third most successful haul in professional league history. The green and white shirt has been worn by many international stars including Faustino Asprilla and Juan Pablo Ángel.

CLUB DEPORTIVO EL NACIONAL

ESTADIO OLIMPICO ATAHUALPA, QUITO, ECUADOR

Owned by the country's military, El Nacional only fields players with Ecuadorian nationality. The team colours represent the three branches of the military. With 13 domestic titles they are jointly Ecuador's most successful team, an honour they share with Barcelona Sporting Club of Guayaquil.

ALIANZA LIMA

ESTADIO ALEJANDRO VILLANUEVA, LIMA, PERU

Universitario de Deportes have won more league titles (24) than Alianza (22), but Alianza have only recently recovered after losing their entire team in an air crash in 1987.

RIVER PLATE

EL MONUMENTAL, BUENOS AIRES, ARGENTINA

With 32 championships, River Plate are Argentina's most successful club. As local rivals, River v Boca is one of the great derby games.

Midfielder Marcelo Mattos was part of the great 2005 Corinthians team that included Carlos Tévez and Javier Mascherano.

CARACAS FC

COCODRILOS SPORTS PARK, CARACAS, VENEZUELA

The nine-times domestic league champions are the most successful team in Venzuelan history, with all nine titles coming in the last 15 years. Their nickname is 'Los Rojos' (the Reds). Amazingly, the club only turned professional in 1984.

CORINTHIANS

PACAEMBU, SÃO PAULO, BRAZIL

Sport Club Corinthians Paulista, named after famous English amateur club Corinthian FC, are one of Brazil's most successful teams with an impressive four league titles. They are estimated to have more than 25 million fans around the world.

- MILLIONARIOS (COLOMBIA)
- NEWELL'S OLD BOYS (ARGENTINA)
- OLIMPIA ASUNCION (PARAGUAY)
- ONCE CALDAS (COLOMBIA)
- PALMEIRAS (BRAZIL)
- SAN LORENZO (ARGENTINA)
- SANTOS (BRAZIL)
- THE STRONGEST (BOLIVIA)
- UNIVERSITARIO DE DEPORTES (PERU)

NORTH AMERICA

"WE HAVE COMPETITIVE TEAMS, COMPETITIVE INDIVIDUAL PLAYERS AND A VERY GOOD AND GROWING LEAGUE."

LA GALAXY GENERAL MANAGER AND FORMER USA INTERNATIONAL ALEXEI LALAS

The USA first launched a professional football league in 1968. Known as the NASL (North American Soccer League) it boasted star signings such as Pelé, Franz Beckenbauer and George Best. Although the NASL folded in 1984 it helped to raise football's profile in North America, particularly among young people. Ten years after the demise of the NASL the USA successfully hosted the World Cup Finals, and in 1996 a new MLS (Major League Soccer) was launched. Over the years, the MLS has flourished, attracting big-money sponsorship and world-class players.

LA GALAXY

HOME DEPOT CENTER, CARSON, CALIFORNIA, USA

LA Galaxy mix Hollywood glamour with good, old fashioned successful football. They have won the MLS Championship twice and the CONCACAF Champions' Cup once, in 2000. LA Galaxy were the first MLS club to record a profit.

D.C. UNITED

RFK STADIUM, WASHINGTON DC, USA

The team from the US capital quickly became a power base of the MLS. D.C. United have won four League Championships, including a 1996 league and cup double under coach Bruce Arena and captain John Harkes.

D.C. United's Luciano Emilio celebrates a goal against New England Revolution in 2007.

LA Galaxy hope that English superstar David Beckham (right) will bring further glory to the California team.

TORONTO FC

BMO FIELD, TORONTO, ONTARIO, CANADA

Toronto were the first Canadian entrants to the MLS in 2007. They have arguably the most intense fans in the league and enjoy sell-out crowds at almost every game.

Toronto FC players celebrate their late 2nd half goal, also against New England Revolution, in October 2007.

MLS FAMOUS CLUBS

Houston Dynamo

Chivas USA

FC Dallas

DC United

Toronto FC

LA Galaxy

Real Salt Lake

FC DALLAS

PIZZA HUT PARK, FRISCO, TEXAS, USA

Under their former name Dallas Burn, the Texas team beat D.C. United to the US Open Cup in 1997. In 2007 Dallas signed Brazilian winger Denílson, once the most expensive footballer in the world.

Guatemala's all-time top scorer Carlos Ruíz (above) has been FC Dallas' skipper and inspiration since signing from LA Galaxy in 2005.

HOUSTON DYNAMO

ROBERTSON STADIUM, HOUSTON, TEXAS, USA

MLS new boys Houston Dynamo won the 2006 MLS Cup in their first season and then won it again in 2007. They took over the San Jose Earthquakes franchise which meant they kept the same players, but changed the team's name and moved to a different state (Texas, from California).

Midfielder Corey Ashe heads the ball during a match between Houston Dynamo and Real Salt Lake in September 2007.

CONCACAF CLUBS

CF PACHUCA

ESTADIO HIDALGO, PACHUCA, MEXICO

In the last decade Mexico's oldest club CF Pachuca have outshone rivals Cruz Azul and Club América to win five national championships and three CONCACAF Champions' Cups.

SAPRISSA

ESTADIO RICARDO SAPRISSA AYMÁ, SAN JOSÉ, COSTA RICA

Saprissa have a record haul of 26 domestic titles as well as three CONCACAF Champions' Cups.

Pachuca captain Gabriel Caballero raises the SuperLiga trophy after his team's victory in the 2007 final.

CLUB DEPORTIVO GUADALAJARA

ESTADIO JALISCO, GUADALAJARA, MEXICO

Commonly known as the 'Chivas' (Goats), Guadalajara are the best-supported side in Mexico. A spin-off team, Chivas USA, joined the MLS in 2005.

SV TRANSVAAL

ANDRÉ KAMPERVEEN STADIUM, PARAMARIBO, SURINAM

Transvaal have won the Surinam league 19 times and the CONCACAF Champions Cup twice. SV Robinhood have 23 league titles.

CLUB DEPORTIVO OLIMPIA

ESTADIO MANUEL FERREIRA, ASUNCIÓN, PARAGUAY

Paraguay's oldest club celebrated their centenary in 2002 with their third Copa Libertadores. Cerro Porteño and Libertad have dominated the league so far this century.

Red Bull New York

New England Revolution

Colorado Rapids

Chicago Fire

Kansas City Wizards

Columbus Crew

San Jose Earthquakes

AFRICAN CLUBS

"IT'S ALL ABOUT FOOTBALL, FOOTBALL, FOOTBALL, FOOTBALL – THE WHOLE OF AFRICA, WE LOVE FOOTBALL." NIGERIA CAPTAIN AND STRIKER NWANKWO KANU

Despite some of the greatest talents being tempted away by rich European clubs, Africa has an impressive football culture. Rowdy rivalries, noble histories and some of the loudest, proudest fans on the planet – African club football has all the right ingredients. The African Cup of Champions kicked off in 1964 and became the CAF Champions League in 1997.

RAJA CASABLANCA

STADE MOHAMED V, CASABLANCA, MOROCCO

Founded in 1949, the 'people's club' took 26 years to win a trophy. However, they won the CAF Champions League in 1989, 1997 and 1999. Along with local rivals Wydad Casablanca, they are Morocco's most powerful club.

Defender Abdellatif Jrindou is the current Raja Casablanca captain.

MAMELODI SUNDOWNS

LOFTUS VERSFIELD STADIUM, PRETORIA, SOUTH AFRICA

Having a billionaire owner helps, but Mamelodi Sundowns were already a rising power in South Africa before Patrice Mosepe's 2003 takeover. They have won five league titles since 1998.

CANON YAOUNDÉ

STADE OMNISPORTS, YAOUNDÉ, CAMEROON

Canon Yaoundé are one of the most successful clubs in Cameroon. They have won nine league titles, three CAF Champions Leagues (1971, 1978,1980) and one CAF Cup Winners' Cup.

The Sundowns pipped Orlando Pirates to South Africa's Supa 8 cup in 2007.

EL-AHLY

CAIRO INTERNATIONAL STADIUM, CAIRO, EGYPT

Named the CAF's 'Club of the Century' in 2000, El-Ahly's record of five CAF Champions League titles and 33 Egyptian titles is unrivalled. They did not lose a single game from 1974 to 1977.

Goalkeeper Essam Al Hadari (left) and skipper Shady Mohamed (right) celebrate El-Ahly's 32nd league title in July 2007.

FAMOUS CLUBS

Kaizer Chiefs (South Africa)

Cotonsport Garoua (Cameroon)

Invincible Eleven (Liberia)

ASEC Mimosas (Côte D'Ivoire)

Accra Hearts of Oak Sporting Club (Ghana)

ENYIMBA

ENYIMBA INTERNATIONAL STADIUM, ABA, NIGERIA

In 2003 Enyimba, whose name means 'Elephant', brought the CAF Champions League trophy to Nigeria for the first time, 13 years after turning professional.

Goalkeeper Dele Aiyenugba secured Enyimba's first Nigerian FA Cup in 2005.

HAFIA FC

STADE 28 SEPTEMBRE, CONAKRY, GUINEA

Guinea's greatest got to keep the first African championship trophy after their third win in 1977, and they won the Guinean league 15 times (including titles won under their previous name Conakry II). However, success has eluded Hafia in recent years, with clubs such as Horoya AC and AS Kaloum Star rising to the top instead.

ÉTOILE SPORTIVE DU SAHEL

STADE OLYMPIQUE DE SOUSSE, SOUSSE, TUNISIA

Tunisia's oldest club, Sahel have won an array of CAF trophies to add to eight domestic league titles, thanks to Tunisian heroes such as midfielder Kaies Ghodhbane and Brazil-born striker Francileudo Santos, backed by big-name imports such as Ivoirian forward Kader Keïta.

ACCRA HEARTS OF OAK SPORTING CLUB

OHENE DJAN STADIUM, ACCRA, GHANA

Along with Asante Kotoko, Hearts of Oak have dominated football in Ghana. Although rivals Asante have won 20 league titles, Hearts can boast of being Ghana's oldest club. They have won 19 league titles (including 2006–2007) and one CAF Champions League (2000).

Hearts of Oak defender Charles Vadis beats Enyimba attacker Sunday Mba to the ball during a 2006 CAF Champions League match.

EL ZAMALEK

CAIRO STADIUM, CAIRO

El Zamalek and El-Ahly are Egypt's answer to the Glasgow 'Old Firm' (see p.112–113), and foreign referees are brought in to oversee their fierce derby matches. Zamelek share El-Ahly's record of five CAF Champions League titles and have won the league 11 times. They topped FIFA's club rankings in 2003.

ASEC MIMOSAS

STADE FÉLIX HOUPHOUËT-BOIGNY, ABIDJAN, CÔTE D'IVOIRE

Their 22 league titles to 2007 is an awesome record, but just as impressive is the youth academy created by Jean-Marc Guillou that has produced Emmanuel Eboué, Bonaventure and Salomon Kalou and Kolo and Yaya Touré.

Striker Walid Abdel–Latif in action for El Zamelek in a CAF Champions League match in 2005.

- ASANTE KOTOKO (GHANA)
- AS DOUANES (SENEGAL)
- DC MOTEMA PEMBE (PR CONGO)
- JS KABYLIE (ALGERIA)
- FAR RABAT (MOROCCO)
- ORLANDO PIRATES (SOUTH AFRICA)
- PRIMEIRO DE AGOSTO (ANGOLA)
- STADE MALIEN (MALI)
- TP MAZEMBE (DR CONGO)

ASIA AND OCEANIA

"ASIAN FOOTBALL IS IN THE PROCESS OF MAKING A BIG STEP FORWARD."

FRENCH SUPERSTAR ZINEDINE ZIDANE

The A-League (Australia), J-League (Japan) and K-League (Republic of Korea) are just some of the logically-named club championships of Asia and Oceania. Over the years, their up-and-coming teams have lured many notable players such as Kazuyoshi Miura and Dwight Yorke (Australia), Hristo Stoichkov, Patrick Mboma and Gary Lineker (Japan) and Alpay (Republic of Korea). The future looks bright for this rapidly developing football region.

MELBOURNE VICTORY FC

TELSTRA DOME, MELBOURNE, AUSTRALIA

Australian football is on the way up, with Melbourne Victory leading the charge. Sydney FC won the first A-League in 2006, but captain Kevin Muscat helped take the title to Melbourne the next year and then added the Championship trophy after the top four played off in the Finals Series.

Melbourne striker Archie Thompson is one of a growing number of A-league players to play for the Australian national team.

JEONBUK FC

JEONJU WORLD CUP STADIUM, JEONJU, REPUBLIC OF KOREA

Jeonbuk were the first South Korean team to win the AFC Champions League, in 2006. Despite domestic cup success, they still await their first K-League title as the league has been largely monopolised by Seongnam Ilhwa Chunma.

Jeonbuk's players after winning the AFC Champions League 2006 trophy.

WELLINGTON PHOENIX

WESTPAC STADIUM, WELLINGTON, NEW ZEALAND

Wellington Phoenix were formed in 2007 to replace New Zealand Knights in Australia's A-League.

German-born New Zealand international Shane Smeltz plays for the Phoenix.

DEMPO SPORTS CLUB

JAWAHARLAL NEHRU FATORDA STADIUM, MARGAO, INDIA

Dempo won two of the last three titles of India's National Football League. The NFL finished in 2007 and was replaced by a new professional league called the I-League, which Dempo also won in its first season.

FAMOUS CLUBS

Suwon Samsung Bluewings (South Korea)

Singapore Armed Forces FC (Singapore)

Júbilo Iwata (Japan)

Dalian Shide (China)

Adelaide United (Australia)

Central Coast Mariners (Australia)

DALIAN SHIDE

DALIAN PEOPLE'S STADIUM, DALIAN, CHINA

Dalian Shide are the most successful team in China. They won seven out of ten Jia league titles and have, so far, won the new Super League once.

Midfielder Zhu Ting scores for Dalian during their 2006 A3 Champions Cup match against Japan's JEF United Chiba.

AL-ZAWRAA

AL-ZAWRAA STADIUM, BAGHDAD, IRAQ

Arguably Iraq's best player Ahmed Radhi – 1988 Asian Footballer of the Year – had three jubilant spells with the country's biggest club, Al-Zawraa. A single goal by Japan's Shimizu S-Pulse denied them the Asian Cup Winners' Cup in 2000.

Abdulsalam Abboud (left) of Al-Zawraa vies with Taweeq Abdul Razzaq of UAE club Al-Wahda.

PAKISTAN ARMY FC

ARMY STADIUM, RAWALPINDI, PAKISTAN

Goalkeeper-captain Jaffar Khan and his Pakistan Army team marched to their fourth league title in 2006–2007, However, they remain five behind high-fliers Pakistan International Airlines.

Faheem Riaz (left) plays in midfield for Pakistan Army.

KASHIMA ANTLERS

KASHIMA STADIUM, KASHIMA, JAPAN

Kashima Antlers clinched the J-League's most eye-catching transfer coup by signing Brazilian star Zico in 1993. The five-times league champions peaked in 2000 with a treble of the J-League, J-League Cup and the Emperor's Cup.

Midfielder Mitsuo Ogasawara (left) in action for the Kashima Antlers.

AL-HILAL

KING FAHD INTERNATIONAL STADIUM, RIYADH, SAUDI ARABIA

The Al-Hilal trophy cabinet has been crammed with 47 cups since 1957, thanks to talents such as Brazilian World Cup-winner Rivelino, who played for them from 1978–1981.

ESTEGHLAL FC

AZADI STADIUM, TEHRAN, IRAN

Rivals Persepolis have won a few more league titles while sharing the same 90,000-capacity home, but Esteghlal can boast of being Asian champions in 1991 and runners-up eight years later.

Al-Hilal striker Yasser al-Qahtani is also the captain of the Saudi Arabia national team.

| Melbourne Victory FC (Australia) | Newcastle Jets (Australia) | Perth Glory (Australia) | Queensland Roar (Australia) | Sydney FC (Australia) | Wellington Phoenix (New Zealand) |

WOMEN'S CLUBS

"WE HAVE COME A LONG WAY IN DEVELOPING THE NATIONAL TEAMS – NOW THE TIME HAS COME TO WORK EVEN HARDER TO DEVELOP THE CLUBS."

SUSANNE ERLANDSSON OF THE UEFA
WOMEN'S FOOTBALL COMMITTEE

As relatively recently as the end of the 20th century, women were banned from playing football in many countries, such as Brazil. However, in the 21st century things are slowly improving – the international game is gaining in popularity and domestic leagues are now flourishing, especially in Northern Europe and the USA. Brazil's second place at the 2007 Women's World Cup has even prompted promises to set up a league there.

L-LEAGUE
JAPAN

Introduced in 1989, Japan's amateur L-League thrived thanks to big-money sponsorship and star players such as the USA's Tiffeny Milbrett (Shiroki Serena) and Norway's Hege Riise (Nikko Securities Dream Ladies).

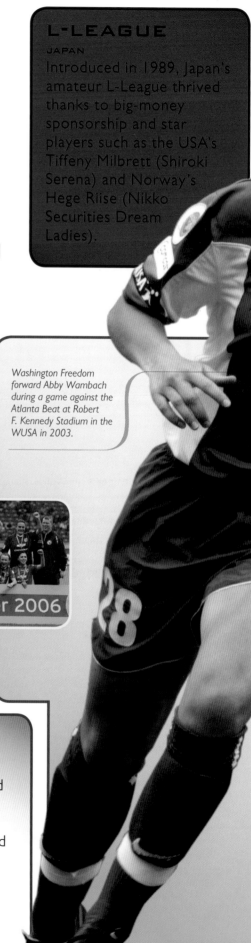

Washington Freedom forward Abby Wambach during a game against the Atlanta Beat at Robert F. Kennedy Stadium in the WUSA in 2003.

FRAUEN-BUNDESLIGA
GERMANY

Two clubs have dominated German women's football since the women's semi-pro league was founded in 1990 – 1. FFC Frankfurt and 1. FFC Turbine Potsdam. Domestic and European success, particularly for Frankfurt, has provided the foundation for Germany's many international triumphs.

Striker Birgit Prinz has collected six league titles, six German Cups and six UEFA club championships since joining Frankfurt in 1998.

DFB-Pokalsieger 2006

1. FFC Turbine Potsdam celebrate winning the 2006 German Cup against Frankfurt.

TOPPSERIEN
NORWAY

Scandinavia has long been a stronghold for women's football and Norway first established a women's league in 1984. It began as three regional divisions which then merged three years later to form a single league. The majority of titles have been shared between Trondheims-Ørn and Asker SK. In fact, during the 1998 season Asker SK won all of their 18 games!

USA W-LEAGUE
USA

The USA made history by setting up the world's first professional league for women in 2001, with 20 founding players including Kristine Lilly and Michelle Akers. However, the WUSA (Women's United Soccer Association) folded after just three seasons, although hopes are high for a 2008 relaunch. For now, attention is back on the amateur W-League, running since 1995 and featuring both international stars and up-and-coming college players.

Canada's Vancouver Whitecaps were W-League champions in 2004 and 2006, but now face a tough challenge from ex-WUSA team Washington Freedom.

SUPERLIGA FEMININA
SPAIN

The women's league clubs in Spain have maintained close links to their male counterparts since kicking off in 1983. As in La Liga's early years, the front-runners are Athletic Bilbao. However, in the women's game, Real Madrid remain absent from the top divison and Barcelona were relegated in 2006–2007.

The FA Women's Cup spcnsored by E.ON 2007 Final

Arsenal Ladies added the league title, League Cup and UEFA trophy to their FA Women's Cup in 2007 (above).

PREMIER LEAGUE
ENGLAND

When Arsenal Ladies beat Sweden's Umeå IK to capture the UEFA Women's Cup in 2007 it was England's first victory in that competiton. It marked a clean sweep of trophies for the London club and also brought positive signs for the development of the women's game in England.

DAMALLSVENSKAN
SWEDEN

Sweden seem to develop women's football better than anywhere else in the world. The Swedish league, known as the Damallsvenskan, dates back to 1973 and has attracted some of the best players from around the world. Stars such as the USA's Kristine Lilly, China's Ma Xiaoxu and Brazil's Marta combine with the finest homegrown talents such as Hanna Ljungberg. Top team Umeå IK have twice been UEFA Women's Cup champions. Despite club success, Sweden remain international football's runners-up, losing four major international finals.

Marta left Brazil for Sweden's Umeå IK in 2004 because Brazil did not have a serious women's league.

RIVELINO
BRAZIL
The midfielder's performances for Brazil between 1965 and 1978 earned him legendary status. Famed for his graceful play and thunderous left foot, Rivelino is unofficially credited with scoring the fastest ever goal – directly from the kick-off.

JAIRZINHO
BRAZIL
This powerful winger scored in every game of the 1970 World Cup tournament, the only player so far ever to achieve this feat. Immensely talented, Jairzinho made his professional debut at 15 and his international debut in 1964, at the age of 19.

BRIAN LAUDRUP
DENMARK
Highly skilled, with devastating pace, attacking midfielder Brian Laudrup was a key member of the Danish team that won the 1992 European Championships. He also helped Glasgow Rangers win nine consecutive league titles, before retiring in 2000.

BIXENTE LIZARAZU
FRANCE
Able to mark tightly, anchor the defence and pass the ball expertly, Lizarazu was widely regarded as one of the finest left backs of all time. He was a key member of the France side that won the 1998 World Cup and 2000 European Championship.

HALL OF FAME

"THE CLEVEREST DO MATHS, THE NEXT-BEST WRITE BOOKS. DANCERS ARE THE CLEVEREST WITH THEIR FEET, NEXT ARE FOOTBALLERS." JOHAN CRUYFF

In this book we have set out to select the greatest players and best teams in world football. Sadly, it is impossible to include absolutely everyone and many footballing legends have not managed to squeeze onto our pages. However, there are some heroes – old and new and from all around the world – that we simply had to find space for. This is our Hall of Fame.

JORGE VALDANO
ARGENTINA
The striker played for his country between 1975 and 1986, and also achieved fame as a player and coach with Real Madrid. Valdano's footballing knowledge and opinions of the game have earned him the nickname 'The Philosopher of Football'.

SÓCRATES
BRAZIL
Skilful, inspirational and a fine reader of the game, Sócrates captained his country in the 1982 and 1986 World Cups. His trademark move was the blind heel pass, which involved passing the ball with his heel whilst looking in the opposite direction.

JOHAN NEESKENS
NETHERLANDS
A technically gifted midfielder, Neeskens provided the base for the master Johan Cruyff to work his magic in the great Dutch 'Total Football' side of the 1970s. He played club football for Ajax and Barcelona and was known for his powerful penalty kicks.

FERNANDO HIERRO
SPAIN
A tough defender with superior passing ability, Hierro was a stalwart for Spain for more than a decade. He scored an impressive 29 goals for his country in 89 appearances and also helped Real Madrid to five league titles between 1989 and 2002.

OLIVER KAHN
GERMANY
This recently-retired goalkeeper was nicknamed 'King Kahn'. He was regarded as the world's number one after the 2002 World Cup Finals when he become the first goalkeeper in history to win the Golden Ball for best player.

OMAR SÍVORI
ARGENTINA/ITALY
A wonderfully-gifted, audacious forward who loved to dribble the ball and delighted in nutmegging defenders, his speed and invention make him one of the finest footballers ever. Sívori played for both Argentina and Italy between 1956 and 1962.

LEV YASHIN
USSR
Voted the best goalkeeper of the 20th century, Yashin was known for his athleticism and reflex saves. He played for the USSR between 1949 and 1967 and spent his entire club career at Dinamo Moscow. He is believed to have saved 150 penalties.

IAN RUSH
WALES
A deadly striker who combined lethal finishing with superb anticipation, 'Rushie' formed half of what many regard as Britain's greatest-ever strike partnership alongside Liverpool team mate Kenny Dalglish. Rush is Liverpool's all-time highest scorer.

ROY KEANE
REPUBLIC OF IRELAND
Central midfielder Keane was seen as one of the best players of the modern era. A competitive and aggressive ball winner whose late runs into the box often led to goals, he achieved most success with Man Utd and has recently moved into club management.

SIR BOBBY CHARLTON
ENGLAND
Graceful, athletic, quick, with a thunderbolt shot and fierce sense of fair play, Bobby Charlton's exploits with Manchester United and England during the 1950s and 1960s make him one of the greatest players of all time. He is still England's top scorer.

JIMMY GREAVES
ENGLAND
In the 1960s, nobody was better at scoring goals than striker Jimmy Greaves. He scored on every debut and netted 44 times in 57 England games – including six hat-tricks. He also played for Chelsea, AC Milan, Tottenham Hotspur and West Ham.

MICHELLE AKERS
USA
Dubbed 'the Pele of women's football' and voted FIFA's Woman Player of the Century in 2002, Akers was part of the first-ever USA women's team in 1985. She was top scorer in the first women's World Cup in 1991, scoring twice in the final win over Norway.

DENIS LAW
SCOTLAND
The only Scotsman ever to be European Footballer of the Year, (in 1964), this fiercely competitive striker was a supreme goalscorer, incisive passer and intelligent reader of the game. A legend at Manchester United, he also played for Manchester City.

FRANCO BARESI
ITALY
Able to play as a central defender or sweeper, Baresi was famous for his tough tackling. He captained Italy at the 1994 World Cup Finals. He was also a rock in the AC Milan defence for 20 years and AC Milan's no. 6 shirt has been retired in his honour.

GEORGE BEST
NORTHERN IRELAND
Possibly Britain's greatest ever player, Best was dazzlingly skilful. Fast, two-footed, an expert dribbler and scorer of sublime goals, Best unfortunately never graced a World Cup Finals. As the saying goes 'Maradona good, Pelé better, George Best'.

SIR STANLEY MATTHEWS
ENGLAND
A classic winger, Matthews played for an astonishing 33 years – until he was 50! He was the first-ever European Footballer of the Year and the first footballer to be knighted. Matthews was a true gentleman of the game and never received a single booking.

MARCEL DESAILLY
FRANCE
One of the top centre-backs in the world between 1993 and 2004, Desailly won every major club and international honour in the game with AC Milan, Chelsea and France. Chelsea fans voted him their greatest ever centre-back, alongside John Terry.

ERIC CANTONA
FRANCE
One of the most influential footballers of the 1980s and 1990s, Cantona had everything. Dubbed 'The King' by Man Utd fans, he could score goals or create them, displayed superb ball control and breathtaking vision – a true entertainer.

ROBERTO AYALA
ARGENTINA

This much-capped central defender is good in the air, a tenacious tackler and an excellent passer of the ball. Ayala inherited the nickname of El Ratón (Mouse) from Argentine 1974 World Cup player Rubén Ayala, although they are not related.

KRISTINE LILLY
USA

The USA's legendary captain has played 340 games for the national side – a world record for men or women. Nicknamed 'Iron Woman', Lilly is a tireless worker who can score and create goals. She is the first woman to play in five World Cup Finals.

TAB RAMOS
USA

One of the most technically gifted players to wear the USA shirt, midfielder Ramos won 81 caps between 1981 and 2000. Born in Uruguay, he was also one of the first US players to find success abroad, playing in both Spain and Mexico.

ALFREDO DI STÉFANO
ARGENTINA/SPAIN

Considered by many the greatest player ever, di Stéfano's fitness and versatility saw him play in most outfield positions. Best known as a deadly centre-forward, he inspired Real Madrid to five successive European Cups between 1956 and 1960.

ROMÁRIO
BRAZIL

This gifted centre-forward, who retired in 2008 at over 40 years old, claimed a career total of more than 1,000 goals. His technique and sharpness in the box fired PSV and Barcelona to success, as well as Brazil. Romário won the Golden Ball at the '94 World Cup Finals.

EUSÉBIO
PORTUGAL

Portuguese but of Mozambican origin, striker Eusébio was the first African football superstar. Playing in the 1960s, Eusébio was fast, powerful, capable of superb ball-control and had a deadly right foot. He is still all-time top scorer for his club Benfica.

ALESSANDRO NESTA
ITALY

A powerful, confident central defender, widely acknowledged as one of the world's best, Nesta has won almost every major honour in the game, including the 2006 World Cup. Still a regular for AC Milan, he has retired from international football.

MAHMOUD EL-KHATIB
EGYPT

A true legend of Egyptian football, striker El-Khatib was an accomplished goalscorer between 1972 and 1988. Nicknamed 'Bibo', El-Khatib holds the dubious honour of sustaining the most injuries in the history of the Egyptian game.

HRISTO STOICHKOV
BULGARIA

Probably his country's greatest player, this left-sided attacker could accelerate at speed, dribble superbly and unleash powerful shots from unpredictable situations. He inspired Bulgaria to fourth at the 1994 World Cup, and Barcelona to four league titles.

DINO ZOFF
ITALY

One of the finest goalkeepers ever, Zoff holds the record for not conceding an international goal – 1142 minutes between 1972 and 1974. He captained Italy, most famously at the 1982 World Cup, and was a key member of the great Juventus team of the 1970s.

'JAY-JAY' OKOCHA
NIGERIA

A skilful midfielder reknowned for his dazzling step-overs, Okocha helped establish his country as a world force in the 1990s and played for club sides across Europe. His fans at Bolton Wanderers used to say, he's "so good they named him twice".

'DOCTOR' KHUMALO
SOUTH AFRICA

The man who made his country and his club side, Kaizer Chiefs, tick in the 1980 and 1990s, Khumalo's passing and movement were so good that he could run the game from his midfield position. He was also an accomplished ball-juggler!

TONY VIDMAR
AUSTRALIA
One of the most successful Australians in club football, this left-sided defender achieved most success with Glasgow Rangers between 1997 and 2002. Versatile enough to play across the back line, he could also push up the left wing to support attacks.

RUUD KROL
NETHERLANDS
A legend of the 1970s 'Total Football' sides of Ajax and the Netherlands, Krol was a technically gifted defender who could play across the back line, as a sweeper or defensive midfielder. He captained his country after Johan Cruyff retired.

KARL-HEINZ RUMMENIGGE
GERMANY
A prolific goalscorer for his country and club Bayern Munich, Rummenigge was Germany's football superstar after Franz Beckenbauer retired. Twice European Footballer of the Year (in 1980 and 1981), he retired from the game in 1989.

JUAN ROMÁN RIQUELME
ARGENTINA
With great ball control, pinpoint passing and incisive vision, attacking midfielder Riquelme is considered by some to be the world's best current player. Watching him run with the ball is a joy, and he scores spectacular goals, often from free-kicks.

FRANCISCO GENTO
SPAIN
Gento's ability to run with the ball and eye for goal were central to the success of the Real Madrid side of the 1950s and 1960s. He is still the only man to win six European Cups and was also part of Spain's 1964 European Championship winning side.

FRITZ WALTER
GERMANY
Named by the German football associations as the country's most outstanding player, this forward captained Germany to its first World Cup success in 1954. His ability to read the game and to control the ball kept him two steps ahead of opponents.

LI MING
CHINA
Hard-working midfielder Li Ming's reputation for striking the right balance between attack and defence made him a key part of the Dalian Shide team that won six Chinese league titles in the 1990s. He is also China's most-capped player.

PAULINO ALCÁNTARA
PHILIPPINES
Born in the Philippines to a Spanish father, striker Alcántara scored a remarkable 357 goals in 357 games for Barcelona between 1912 and 1927. The first Asian footballer ever to play for a European club, Alcántara is still Barcelona's top scorer.

SALIF KEÏTA
MALI
A hugely-talented striker, Keïta was also a football pioneer. He was the first African Footballer of the Year (in 1970) and one of the first African footballers to play in Europe. In 2005, Keïta was elected president of the Malian Federation of Football (FEMAFOOT).

KARIM ABDUL RAZAK
GHANA
Midfielder Razak was blessed with superb ball control and ability to read the game. He was African Footballer of the Year in 1978 and was a key part of the Ghana team that won the African Cup of Nations in the same year. Razak is now a top coach in Ghana.

MASAMI IHARA
JAPAN
An accomplished sweeper and central defender, Ihara was a fixture in the national team throughout the 1990s. What he lacked in pace he made up for in awareness. His phenomenal record of 122 caps may never be equalled.

MOHAMMED AL-DEAYEA
SAUDI ARABIA
A goalkeeper who played for his country in four World Cup Finals, Al-Deayea holds 181 caps, a record for a male player. His penalty saves in the 1996 Asian Cup final helped Saudi Arabia to victory. Al-Deayea has now retired from international football.

INTERNATIONAL STATS

FIFA WORLD CUP

A competition for national teams of member nations of FIFA, the international ruling body of football.

2006	Italy
2002	Brazil
1998	France
1994	Brazil
1990	West Germany
1986	Argentina
1982	Italy
1978	Argentina
1974	West Germany
1970	Brazil
1966	England
1962	Brazil
1958	Brazil
1954	West Germany
1950	Uruguay
1938	Italy
1934	Italy
1930	Uruguay

FIFA WOMEN'S WORLD CUP

2007	Germany
2003	Germany
1999	USA
1995	Norway
1991	USA

UEFA EUROPEAN CHAMPIONSHIP

A competition for national teams of nations governed by UEFA, the ruling body of European football.

2004	Greece
2000	France
1996	Germany
1992	Denmark
1988	Netherlands
1984	France
1980	West Germany
1976	Czechoslovakia*
1972	West Germany
1968	Italy
1964	Spain
1960	USSR

UEFA WOMEN'S CHAMPIONSHIPS

2005	Germany
2001	Germany
1997	Germany
1995	Germany
1993	Norway
1991	Germany

* See p.45 for the current name of Czechoslovakia.

CONMEBOL COPA AMÉRICA

A competition for national teams of nations governed by CONMEBOL, the ruling body of South American football.

2007	Brazil
2004	Brazil
2001	Colombia
1999	Brazil
1997	Brazil
1995	Uruguay
1993	Argentina
1991	Argentina
1989	Brazil
1987	Uruguay
1983	Uruguay
1979	Paraguay
1975	Peru
1967	Uruguay
1963	Bolivia
1959	Uruguay (December)
1959	Argentina (April)
1957	Argentina
1956	Uruguay
1955	Argentina
1953	Paraguay
1949	Brazil
1947	Argentina
1946	Argentina
1945	Argentina
1942	Uruguay
1941	Argentina
1939	Peru
1937	Argentina
1935	Uruguay
1929	Argentina
1927	Argentina
1926	Uruguay
1925	Argentina
1924	Uruguay
1923	Uruguay
1922	Brazil
1921	Argentina
1920	Uruguay
1919	Brazil
1917	Uruguay
1916	Uruguay

CONCACAF GOLD CUP*

A competition for national teams of countries governed by CONCACAF, the ruling body of football in North America, Central America and the Caribbean.

2007	USA
2005	USA
2003	Mexico
2002	USA
2000	Canada
1998	Mexico
1996	Mexico
1993	Mexico
1991	USA
1989	Costa Rica
1985	Canada
1981	Honduras
1977	Mexico
1973	Haiti
1971	Mexico
1969	Costa Rica
1967	Guatemala
1965	Mexico
1963	Costa Rica

*1963–1989 competition known as CONCACAF Championship; 1991– present competition known as CONCACAF Gold Cup.

CAF AFRICAN CUP OF NATIONS

A competition for national teams of African countries, sanctioned by CAF.

2008	Egypt
2006	Egypt
2004	Tunisia
2002	Cameroon
2000	Cameroon
1998	Egypt
1996	South Africa
1994	Nigeria
1992	Côte d'Ivoire
1990	Algeria
1988	Cameroon
1986	Egypt
1984	Cameroon
1982	Ghana
1980	Nigeria
1978	Ghana
1976	Morocco
1974	Zaire
1972	Congo
1970	Sudan
1968	Congo Kinshasa (now DR Congo)
1965	Ghana
1963	Ghana
1962	Ethiopia
1959	Egypt
1957	Egypt

AFC ASIAN CUP

A competition for national teams of Asian countries, organised by AFC.

2007	Iraq
2004	Japan
2000	Japan
1996	United Arab Emirates
1992	Japan
1988	Saudi Arabia
1984	Saudi Arabia
1980	Kuwait
1976	Iran
1972	Iran
1968	Iran
1964	Israel
1960	Republic of Korea
1956	Republic of Korea

OFC NATIONS CUP (OCEANIA)

A competition for national teams of member countries of OFC.

2004	Australia
2002	New Zealand
2000	Australia
1998	New Zealand
1996	Australia
1980	Australia
1973	New Zealand

FIFA CONFEDERATIONS CUP

A competition for winners of the the AFC Asian Cup, the CAF African Cup of Nations, the CONCACAF Gold Cup, the CONMEBOL Copa America, the OFC Nations Cup, the UEFA European Championships, and the World Cup champions and host country.

2005	Brazil
2003	France
2001	France
1999	Mexico
1996	Brazil
1994	Denmark
1992	Argentina

OLYMPIC GAMES – MEN'S FOOTBALL

A football competition that is part of an international event made up of multiple sporting competitions.

2004	Argentina
2000	Cameroon
1996	Nigeria
1992	Spain
1988	USSR
1984	France
1980	Czechoslovakia*
1976	East Germany**
1972	Poland
1968	Hungary
1964	Hungary
1960	Yugoslavia***
1956	USSR****
1952	Hungary
1948	Sweden
1936	Italy
1928	Uruguay
1924	Uruguay
1920	Belgium
1912	Great Britain
1908	Great Britain
1904	Canada
1900	Great Britain

*, ***, **** See p.45 for the current names of Czechoslovakia, Yugoslavia and the USSR.
** See p.38 and 39 for the current name of East Germany.

OLYMPIC GAMES – WOMEN'S FOOTBALL

2004	USA
2000	Norway
1996	USA

FIFA WORLD PLAYER OF THE YEAR*

2007	Kaká (AC Milan and Brazil)
2006	Fabio Cannavaro (Juventus, Real Madrid and Italy)
2005	Ronaldinho (Barcelona and Brazil)
2004	Ronaldinho (Barcelona and Brazil)
2003	Zinedine Zidane (Real Madrid and France)
2002	Ronaldo (Internazionale, Real Madrid and Brazil)
2001	Luis Figo (Real Madrid and Portugal)
2000	Zinedine Zidane (Juventus and France)
1999	Rivaldo (Barcelona and Brazil)
1998	Zinedine Zidane (Juventus and France)
1997	Ronaldo (Barcelona, Internazionale and Brazil)
1996	Ronaldo (PSV Eindhoven, Barcelona and Brazil)
1995	George Weah (AC Milan and Liberia)
1994	Romário (Barcelona and Brazil)
1993	Roberto Baggio (Juventus and Italy)
1992	Marco van Basten (AC Milan and Netherlands)
1991	Lothar Matthäus (Internazionale and Germany)

*As voted by coaches and captains of international teams.

EUROPEAN FOOTBALLER OF THE YEAR*

2007	Kaká (AC Milan and Brazil)
2006	Fabio Cannavaro (Real Madrid and Italy)
2005	Ronaldinho (Barcelona and Brazil)
2004	Andriy Shevchenko (AC Milan and Ukraine)
2003	Pavel Nedved (Juventus and Czech Republic)
2002	Ronaldo (Internazionale, Real Madrid and Brazil)
2001	Michael Owen (Liverpool and England)
2000	Luís Figo (Real Madrid and Portugal)
1999	Rivaldo (Barcelona and Brazil)
1998	Zinedine Zidane (Juventus and France)
1997	Ronaldo (Barcelona, Internazionale and Brazil)
1996	Matthias Sammer (Borussia Dortmund and Germany)
1995	George Weah (Paris Saint-Germain, AC Milan and Liberia)
1994	Hristo Stoichkov (Barcelona and Bulgaria)
1993	Roberto Baggio (Juventus and Italy)
1992	Marco van Basten (AC Milan and Netherlands)
1991	Jean-Pierre Papin (Marseille and France)
1990	Lothar Matthäus (Internazionale and West Germany)
1989	Marco van Basten (AC Milan and Netherlands)
1988	Marco van Basten (AC Milan and Netherlands)

OLYMPIC GAMES

Olympic football, at least for men, has never quite enjoyed the prestige of other international tournaments, such as the World Cup. In 1992 FIFA ruled that Olympic players must be under 23 (with three exceptions allowed per squad). This has changed the nature of the tournament and allowed teams such as Cameroon and Nigeria to shine at the Olympics.

In the 2004 Olympic final, Argentina beat Paraguay 1–0. Argentina's Javier Mascherano (right) and Paraguay's Osvaldo Díaz (left) battle for the ball.

1987	Ruud Gullit (PSV Eindhoven, Ajax and Netherlands)
1986	Igor Belanov (Dinamo Kiev and USSR)
1985	Michel Platini (Juventus and France)
1984	Michel Platini (Juventus and France)
1983	Michel Platini (Juventus and France)
1982	Paolo Rossi (Juventus and Italy)
1981	Karl-Heinz Rummenigge (Bayern Munich and West Germany)
1980	Karl-Heinz Rummenigge (Bayern Munich and West Germany)
1979	Kevin Keegan (Hamburg and England)
1978	Kevin Keegan (Hamburg and England)
1977	Allan Simonsen (Borussia Mönchengladbach and Denmark)
1976	Franz Beckenbauer (Bayern Munich and West Germany)
1975	Oleg Blokhin (Dinamo Kiev and USSR)
1974	Johan Cruyff (Barcelona and Netherlands)
1973	Johan Cruyff (Ajax, Barcelona and Netherlands)
1972	Franz Beckenbauer (Bayern Munich and West Germany)
1971	Johan Cruyff (Ajax and Netherlands)
1970	Gerd Müller (Bayern Munich and West Germany)
1969	Gianni Rivera (AC Milan and Italy)
1968	George Best (Manchester United and Northern Ireland)
1967	Flórián Albert (Ferencvaros and Hungary)
1966	Bobby Charlton (Manchester United and England)
1965	Eusébio (Benfica and Portugal)
1964	Denis Law (Manchester United and Scotland)
1963	Lev Yashin (Dinamo Moscow and USSR)
1962	Josef Masopust (Dukla Prague and Czechoslovakia)
1961	Omar Sívori (Juventus and Italy)
1960	Luis Suárez (Barcelona and Spain)
1959	Alfredo di Stéfano (Real Madrid and Spain)
1958	Raymond Kopa (Real Madrid and France)
1957	Alfredo di Stéfano (Real Madrid and Spain)
1956	Stanley Matthews (Blackpool and England)

*As voted by France Football magazine.

SOUTH AMERICAN FOOTBALLER OF THE YEAR*

2007 Salvador Cabañas (Club América and Paraguay)
2006 Matías Fernández (Colo-Colo and Chile)
2005 Carlos Tevéz (Corinthians and Argentina)
2004 Carlos Tevéz (Boca Juniors and Argentina)
2003 Carlos Tevéz (Boca Juniors and Argentina)
2002 José Cardozo (Toluca and Paraguay)
2001 Juan Román Riquelme (Boca Juniors and Argentina)
2000 Romário (Vasco da Gama and Brazil)
1999 Javier Saviola (River Plate and Argentina)
1998 Martín Palermo (Boca Juniors and Argentina)
1997 Marcelo Salas (River Plate and Chile)
1996 José Luis Chilavert (Vélez Sársfield and Paraguay)
1995 Enzo Francescoli (River Plate and Uruguay)
1994 Cafú (São Paulo and Brazil)
1993 Carlos Valderrama (Atlético Junior and Colombia)
1992 Raí (São Paulo and Brazil)
1991 Oscar Ruggeri (Vélez Sársfield and Argentina)
1990 Raúl Vicente Amarilla (Olimpia and Paraguay)
1989 Bebeto (Vasco da Gama and Brazil)
1988 Rubén Paz (Racing Club and Uruguay)
1987 Carlos Valderrama (Deportivo Cali and Colombia)
1986 Antonio Alzamendi (River Plate and Uruguay)
1985 Romerito (Fluminense and Paraguay)
1984 Enzo Francescoli (River Plate and Uruguay)
1983 Sócrates (Corinthians and Brazil)
1982 Zico (Flamengo and Brazil)
1981 Zico (Flamengo and Brazil)
1980 Diego Maradona (Argentinos Juniors and Argentina)
1979 Diego Maradona (Argentinos Juniors and Argentina)
1978 Mario Kempes (Valencia and Argentina)
1977 Zico (Flamengo and Brazil)
1976 Elías Figueroa (Internacional and Chile)
1975 Elías Figueroa (Internacional and Chile)
1974 Elías Figueroa (Internacional and Chile)
1973 Pelé (Santos and Brazil)
1972 Teófilo Cubillas (Alianza Lima and Peru)
1971 Tostão (Cruzeiro and Brazil)

*As voted by El Mundo magazine 1971–1986 and El País 1987–present.

AFRICAN FOOTBALLER OF THE YEAR*

2007 Frédéric Kanouté (Sevilla and Mali)
2006 Didier Drogba (Chelsea and Côte d'Ivoire)
2005 Samuel Eto'o (Barcelona and Cameroon)
2004 Samuel Eto'o (Real Mallorca, Barcelona and Cameroon)
2003 Samuel Eto'o (Real Mallorca and Cameroon)
2002 El Hadji Diouf (Lens, Liverpool and Senegal)
2001 El Hadji Diouf (Lens and Senegal)
2000 Patrick Mboma (Parma and Cameroon)
1999 Nwankwo Kanu (Arsenal and Nigeria)
1998 Mustapha Hadji (Deportivo La Coruña and Morocco)
1997 Viktor Ikpeba (Monaco and Nigeria)
1996 Nwankwo Kanu (Ajax, Internazionale and Nigeria)
1995 George Weah (Milan and Liberia)
1994 Emmanuel Amuneke (Zamalek, Sporting Lisbon and Nigeria)
1993 Rashidi Yekini (Vitória Setubal and Nigeria)
1992 Abédi 'Pelé' Ayew (Lille and Ghana)
1991 Abédi 'Pelé' Ayew (Marseille and Ghana)
1990 Roger Milla (Cameroon)
1989 George Weah (Monaco and Liberia)
1988 Kalusha Bwalya (Cercle Brugge and Zambia)
1987 Rabah Madjer (Porto and Algeria)
1986 Badou Zaki (Real Mallorca and Morocco)
1985 Mohamed Timoumi (FAR Rabat and Morocco)
1984 Théophile Abega (Toulouse and Cameroon)
1983 Mahmoud El-Khatib (Al-Ahly and Egypt)
1982 Thomas Nkono (Espanyol and Cameroon)
1981 Lakhdar Belloumi (GCR Mascara and Algeria)
1980 Jean Manga-Onguene (Canon Yaoundé and Cameroon)
1979 Thomas Nkono (Canon Yaoundé and Cameroon)
1978 Abdul Razak (Asante Kotoko and Ghana)

1977 Tarak Dhiab (Espérance and Tunisia)
1976 Roger Milla (Canon Yaoundé and Cameroon)
1975 Ahmed Faras (SC Chabab Mohammedia and Morocco)
1974 Paul Moukila (CARA Brazzaville and People's Republic of Congo)
1973 Tshimen Bwanga (TP Mazembe and Zaire)
1972 Cherif Souleymane (Hafia Conakry and Guinea)
1971 Ibrahim Sunday (Asante Kotoko and Ghana)
1970 Salif Keita (Saint-Étienne/Mali)

*as voted by France Football magazine 1970–1992 and CAF 1992–present.

ASIAN FOOTBALLER OF THE YEAR*

2007 Yasser Al-Qahtani (Al-Hilal and Saudi Arabia)
2006 Khalfan Ibrahim (Al-Sadd and Qatar)
2005 Hamad Al-Montashari (Al-Ittihad and Saudi Arabia)
2004 Ali Karimi (Al-Ahli and Iran)
2003 Mehdi Mahdavikia (Hamburg and Iran)
2002 Shinji Ono (Feyenoord and Japan)
2001 Fan Zhiyi (Dundee and China)
2000 Nawaf Al-Temyat (Al-Hilal and Saudi Arabia)
1999 Ali Daei (Hertha Berlin and Iran)
1998 Hidetoshi Nakata (Perugia and Japan)
1997 Hidetoshi Nakata (Bellmare Hiratsuka and Japan)
1996 Khodadad Azizi (Bahman and Iran)
1995 Masami Ihara (Yokohama Marinos and Japan)
1994 Saeed Al-Owairan (Al-Shabab and Saudi Arabia)
1993 Kazuyoshi Miura (Verdy Kawasaki and Japan)
1992 Not awarded
1991 Kim Joo-Sung (Daewoo Royals and Republic of Korea)
1990 Kim Joo-Sung (Daewoo Royals and Republic of Korea)
1989 Kim Joo-Sung (Daewoo Royals and Republic of Korea)
1988 Ahmed Radhi (Al-Rasheed and Iraq)

*Awarded by AFC.

OCEANIA FOOTBALLER OF THE YEAR*

2004 Tim Cahill (Millwall, Everton and Australia)
2003 Harry Kewell (Leeds United, Liverpool and Australia)
2002 Brett Emerton (Feyenoord and Australia)
2001 Harry Kewell (Leeds United and Australia)
2000 Mark Viduka (Celtic, Leeds United and Australia)
1999 Harry Kewell (Leeds United and Australia)
1998 Christian Karembeu (Sampdoria and New Caledonia)
1997 Mark Bosnich (Aston Villa and Australia)
1996 Paul Okon (Club Brugge, Lazio and Australia)
1995 Christian Karembeu (Nantes, Atlantique and New Caledonia)
1994 Aurelio Vidmar (KSV Waregem, Standard Liége and Australia)
1993 Robbie Slater (Anderlecht and Australia)
1992 Wynton Rufer (Werder Bremen and New Zealand)
1991 Robbie Slater (Anderlecht and Australia)
1990 Wynton Rufer (Werder Bremen and New Zealand)
1989 Wynton Rufer (Grasshopper Zurich, Werder Bremen and New Zealand)
1988 Frank Farina (Marconi Fairfield, Club Brugge and Australia)

*As voted by a forum of journalists.

UEFA CHAMPIONS LEAGUE/EUROPEAN CUP

A competition for the most successful football clubs in Europe, organised by UEFA.

2008	Manchester United (England)
2007	AC Milan (Italy)
2006	Barcelona (Spain)
2005	Liverpool (England)
2004	Porto (Portugal)
2003	AC Milan (Italy)
2002	Real Madrid (Spain)
2001	Bayern Munich (Germany)
2000	Real Madrid (Spain)
1999	Manchester United (England)
1998	Real Madrid (Spain)
1997	Borussia Dortmund (Germany)
1996	Juventus (Italy)
1995	Ajax (Netherlands)
1994	AC Milan (Italy)
1993	Marseille (France)
1992	Barcelona (Spain)
1991	Red Star Belgrade (Yugoslavia*)
1990	AC Milan (Italy)
1989	AC Milan (Italy)
1988	PSV Eindhoven (Netherlands)
1987	Porto (Portugal)
1986	Steaua Bucharest (Romania)
1985	Juventus (Italy)
1984	Liverpool (England)
1983	Hamburg (West Germany)
1982	Aston Villa (England)
1981	Liverpool (England)
1980	Nottingham Forest (England)
1979	Nottingham Forest (England)
1978	Liverpool (England)
1977	Liverpool (England)
1976	Bayern Munich (West Germany)
1975	Bayern Munich (West Germany)
1974	Bayern Munich (West Germany)
1973	Ajax (Netherlands)
1972	Ajax (Netherlands)
1971	Ajax (Netherlands)
1970	Feyenoord (Netherlands)
1969	AC Milan (Italy)
1968	Manchester United (England)
1967	Celtic (Scotland)
1966	Real Madrid (Spain)
1965	Internazionale (Italy)
1964	Internazionale (Italy)
1963	AC Milan (Italy)
1962	Benfica (Portugal)
1961	Benfica (Portugal)
1960	Real Madrid (Spain)
1959	Real Madrid (Spain)
1958	Real Madrid (Spain)
1957	Real Madrid (Spain)
1956	Real Madrid (Spain)

*See p.45 for current name of Yugoslavia.

UEFA CUP*

A competition for European football clubs, organised by UEFA.

2007–2008	Zenit St Petersburg (Russia)
2006–2007	Sevilla (Spain)
2005–2006	Sevilla (Spain)
2004–2005	CSKA Moscow (Russia)
2003–2004	Valencia (Spain)
2002–2003	Porto (Portugal)
2001–2002	Feyenoord (Netherlands)
2000–2001	Liverpool (England)
1999–2000	Galatasaray (Turkey)
1998–1999	Parma (Italy)
1997–1998	Internazionale (Italy)
1996–1997	Schalke (Germany)
1995–1996	Bayern Munich (Germany)
1994–1995	Parma (Italy)
1993–1994	Internazionale (Italy)
1992–1993	Juventus (Italy)
1991–1992	Ajax (Netherlands)
1990–1991	Internazionale (Italy)
1989–1990	Juventus (Italy)
1988–1989	Napoli (Italy)
1987–1988	Bayer Leverkusen (West Germany)
1986–1987	IFC Gothenburg (Sweden)
1985–1986	Real Madrid (Spain)
1984–1985	Real Madrid (Spain)
1983–1984	Tottenham Hotspur (England)
1982–1983	Anderlecht (Belgium)
1981–1982	IFK Gothenburg (Sweden)
1980–1981	Ipswich Town (England)
1979–1980	Eintracht Frankfurt (West Germany)
1978–1979	Borussia Mönchengladbach (West Germany)
1977–1978	PSV Eindhoven (Netherlands)
1976–1977	Juventus (Italy)
1975–1976	Liverpool (England)
1974–1975	Borussia Mönchengladbach (West Germany)
1973–1974	Feyenoord (Netherlands)
1972–1973	Liverpool (England)
1971–1972	Tottenham Hotspur (England)
1970–1971	Leeds United (England)
1969–1970	Arsenal (England)
1968–1969	Newcastle United (England)
1967–1968	Leeds United (England)
1966–1967	Dinamo Zagreb (Yugoslavia)
1965–1966	Barcelona (Spain)
1964–1965	Ferencvaros (Hungary)
1963–1964	Real Zaragoza (Spain)
1962–1963	Valencia (Spain)
1961–1962	Valencia (Spain)
1960–1961	Roma (Italy)
1958–1960	Barcelona (Spain)
1955–1958	Barcelona (Spain)

*Before 1971 competition was known as the Inter-Cities Fairs Cup.

EUROPEAN CUP WINNERS' CUP

A club competition for recent winners of European cup competitions, organised by UEFA.

1998–1999	Lazio (Italy)
1997–1998	Chelsea (England)
1996–1997	Barcelona (Spain)
1995–1996	Paris Saint-Germain (France)
1994–1995	Real Zaragoza (Spain)
1993–1994	Arsenal (England)
1992–1993	Parma (Italy)
1991–1992	Werder Bremen (Germany)
1990–1991	Manchester United (England)
1989–1990	Sampdoria (Italy)
1988–1989	Barcelona (Spain)
1987–1988	Mechelen (Belgium)
1986–1987	Ajax (Netherlands)
1985–1986	Dinamo Kiev (USSR)
1984–1985	Everton (England)
1983–1984	Juventus (Italy)
1982–1983	Aberdeen (Scotland)
1981–1982	Barcelona (Spain)
1980–1981	Dinamo Tbilisi (USSR)
1979–1980	Valencia (Spain)
1978–1979	Barcelona (Spain)
1977–1978	Anderlecht (Belgium)
1976–1977	Hamburg (West Germany)
1975–1976	Anderlecht (Belgium)
1974–1975	Dinamo Kiev (USSR)
1972–1973	AC Milan (Italy)
1973–1974	1. FC Magdeburg (East Germany)
1971–1972	Rangers (Scotland)
1970–1971	Chelsea (England)
1969–1970	Manchester City (England)
1968–1969	Slovan Bratislava (Czechoslovakia)
1967–1968	AC Milan (Italy)
1966–1967	Bayern Munich (West Germany)
1965–1966	Borussia Dortmund (West Germany)
1964–1965	West Ham United (England)
1963–1964	Sporting Lisbon (Portugal)
1962–1963	Tottenham Hotspur (England)
1961–1962	Atlético Madrid (Spain)
1960–1961	Fiorentina (Italy)

EUROPEAN SUPER CUP

An annual football match played between the current champions of the UEFA Cup and the Champions League.

2007	AC Milan (Italy)
2006	Sevilla (Spain)
2005	Liverpool (England)
2004	Valencia (Spain)
2003	AC Milan (Italy)
2002	Real Madrid (Spain)
2001	Liverpool (England)
2000	Galatasaray (Turkey)
1999	Lazio (Italy)
1998	Chelsea (England)
1997	Barcelona (Spain)
1996	Juventus (Italy)
1995	Ajax (Netherlands)
1994	AC Milan (Italy)
1993	Parma (Italy)
1992	Barcelona (Spain)
1991	Manchester United (England)
1990	AC Milan (Italy)
1989	AC Milan (Italy)
1988	Mechelen (Belgium)
1987	Porto (Portugal)
1986	Steaua Bucharest (Romania)
1985	Not played
1984	Juventus (Italy)
1983	Aberdeen (Scotland)
1982	Aston Villa (England)
1981	Not played
1980	Valencia (Spain)
1979	Nottingham Forest (England)
1978	Anderlecht (Belgium)
1977	Liverpool (England)
1976	Anderlecht (Belgium)
1975	Dinamo Kiev (USSR)
1974	Not played
1973	Ajax (Netherlands)
1972	Ajax (Netherlands)

Qatar's Khalfan Ibrahim was the 2006 Asian Footballer of the Year. The striker is famous for his tricks with the ball and is often compared to Ronaldinho.

CONMEBOL COPA LIBERTADORES

A competition for the most successful football clubs in South America, organised by CONMEBOL.

2007	Boca Juniors (Argentina)
2006	Internacional (Brazil)
2005	São Paulo (Brazil)
2004	Once Caldas (Colombia)
2003	Boca Juniors (Argentina)
2002	Olimpia (Paraguay)
2001	Boca Juniors (Argentina)
2000	Boca Juniors (Argentina)
1999	Palmeiras (Brazil)
1998	Vasco da Gama (Brazil)
1997	Cruzeiro (Brazil)
1996	River Plate (Argentina)
1995	Grêmio (Brazil)
1994	Vélez Sársfield (Argentina)
1993	São Paulo (Brazil)
1992	São Paulo (Brazil)
1991	Colo-Colo (Chile)
1990	Olimpia (Paraguay)
1989	Atlético Nacional (Colombia)
1988	Nacional (Uruguay)
1987	Peñarol (Uruguay)
1986	River Plate (Argentina)
1985	Argentinos Juniors (Argentina)
1984	Independiente (Argentina)
1983	Grêmio (Brazil)
1982	Peñarol (Uruguay)
1981	Flamengo (Brazil)
1980	Nacional (Uruguay)
1979	Olimpia (Paraguay)
1978	Boca Juniors (Argentina)
1977	Boca Juniors (Argentina)
1976	Cruzeiro (Brazil)
1975	Independiente (Argentina)
1974	Independiente (Argentina)
1973	Independiente (Argentina)
1972	Independiente (Argentina)
1971	Nacional (Uruguay)
1970	Estudiantes (Argentina)
1969	Estudiantes (Argentina)
1968	Estudiantes (Argentina)
1967	Racing Club (Argentina)
1966	Peñarol (Uruguay)
1965	Independiente (Argentina)
1964	Independiente (Argentina)
1963	Santos (Brazil)
1962	Santos (Brazil)
1961	Peñarol (Uruguay)
1960	Peñarol (Uruguay)

FIFA CLUB WORLD CUP

A competition between the winners of the 6 continental federations: UEFA, CONMEBOL, CONCACAF, CAF, AFC and OFC.

2007	AC Milan (Italy)
2006	Internacional (Brazil)
2005	São Paulo (Brazil)
2001–2004	Not played until merged with Intercontinental Cup in 2005

INTERCONTINENTAL CUP*

A competition between the winners of the UEFA Champions League and the Copa Libertadores.

2004	Porto (Portugal)
2003	Boca Juniors (Argentina)
2002	Real Madrid (Spain)
2001	Bayern Munich (Germany)
2000	Boca Juniors (Argentina)
1999	Manchester United (England)
1998	Real Madrid (Spain)
1997	Borussia Dortmund (Germany)
1996	Juventus (Italy)
1995	Ajax (Netherlands)
1994	Vélez Sársfield (Argentina)
1993	São Paulo (Brazil)
1992	São Paulo (Brazil)
1991	Red Star Belgrade (Yugoslavia**)
1990	AC Milan (Italy)
1989	AC Milan (Italy)
1988	Nacional (Uruguay)
1987	Porto (Portugal)
1986	River Plate (Argentina)
1985	Juventus (Italy)
1984	Independiente (Argentina)
1983	Grêmio (Brazil)
1982	Peñarol (Uruguay)
1981	Flamengo (Brazil)
1980	Nacional (Uruguay)
1979	Olimpia (Paraguay)
1978	Not played
1977	Boca Juniors (Argentina)
1976	Bayern Munich (West Germany)
1975	Not played
1974	Atlético Madrid (Spain)
1973	Independiente (Argentina)
1972	Ajax (Netherlands)
1971	Nacional (Uruguay)
1970	Feyenoord (Netherlands)
1969	AC Milan (Italy)
1968	Estudiantes (Argentina)
1967	Racing Club (Argentina)
1966	Peñarol (Uruguay)
1965	Internazionale (Italy)
1964	Internazionale (Italy)
1963	Santos (Brazil)
1962	Santos (Brazil)
1961	Peñarol (Uruguay)
1960	Real Madrid (Spain)

* Known as the World Club Championship until 2000. From 2005, competition replaced by FIFA Club World Cup.

** See p.45 for the current name of Yugoslavia.

CONCACAF CHAMPIONS' CUP

A competition for the most successful football clubs in North America, Central America and the Caribbean, organised by CONCACAF.

2008	Pachuca (Mexico)
2007	Pachuca (Mexico)
2006	Club América (Mexico)
2005	Deportivo Saprissa (Costa Rica)
2004	Alajuelense (Costa Rica)
2003	Toluca (Mexico)
2002	Pachuca (Mexico)
2001	Not played
2000	Los Angeles Galaxy (USA)
1999	Necaxa (Mexico)
1998	DC United (USA)
1997	Cruz Azul (Mexico)
1996	Cruz Azul (Mexico)
1995	Deportivo Saprissa (Costa Rica)
1994	CS Cartaginés (Costa Rica)
1993	Deportivo Saprissa (Costa Rica)
1992	Club América (Mexico)
1991	Puebla (Mexico)
1990	Club America (Mexico)
1989	UNAM Pumas (Mexico)
1988	Olimpia (Honduras)
1987	Club América (Mexico)
1986	Alajuelense (Costa Rica)
1985	Defence Force (Trinidad and Tobago)
1984	Violette AC (Haiti) awarded the trophy after Guadalajara (Mexico) and New York Freedoms (USA) were disqualified
1983	Atlante (Mexico)
1982	UNAM Pumas (Mexico)
1981	Transvaal (Surinam)
1980	UNAM Pumas (Mexico)
1979	FAS (El Salvador)
1978	Universidad de Guadalajara (Mexico) awarded the trophy
1977	Club America (Mexico)
1976	Aguila (El Salvador)
1975	Atlético Español (Mexico)
1974	CSD Municipal (Guatemala) won 4–2 on aggregate
1973	Transvaal (Surinam) awarded the trophy after Northern and Central region teams withdrew
1972	Olimpia (Honduras)
1971	Cruz Azul (Mexico)
1970	Cruz Azul (Mexico) awarded the trophy after Transvaal (Surinam) and Deportivo Saprissa (Costa Rica) withdrew
1969	Cruz Azul (Mexico)
1968	Toluca (Mexico) awarded a walkover win after Aurora (Guatemala) and Transvaal (Surinam) were suspended
1967	Alianza (El Salvador)
1964–1966	Not played
1963	Racing Club (Haiti) awarded the cup after Guadalajara withdrew
1962	Guadalajara (Mexico)

CAF AFRICAN CHAMPIONS LEAGUE*

A competition for the most successful football clubs in Africa, organised by CAF.

2007	Étoile de Sahel (Tunisia)
2006	Al-Ahly (Egypt)
2005	Al-Ahly (Egypt)
2004	Enyimba (Nigeria)
2003	Enyimba (Nigeria)
2002	Zamalek (Egypt)
2001	Al-Ahly (Egypt)
2000	Hearts of Oak (Ghana)
1999	Raja Casablanca (Morocco)
1998	ASEC Abidjan (Côte d'Ivoire)
1997	Raja Casablanca (Morocco)
1996	Zamalek (Egypt)
1995	Orlando Pirates (South Africa)
1994	Espérance (Tunisia)
1993	Zamalek (Egypt)
1992	Wydad Casablanca (Morocco)
1991	Club Africain (Algeria)
1990	JS Kabylie (Algeria)
1989	Raja Casablanca (Morocco)
1988	EP Sétif (Algeria)
1987	Al-Ahly (Egypt)
1986	Zamalek (Egypt)
1985	FAR Rabat (Morocco)
1984	Zamalek (Egypt)
1983	Asante Kotoko (Ghana)
1982	Al-Ahly (Egypt)
1981	JE Tizi-Ouzou (Algeria)
1980	Canon Yaoundé (Cameroon)
1979	Union Douala (Cameroon)
1978	Canon Yaoundé (Cameroon)
1977	Hafia Conakry (Ghana)
1976	MC Algiers (Algeria)
1975	Hafia Conakry (Ghana)
1974	CARA Brazzaville (Congo)
1973	As Vita Club (Zaire)
1972	Hafia Conakry (Ghana)
1971	Canon Yaoundé (Cameroon)
1970	Asante Kotoko (Ghana)
1969	Ismaily (Egypt)
1968	TP Englebert (Zaire)
1967	Trophy awarded to TP Englebert (Zaire) after Asante Kotoko (Ghana) refused to take part in a play-off
1966	Stade Abidjan (Côte d'Ivoire)
1965	Not played
1964	Oryz Douala (Cameroon)

*Known as the African Cup of Champions until 1997, and since then as the CAF Champions League.

CAF AFRICAN CONFEDERATION CUP*

A competition for African Football clubs, organised by CAF.

2007	CS SFaxien (Tunisia)
2006	Étoile du Sahel (Tunisia)
2005	FAR Rabat (Morocco)
2004	Hearts of Oak (Ghana)

*Competition was formed when the CAF Cup and the CAF African Cup Winners' Cup merged.

CAF CUP

A competition for African clubs, organised by CAF.

2003	Raja Casablanca (Morocco)
2002	JS Kabylie (Algeria)
2001	JS Kabylie (Algeria)
2000	JS Kabylie (Algeria)
1999	Étoile du Sahel (Tunisia)
1998	CS Sfaxien (Tunisia)
1997	Espérance (Tunisia)
1996	Kawkab Marrakech (Morocco)
1995	Étoile du Sahel (Tunisia)
1994	Bendel Insurance (Nigeria)
1993	Stella Abidjan (Côte d'Ivoire)
1992	Shooting Stars (Nigeria)

CAF AFRICAN CUP WINNERS' CUP

A competition for African clubs who were winners of national competitions, organised by CAF.

2003	Étoile du Sahel (Tunisia)
2002	Wydad Casablanca (Morocco)
2001	Kaizer Chiefs (South Africa)
2000	Zamalek (Egypt)
1999	Africa Sports (Côte d'Ivoire)
1998	Espérance (Tunisia)
1997	Étoile du Sahel (Tunisia)
1996	Al-Mokawloon al-Arab (Egypt)
1995	JS Kabylie (Algeria)
1994	DC Motemba Pemba (Zaire)
1993	Al-Ahly (Egypt)
1992	Africa Sports (Côte d'Ivoire)
1991	Power Dynamos (Zambia)
1990	BBC Lions (Nigeria)
1989	Al-Merrick (Sudan)
1988	CA Bizertin (Algeria)
1987	Gor Mahia (Kenya)
1986	Al-Ahly (Egypt)
1985	Al-Ahly (Egypt)
1984	Al-Ahly (Egypt)
1983	Al-Mokawloon al-Arab (Egypt)
1982	Al-Mokawloon al-Arab (Egypt)
1981	Union Douala (Cameroon)
1980	TP Mazembe (Zaire)
1979	Canon Yaoundé (Cameroon)
1978	Horoya AC (Guinea)
1977	Enugu Rangers (Nigeria)
1976	Shooting Stars (Nigeria)
1975	Tonnerre Yaoundé (Cameroon)

CAF AFRICAN SUPER CUP

A competition match between the current champions of the CAF Confederation Cup and the CAF Champions League.

2008	Étoile du Sahel (Tunisia)
2007	Al-Ahly (Egypt)
2006	Al-Ahly (Egypt)
2005	Enyimba (Nigeria)
2004	Enyimba (Nigeria)
2003	Zamalek (Egypt)
2002	Al-Ahly (Egypt)
2001	Hearts of Oak (Ghana)

2000	Raja Casablanca (Morocco)
1999	ASEC Abidjan (Côte d'Ivoire)
1998	Étoile du Sahel (Tunisia)
1997	Zamalek (Egypt)
1996	Orlando Pirates (South Africa)
1995	Espérance (Tunisia)
1994	Zamalek (Egypt)
1993	Africa Sports (Côte d'Ivoire)

AFC ASIAN CHAMPIONS LEAGUE*

A competition between champions and cup winners of the top 14 Asian leagues.

2006–2007	Urawa Red Diamonds (Japan)
2005–2006	Jeonbuk Hyundai Motors (Republic of Korea)
2004–2005	Al-Ittihad (Saudi Arabia)
2003–2004	Al-Ittihad (Saudi Arabia)
2002–2003	Al Ain (United Arab Emirates)

*Competition formed when the Asian Cup Winners' Cup and the Asian Champions Cup merged.

AFC ASIAN CUP WINNERS' CUP

A competition for Asian domestic cup winners, organised by AFC.

2001–2002	Al-Hilal (Saudi Arabia)
2000–2001	Al-Shabab (Saudi Arabia)
1999–2000	Shimizu S-Pulse (Japan)
1998–1999	Al-Ittihad (Saudi Arabia)
1997–1998	Al-Nasr (Saudi Arabia)
1996–1997	Al-Hilal (Saudi Arabia)
1995–1996	Bellmare Hiratsuka (Japan)
1994–1995	Yokohama Flügels (Japan)
1993–1994	Al-Qadisiya (Saudi Arabia)
1992–1993	Yokohama Marinos (formerly Nissan)
1991–1992	Nissan (Japan)
1990–1991	Persepolis (Iran)

AFC ASIAN CHAMPIONS CUP*

A competition for champions of Asian leagues.

2001–2002	Suwon Samsung Bluewings (Republic of Korea)
2000–2001	Suwon Samsung Bluewings (Republic of Korea)
1999–2000	Al-Hilal (Saudi Arabia)
1998–1999	Júbilo Iwata (Japan)
1997–1998	Pohang Steelers (South Korea)
1996–1997	Pohang Steelers (Republic of Korea)
1995–1996	Ilhwa Chunma (South Korea)
1994–1995	Thai Farmers Bank (Thailand)

1993–1994	Thai Farmers Bank (Thailand)
1991–1992	Al-Hilal (Saudi Arabia)
1990–1991	Esteghlal (Iran)
1989–1990	Liaoning (China)
1988–1989	Al-Sadd (Qatar)
1987–1988	Yomiuri (Japan) awarded the trophy after Al-Hilal (Saudi Arabia) withdrew
1986–1987	Furukawa Electric (Japan)
1985–1986	Daewoo Royals (South Korea)
1972–1984	Not played
1970–1971	Maccabi Tel Aviv (Israel) awarded the trophy after Al Shorta (Iraq) withdrew
1969–1970	Taj (Iran)
1968–1969	Maccabi Tel Aviv (Israel)
1966–1967	Hapoel Tel Aviv (Israel)

* 1967–1971 known as the Asian Club Championship; 1985–2002 known as the Asian Champions Cup. Not played 1967–1968 and 1972–1984.

AFC ASIAN SUPER CUP

A competition between the winners of the Asian Champions Cup and the Asian Cup Winners' Cup. Came to an end after the Asian Champions League was formed.

2002	Suwon Samsung Bluewings (Republic of Korea)
2001	Suwon Samsung Bluewings (Republic of Korea)
2000	Al-Hilal (Saudi Arabia)
1999	Júbilo Iwata (Japan)
1998	Al-Nasr (Saudi Arabia)
1997	Al-Hilal (Saudi Arabia)
1996	Ilhwa Chunma (Republic of Korea)
1995	Yokohama Flugels (Japan)

ARAB CHAMPIONS LEAGUE*

A competition for clubs in the Arab world.

2008	ES Sétif (Algeria)
2007	ES Sétif (Algeria)
2006	Raja Casablanca (Morocco)
2005	Al-Ittihad (Saudi Arabia)
2004	CS Sfaxien (Tunisia)
2003	Zamalek (Egypt)
2002	Al-Ahli (Saudi Arabia)
2001	Al-Sadd (Qatar)
2000	CS Sfaxien (Tunisia)
1999	Al-Shabab (Saudi Arabia)
1998	WA Tlemcen (Algeria)
1997	Club Africain (Algeria)
1996	Al-Ahly (Egypt)
1995	Al-Hilal (Saudi Arabia)
1994	Al-Hilal (Saudi Arabia)
1993	Espérance (Tunisia)
1992	Al-Shabab (Saudi Arabia)
1991	Not played
1990	Not played
1989	Wydad Casablanca (Morocco)

1988	Al-Ittifaq (Saudi Arabia)
1987	Al-Rasheed (Iraq)
1986	Al-Rasheed (Iraq)
1985	Al-Rasheed (Iraq)
1984	Al-Ittifaq (Saudi Arabia)
1983	Not played
1982	Al-Shorta (Iraq)

* Known as the Arab Club Champions Cup until 2001, when it merged with the Arab Cup Winners' Cup. New tournament known as the Prince Faysal bin Fahad Tournament for Arab Clubs until 2003.

ARAB CUP WINNERS' CUP*

A competition between winners of national club competitions in Arab nations.

2001–2002	Stade Tunisien (Tunisia)
2000–2001	Al-Hilal (Saudi Arabia)
1999–2000	Al Ittihad (Qatar)
1998–1999	MC Oran (Algeria)
1997–1998	MC Oran (Algeria)
1996–1997	OC Khouribga (Morocco)
1995–1996	Club Africain (Tunisia)
1994–1995	Al-Ahly (Egypt)
1993–1994	Olympique Casablanca (Morocco)
1992–1993	Olympique Casablanca (Morocco)
1991–1992	Olympique Casablanca (Morocco)
1989–1990	Stade Tunisien (Tunisia)

* 1990–1991 not played.

OCEANIA CHAMPIONS LEAGUE*

A competition for Oceanian football clubs, organised by OFC.

2008	Waitakere United (New Zealand)
2007	Waitakere United (New Zealand)
2006	Auckland City (New Zealand)
2004–2005	Sydney (Australia)
2001–2004	Not played
2000–2001	Wollongong Wolves (Australia)
1999	South Melbourne (Australia)
1987	Adelaide City (Australia)

*Known as Oceania Club Championship until 2007.

UEFA WOMENS CUP

2006–2007	Arsenal (England)
2005–2006	1. FFC Frankfurt (Germany)
2004–2005	Turbine Potsdam (Germany)
2003–2004	Umeå IK (Sweden)
2002–2003	Umeå IK (Sweden)
2001–2002	1. FFC Frankfurt (Germany)

DOMESTIC STATS

ENGLAND: PREMIER LEAGUE*

Season	Champion
2007–2008	Manchester United
2006–2007	Manchester United
2005–2006	Chelsea
2004–2005	Chelsea
2003–2004	Arsenal
2002–2003	Manchester United
2001–2002	Arsenal
2000–2001	Manchester United
1999–2000	Manchester United
1998–1999	Manchester United
1997–1998	Arsenal
1996–1997	Manchester United
1995–1996	Manchester United
1994–1995	Blackburn Rovers
1993–1994	Manchester United
1992–1993	Manchester United
1991–1992	Leeds United
1990–1991	Arsenal
1989–1990	Liverpool
1988–1989	Arsenal
1987–1988	Liverpool
1986–1987	Everton
1985–1986	Liverpool
1984–1985	Everton
1983–1984	Liverpool
1982–1983	Liverpool
1981–1982	Liverpool
1980–1981	Aston Villa
1979–1980	Liverpool
1978–1979	Liverpool
1977–1978	Nottingham Forest
1976–1977	Liverpool
1975–1976	Liverpool
1974–1975	Derby County
1973–1974	Leeds United
1972–1973	Liverpool
1971–1972	Derby County
1970–1971	Arsenal
1969–1970	Everton
1968–1969	Leeds United
1967–1968	Manchester City
1966–1967	Manchester United
1965–1966	Liverpool
1964–1965	Manchester United
1963–1964	Liverpool
1962–1963	Everton
1961–1962	Ipswich Town
1960–1961	Tottenham Hotspur
1959–1960	Burnley
1958–1959	Wolverhampton Wanderers
1957–1958	Wolverhampton Wanderers
1956–1957	Manchester United
1955–1956	Manchester United
1954–1955	Chelsea
1953–1954	Wolverhampton Wanderers
1952–1953	Arsenal
1951–1952	Manchester United
1950–1951	Tottenham Hotspur
1949–1950	Portsmouth
1948–1949	Portsmouth
1947–1948	Arsenal
1946–1947	Liverpool
1938–1939	Everton
1937–1938	Arsenal
1936–1937	Manchester City
1935–1936	Sunderland
1934–1935	Arsenal
1933–1934	Arsenal
1932–1933	Arsenal
1931–1932	Everton
1930–1931	Arsenal
1929–1930	Sheffield Wednesday
1928–1929	Sheffield Wednesday
1927–1928	Everton
1926–1927	Newcastle United
1925–1926	Huddersfield Town
1924–1925	Huddersfield Town
1923–1924	Huddersfield Town
1922–1923	Liverpool
1921–1922	Liverpool
1920–1921	Burnley
1919–1920	West Bromwich Albion
1914–1915	Everton
1913–1914	Blackburn Rovers
1912–1913	Sunderland
1911–1912	Blackburn Rovers
1910–1911	Manchester United
1909–1910	Aston Villa
1908–1909	Newcastle United
1907–1908	Manchester United
1906–1907	Newcastle United
1905–1906	Liverpool
1904–1905	Newcastle United
1903–1904	Sheffield Wednesday
1902–1903	Sheffield Wednesday
1901–1902	Sunderland
1900–1901	Liverpool
1899–1900	Aston Villa
1898–1899	Aston Villa
1897–1898	Sheffield United
1896–1897	Aston Villa
1895–1896	Aston Villa
1894–1895	Sunderland
1893–1894	Aston Villa
1892–1893	Sunderland
1891–1892	Sunderland
1890–1891	Everton
1889–1890	Preston North End
1888–1889	Preston North End

* Known as First Division 1888–1992. Not played 1916–1919 due to the First World War and 1940–1946 due to the Second World War.

ENGLAND: FA CUP*

Season	Winner
2007–2008	Portsmouth
2006–2007	Chelsea
2005–2006	Liverpool
2004–2005	Arsenal
2003–2004	Manchester United
2002–2003	Arsenal
2001–2002	Arsenal
2000–2001	Liverpool
1999–2000	Chelsea
1998–1999	Manchester United
1997–1998	Arsenal
1996–1997	Chelsea
1995–1996	Manchester United
1994–1995	Everton
1993–1994	Manchester United
1992–1993	Arsenal
1991–1992	Liverpool
1990–1991	Tottenham Hotspur
1989–1990	Manchester United
1988–1989	Liverpool
1987–1988	Wimbledon
1986–1987	Coventry City
1985–1986	Liverpool
1984–1985	Manchester United
1983–1984	Everton
1982–1983	Manchester United
1981–1982	Tottenham Hotspur
1980–1981	Tottenham Hotspur
1979–1980	West Ham United
1978–1979	Arsenal
1977–1978	Ipswich Town
1976–1977	Manchester United
1975–1976	Southampton
1974–1975	West Ham United
1973–1974	Liverpool
1972–1973	Sunderland
1971–1972	Leeds United
1970–1971	Arsenal
1969–1970	Chelsea
1969–1960	Wanderers
1968–1969	Manchester City
1967–1968	West Bromwich Albion
1966–1967	Tottenham Hotspur
1965–1966	Everton
1964–1965	Liverpool
1963–1964	West Ham United
1962–1963	Manchester United
1961–1962	Tottenham Hotspur
1960–1961	Tottenham Hotspur
1958–1959	Nottingham Forest
1957–1958	Bolton Wanderers
1956–1957	Aston Villa
1955–1956	Manchester City
1954–1955	Newcastle United
1953–1954	West Bromwich Albion
1952–1953	Blackpool
1951–1952	Newcastle United
1950–1951	Newcastle United
1949–1950	Arsenal
1948–1949	Wolverhampton Wanderers
1947–1948	Manchester City
1946–1947	Charlton Athletic
1945–1946	Derby County
1938–1939	Portsmouth
1937–1938	Preston North End
1936–1937	Sunderland
1935–1936	Arsenal
1934–1935	Sheffield Wednesday
1933–1934	Manchester City
1932–1933	Everton
1931–1932	Newcastle United
1930–1931	West Bromwich Albion
1929–1930	Arsenal
1928–1929	Bolton Wanderers
1927–1928	Blackburn Rovers
1926–1927	Cardiff City
1925–1926	Bolton Wanderers
1924–1925	Sheffield United
1923–1924	Newcastle United
1922–1923	Bolton Wanderers
1921–1922	Huddersfield Town
1920–1921	Tottenham Hotspur
1919–1920	Aston Villa
1914–1915	Sheffield United
1913–1914	Burnley
1912–1913	Aston Villa
1911–1912	Barnsley
1910–1911	Bradford City
1909–1910	Newcastle United
1908–1909	Manchester United
1907–1908	Wolverhampton Wanderers
1906–1907	Sheffield Wednesday
1905–1906	Everton
1904–1905	Aston Villa
1903–1904	Manchester City
1902–1903	Bury
1901–1902	Sheffield United
1900–1901	Tottenham Hotspur
1899–1900	Bury
1898–1899	Sheffield United
1897–1898	Nottingham Forest
1896–1897	Aston Villa
1895–1896	Sheffield Wednesday
1894–1895	Aston Villa
1893–1894	Notts County
1892–1893	Wolverhampton Wanderers
1891–1892	West Bromwich Albion
1890–1891	Blackburn Rovers
1889–1890	Blackburn Rovers
1888–1889	Preston North End
1887–1888	West Bromwich Albion
1886–1887	Aston Villa
1885–1886	Blackburn Rovers
1884–1885	Blackburn Rovers
1883–1884	Blackburn Rovers
1882–1883	Blackburn Olympic
1881–1882	Old Etonians
1880–1881	Old Carthusians
1879–1880	Clapham Rovers
1878–1879	Old Etonians
1877–1878	Wanderers
1876–1877	Wanderers
1875–1876	Wanderers
1874–1875	Royal Engineers
1873–1874	Oxford University
1872–1873	Wanderers
1871–1872	Wanderers

* Not played 1915–1919 due to the First World War and 1939–1945 due to the Second World War.

ENGLAND: LEAGUE CUP

Season	Winner
2007–2008	Tottenham Hotspur
2006–2007	Chelsea
2005–2006	Manchester United
2004–2005	Chelsea
2003–2004	Middlesbrough
2002–2003	Liverpool
2001–2002	Blackburn Rovers
2000–2001	Liverpool
1999–2000	Leicester City
1998–1999	Tottenham Hotspur
1997–1998	Chelsea
1996–1997	Leicester City
1995–1996	Aston Villa
1994–1995	Liverpool

1993–1994	Aston Villa
1992–1993	Arsenal
1991–1992	Manchester United
1990–1991	Sheffield Wednesday
1989–1990	Nottingham Forest
1988–1989	Nottingham Forest
1987–1988	Luton Town
1986–1987	Arsenal
1985–1986	Oxford United
1984–1985	Norwich City
1983–1984	Liverpool
1982–1983	Liverpool
1981–1982	Liverpool
1980–1981	Liverpool
1979–1980	Wolverhampton Wanderers
1978–1979	Nottingham Forest
1977–1978	Nottingham Forest
1976–1977	Aston Villa
1975–1976	Manchester City
1974–1975	Aston Villa
1973–1974	Wolverhampton Wanderers
1972–1973	Tottenham Hotspur
1971–1972	Stoke City
1970–1971	Tottenham Hotspur
1969–1970	Manchester City
1968–1969	Swindon Town
1967–1968	Leeds United
1966–1967	Queens Park Rangers
1965–1966	West Bromwich Albion
1964–1965	Chelsea
1963–1964	Leicester City
1962–1963	Birmingham City
1961–1962	Norwich City
1960–1961	Aston Villa

ENGLAND: LEAGUE TOP SCORERS*

2007–2008	Cristiano Ronaldo (Manchester United) 31
2006–2007	Didier Drogba (Chelsea) 20
2005–2006	Thierry Henry (Arsenal) 27
2004–2005	Thierry Henry (Arsenal) 25
2003–2004	Thierry Henry (Arsenal) 30
2002–2003	Ruud van Nistelrooy (Manchester United) 25
2001–2002	Thierry Henry (Arsenal) 24
2000–2001	Jimmy Floyd Hasselbaink (Chelsea) 23
1999–2000	Kevin Philips (Sunderland) 30
1998–1999	Jimmy Floyd Hasselbaink (Leeds United) 18
	Michael Owen (Liverpool) 18
	Dwight Yorke (Manchester United) 18
1997–1998	Chris Sutton (Blackburn Rovers) 18
	Dion Dublin (Coventry City) 18
	Michael Owen (Liverpool) 18
1996–1997	Alan Shearer (Newcastle United) 25

1995–1996	Alan Shearer (Blackburn Rovers) 31
1994–1995	Alan Shearer (Blackburn Rovers) 34
1993–1994	Andy Cole (Newcastle United) 34
1992–1993	Teddy Sheringham (Tottenham Hotspur) 22
1991–1992	Ian Wright (Crystal Palace and Arsenal) 29
1990–1991	Alan Smith (Arsenal) 22
1989–1990	Gary Lineker (Tottenham Hotspur) 24
1988–1989	Alan Smith (Arsenal) 23
1987–1988	John Aldridge (Liverpool) 26
1986–1987	Clive Allen (Tottenham Hotspur) 33
1985–1986	Gary Lineker (Everton) 30
1984–1985	Kerry Dixon (Chelsea) 24
	Gary Lineker (Leicester City) 24
1983–1984	Ian Rush (Liverpool) 32
1982–1983	Luther Blissett (Watford) 27
1981–1982	Kevin Keegan (Southampton) 26
1980–1981	Peter Withe (Aston Villa) 20
	Steve Archibald (Tottenham Hotspur) 20
1979–1980	Phil Boyer (Southampton) 23
1978–1979	Frank Worthington (Bolton Wanderers) 24
1977–1978	Bob Latchford (Everton) 30
1976–1977	Malcolm Macdonald (Arsenal) 25
	Andy Gray (Aston Villa) 25
1975–1976	Ted MacDougall (Norwich City) 23
1974–1975	Malcolm Macdonald (Newcastle United) 21
1973–1974	Mick Channon (Southampton) 21
1972–1973	Bryan "Pop" Robson (West Ham United) 28
1971–1972	Francis Lee (Manchester City) 33
1970–1971	Tony Brown (West Bromwich Albion) 28
1969–1970	Jeff Astle (West Bromwich Albion) 25
1968–1969	Jimmy Greaves (Tottenham Hotspur) 27
1967–1968	George Best (Manchester United) 28
	Ron Davies (Southampton) 28
1966–1967	Ron Davies (Southampton) 37
1965–1966	Willie Irvine (Burnley) 29
1964–1965	Andy McEvoy (Blackburn Rovers) 29
	Jimmy Greaves (Tottenham Hotspur) 29
1963–1964	Jimmy Greaves

	(Tottenham Hotspur) 35
1962–1963	Jimmy Greaves (Tottenham Hotspur) 37
1961–1962	Ray Crawford (Ipswich Town) 33
	Derek Kevan (West Bromwich Albion) 33
1960–1961	Jimmy Greaves (Chelsea) 41
1959–1960	Dennis Viollet (Manchester United) 32
1958–1959	Jimmy Greaves (Chelsea) 33
1957–1958	Bobby Smith (Tottenham Hotspur) 36
1956–1957	John Charles (Leeds United) 38
1955–1956	Nat Lofthouse (Bolton Wanderers) 33
1954–1955	Ronnie Allen (West Bromwich Albion) 27
1953–1954	Jimmy Glazzard (Huddersfield Town) 29
1952–1953	Charlie Wayman (Preston North End) 24
1951–1952	George Robledo (Newcastle United) 33
1950–1951	Stan Mortensen (Blackpool) 30
1949–1950	Dickie Davis (Sunderland) 25
1948–1949	Willie Moir (Bolton Wanderers) 25
1947–1948	Ronnie Rooke (Arsenal) 33
1946–1947	Dennis Westcott (Wolverhampton Wanderers) 37
1938–1939	Tommy Lawton (Everton) 35
1937–1938	Tommy Lawton (Everton) 28
1936–1937	Freddie Steel (Stoke City) 33
1935–1936	Pat Glover (Grimsby Town) 31
	Raich Carter (Sunderland) 31
	Bobby Gurney (Sunderland) 31
1934–1935	Ted Drake (Arsenal) 42
1933–1934	Jack Bowers (Derby County) 34
1932–1933	Jack Bowers (Derby County) 35
1931–1932	Dixie Dean (Everton) 44
1930–1931	Tom "Pongo" Waring (Aston Villa) 49
1929–1930	Vic Watson (West Ham United) 41
1928–1929	Dave Halliday (Sunderland) 43
1927–1928	Dixie Dean (Everton) 60
1926–1927	Jimmy Trotter (Sheffield Wednesday) 37
1925–1926	Ted Harper (Blackburn Rovers) 43
1924–1925	Frank Roberts (Manchester City) 31
1923–1924	Wilf Chadwick (Everton) 28

1922–1923	Charlie Buchan (Sunderland) 30
1921–1922	Andy Wilson (Middlesbrough) 31
1920–1921	Joe Smith (Bolton Wanderers) 38
1919–1920	Fred Morris (West Bromwich Albion) 37
1914–1915	Bobby Parker (Everton) 35
1913–1914	George Elliot (Middlesbrough) 32
1912–1913	David McLean (Sheffield Wednesday) 30
1911–1912	Harry Hampton (Aston Villa) 25
	George Holley (Sunderland) 25
	David McLean (Sheffield Wednesday) 25
1910–1911	Albert Shepherd (Newcastle United) 25
1909–1910	Jack Parkinson (Liverpool) 30
1908–1909	Bert Freeman (Everton) 38
1907–1908	Enoch West (Nottingham Forest) 27
1906–1907	Alf Young (Everton) 30
1905–1906	Albert Shepherd (Bolton Wanderers) 26
1904–1905	Arthur Brown (Sheffield United) 22
1903–1904	Steve Bloomer (Derby County) 20
1902–1903	Sam Raybould (Liverpool) 31
1901–1902	Jimmy Settle (Everton) 18
1900–1901	Steve Bloomer (Derby County) 23
1899–1900	Billy Garraty (Aston Villa) 27
1898–1899	Steve Bloomer (Derby County) 23
1897–1898	Fred Wheldon (Aston Villa) 21
1896–1897	Steve Bloomer (Derby County) 22
1895–1896	Johnny Campbell (Aston Villa) 20
	Steve Bloomer (Derby County) 20
1894–1895	Johnny Campbell (Sunderland) 22
1893–1894	Jack Southworth (Everton) 27
1892–1893	Johnny Campbell (Sunderland) 31
1891–1892	Johnny Campbell (Sunderland 32)
1890–1891	Jack Southworth (Blackburn Rovers) 26
1889–1890	Jimmy Ross (Preston North End) 24
1888–1889	John Goodall (Preston North End) 21

* Not played 1916–1919 due to the First World War and 1940–1946 due to the Second World War.

135

DOMESTIC STATS

SCOTLAND: LEAGUE CHAMPIONS* **

Season	Champion
2007–2008	Celtic
2006–2007	Celtic
2005–2006	Celtic
2004–2005	Rangers
2003–2004	Celtic
2002–2003	Rangers
2001–2002	Celtic
2000–2001	Celtic
1999–2000	Rangers
1998–1999	Rangers
1997–1998	Celtic
1996–1997	Rangers
1995–1996	Rangers
1994–1995	Rangers
1993–1994	Rangers
1992–1993	Rangers
1991–1992	Rangers
1990–1991	Rangers
1989–1990	Rangers
1988–1989	Rangers
1987–1988	Celtic
1986–1987	Rangers
1985–1986	Celtic
1984–1985	Aberdeen
1983–1984	Aberdeen
1982–1983	Dundee United
1981–1982	Celtic
1980–1981	Celtic
1979–1980	Aberdeen
1978–1979	Celtic
1977–1978	Rangers
1976–1977	Celtic
1975–1976	Rangers
1974–1975	Rangers
1973–1974	Celtic
1972–1973	Celtic
1971–1972	Celtic
1970–1971	Celtic
1969–1970	Celtic
1968–1969	Celtic
1967–1968	Celtic
1966–1967	Celtic
1965–1966	Celtic
1964–1965	Kilmarnock
1963–1964	Rangers
1962–1963	Rangers
1961–1962	Dundee
1960–1961	Rangers
1959–1960	Heart of Midlothian
1958–1959	Rangers
1957–1958	Heart of Midlothian
1956–1957	Rangers
1955–1956	Rangers
1954–1955	Aberdeen
1953–1954	Celtic
1952–1953	Rangers
1951–1952	Hibernian
1950–1951	Hibernian
1949–1950	Rangers
1948–1949	Rangers
1947–1948	Hibernian
1946–1947	Rangers
1938–1939	Rangers
1937–1938	Celtic
1936–1937	Rangers
1935–1936	Celtic
1934–1935	Rangers
1933–1934	Rangers
1932–1933	Rangers
1931–1932	Motherwell
1930–1931	Rangers
1929–1930	Rangers
1920–1929	Rangers
1927–1928	Rangers
1926–1927	Rangers
1925–1926	Celtic
1924–1925	Rangers
1923–1924	Rangers
1922–1923	Rangers
1921–1922	Celtic
1920–1921	Rangers
1919–1920	Rangers
1918–1919	Celtic
1917–1918	Rangers
1916–1917	Celtic
1915–1916	Celtic
1914–1915	Celtic
1913–1914	Celtic
1912–1913	Rangers
1911–1912	Rangers
1910–1911	Rangers
1909–1910	Celtic
1908–1909	Celtic
1907–1908	Celtic
1906–1907	Celtic
1905–1906	Celtic
1904–1905	Celtic
1903–1904	Third Lanark
1902–1903	Hibernian
1901–1902	Rangers
1900–1901	Rangers
1899–1900	Rangers
1898–1899	Rangers
1897–1898	Celtic
1896–1897	Heart of Midlothian
1895–1896	Celtic
1894–1895	Heart of Midlothian
1893–1894	Celtic
1892–1893	Celtic
1891–1892	Dumbarton
1890–1891	Dumbarton/Rangers (shared title)

* Top league known as the First Division until 1975.
** Not played 1940–1946 due to the Second World War.

SCOTLAND: FA CUP*

Season	Winner
2007–2008	Rangers
2006–2007	Celtic
2005–2006	Heart of Midlothian
2004–2005	Celtic
2003–2004	Celtic
2002–2003	Rangers
2001–2002	Rangers
2000–2001	Celtic
1999–2000	Rangers
1998–1999	Rangers
1997–1998	Heart of Midlothian
1996–1997	Kilmarnock
1995–1996	Rangers
1994–1995	Celtic
1993–1994	Dundee United
1992–1993	Rangers
1991–1992	Rangers
1990–1991	Motherwell
1989–1990	Aberdeen
1988–1989	Celtic
1987–1988	Celtic
1986–1987	St Mirren
1985–1986	Aberdeen
1984–1985	Celtic
1983–1984	Aberdeen
1982–1983	Aberdeen
1981–1982	Aberdeen
1980–1981	Rangers
1979–1980	Celtic
1978–1979	Rangers
1977–1978	Rangers
1976–1977	Celtic
1975–1976	Rangers
1974–1975	Celtic
1973–1974	Celtic
1972–1973	Rangers
1971–1972	Celtic
1970–1971	Celtic
1969–1970	Aberdeen
1968–1969	Celtic
1967–1968	Dunfermline Athletic
1966–1967	Celtic
1965–1966	Rangers
1964–1965	Celtic
1963–1964	Rangers
1962–1963	Rangers
1961–1962	Rangers
1960–1961	Dunfermline Athletic
1959–1960	Rangers
1958–1959	St Mirren
1957–1958	Clyde
1956–1957	Falkirk
1955–1956	Heart of Midlothian
1954–1955	Clyde
1953–1954	Celtic
1952–1953	Rangers
1951–1952	Motherwell
1950–1951	Celtic
1949–1950	Rangers
1948–1949	Rangers
1947–1948	Rangers
1946–1947	Aberdeen
1938–1939	Clyde
1937–1938	East Fife
1936–1937	Celtic
1935–1936	Rangers
1934–1935	Rangers
1933–1934	Rangers
1932–1933	Celtic
1931–1932	Rangers
1930–1931	Celtic
1929–1930	Rangers
1928–1929	Kilmarnock
1927–1928	Rangers
1926–1927	Celtic
1925–1926	St Mirren
1924–1925	St Mirren
1923–1924	Airdrieonians
1922–1923	Celtic
1921–1922	Morton
1920–1921	Partick Thistle
1919–1920	Kilmarnock
1913–1914	Celtic
1912–1913	Falkirk
1911–1912	Celtic
1910–1911	Celtic
1909–1910	Dundee
1908–1909	Trophy withheld after a riot during Celtic vs Rangers
1907–1908	Celtic
1906–1907	Celtic
1905–1906	Heart of Midlothian
1904–1905	Third Lanark
1903–1904	Celtic
1902–1903	Rangers
1901–1902	Hibernian
1900–1901	Heart of Midlothian
1899–1900	Celtic
1898–1899	Celtic
1897–1898	Rangers
1896–1897	Rangers
1895–1896	Heart of Midlothian
1894–1895	St Bernard's
1893–1894	Rangers
1892–1893	Queen's Park
1891–1892	Celtic
1890–1891	Heart of Midlothian
1889–1890	Queen's Park
1888–1889	Third Lanark
1887–1888	Renton
1886–1887	Hibernian
1885–1886	Queen's Park
1884–1885	Renton
1883–1884	Queen's Park
1882–1883	Dumbarton
1881–1882	Queen's Park
1880–1881	Queen's Park
1879–1880	Queen's Park
1878–1879	Vale of Leven
1877–1878	Vale of Leven
1876–1877	Vale of Leven
1875–1876	Queen's Park
1874–1875	Queen's Park
1873–1874	Queen's Park

* Not played 1914–1919 due to the First World War and 1939–1946 due to the Second World War.

SCOTTISH LEAGUE CUP*

2007–2008	Rangers
2006–2007	Hibernian
2005–2006	Celtic
2004–2005	Rangers
2003–2004	Livingston
2002–2003	Rangers
2001–2002	Rangers
2000–2001	Celtic
1999–2000	Celtic
1998–1999	Rangers
1997–1998	Celtic
1996–1997	Rangers
1995–1996	Aberdeen
1994–1995	Raith Rovers
1993–1994	Rangers
1992–1993	Rangers
1991–1992	Hibernian
1990–1991	Rangers

1989–1990	Aberdeen
1988–1989	Rangers
1987–1988	Rangers
1986–1987	Rangers
1985–1986	Aberdeen
1984–1985	Rangers
1983–1984	Rangers
1982–1983	Celtic
1981–1982	Rangers
1980–1981	Dundee United
1979–1980	Dundee United
1978–1979	Rangers
1977–1978	Rangers
1976–1977	Aberdeen
1975–1976	Rangers
1974–1975	Celtic
1973–1974	Dundee
1972–1973	Hibernian
1971–1972	Partick Thistle
1970–1971	Rangers
1969–1970	Celtic
1968–1969	Celtic
1967–1968	Celtic
1966–1967	Celtic
1965–1966	Celtic
1964–1965	Rangers
1963–1964	Rangers
1962–1963	Heart of Midlothian
1961–1962	Rangers
1960–1961	Rangers
1959–1960	Heart of Midlothian
1958–1959	Heart of Midlothan
1957–1958	Celtic
1956–1957	Celtic
1955–1956	Aberdeen
1954–1955	Heart of Midlothian
1953–1954	East Fife
1952–1953	Dundee
1951–1952	Dundee
1950–1951	Motherwell
1949–1950	East Fife
1948–1949	Rangers
1947–1948	East Fife
1946–1947	Rangers

SCOTLAND: LEAGUE TOP SCORERS

2007–2008	Scott McDonald (Celtic) 25
2006–2007	Kris Boyd (Rangers) 19
2005–2006	Kris Boyd (Rangers) 32
2004–2005	John Hartson (Celtic) 25
2003–2004	Henrik Larsson (Celtic) 30
2002–2003	Henrik Larsson (Celtic) 28
2001–2002	Henrik Larsson (Celtic) 29
2000–2001	Henrik Larsson (Celtic) 35
1999–2000	Mark Viduka (Celtic) 25
1998–1999	Henrik Larsson (Celtic) 29
1997–1998	Marco Negri (Rangers) 32
1996–1997	Jorge Cadete (Celtic) 25
1995–1996	Pierre van Hooijdonk (Celtic) 26
1994–1995	Tommy Coyne (Motherwell) 16
1993–1994	Mark Hateley (Rangers) 22
1992–1993	Ally McCoist (Rangers) 34
1991–1992	Ally McCoist (Rangers) 34
1990–1991	Tommy Coyne (Celtic) 18
1989–1990	John Robertson (Heart of Midlothian) 17

1988–1989	Mark McGhee (Celtic) 16 Charlie Nicholas (Aberdeen 16)
1987–1988	Tommy Coyne (Dundee) 33
1986–1987	Brian McClair (Celtic) 35
1985–1986	Ally McCoist (Rangers) 24
1984–1985	Frank McDougall (Aberdeen) 22
1983–1984	Brian McClair (Celtic) 23
1982–1983	Charlie Nicholas (Celtic) 29
1981–1982	George McCluskey (Celtic) 21
1980–1981	Frank McGarvey (Celtic) 23
1979–1980	Douglas Somner (St Mirren) 25
1978–1979	Andy Ritchie (Morton) 22
1977–1978	Derek Johnstone (Rangers) 25
1976–1977	Willie Pettigrew (Motherwell) 21
1975–1976	Kenny Dalglish (Celtic) 24
1974–1975	Andy Gray (Motherwell) 20 Willie Pettigrew (Motherwell) 20
1973–1974	John "Dixie" Deans (Celtic) 26
1972–1973	Alan Gordon (Hibernian) 27
1971–1972	Joe Harper (Aberdeen) 33
1970–1971	Harry Hood (Celtic) 22
1969–1970	Colin Stein (Rangers) 24
1968–1969	Kenny Cameron (Dundee United) 26
1967–1968	Bobby Lennox (Celtic) 32
1966–1967	Stevie Chalmers (Celtic) 21
1965–1966	Joe McBride (Celtic) 31 Alex Ferguson (Dunfermline) 31
1964–1965	Jim Forrest (Rangers) 30
1963–1964	Alan Gilzean (Dundee) 32
1962–1963	Jimmy Millar (Rangers) 27
1961–1962	Alan Gilzean (Dundee) 24
1960–1961	Alex Harley (Third Lanark) 42
1959–1960	Joe Baker (Hibernian) 42
1958–1959	Joe Baker (Hibernian) 25
1957–1958	Jimmy Wardhaugh (Heart of Midlothian) 28 Jimmy Murray (Heart of Midlothian) 28
1956–1957	Hugh Baird (Airdrieonians) 33
1955–1956	Jimmy Wardhaugh (Heart of Midlothian) 28
1954–1955	Willie Bauld (Heart of Midlothian) 21
1953–1954	Jimmy Wardhaugh (Heart of Midlothian) 27
1952–1953	Lawrie Reilly (Hibernian) 30 Charles Fleming (East Fife) 30
1951–1952	Lawrie Reilly (Hibernian) 27
1950–1951	Lawrie Reilly (Hibernian) 22
1949–1950	Willie Bauld (Hearts) 30
1948–1949	Alexander Stott (Dundee) 30
1947–1948	Archie Aikman (Falkirk) 20
1946–1947	Bobby Mitchell (Third Lanark) 22
1938–1939	Alex Venters (Rangers) 35
1937–1938	Andy Black (Heart of Midlothian) 40

1936–1937	David Wilson (Hamilton Academical) 34
1935–1936	Jimmy McGrory (Celtic) 50
1934–1935	Dave McCulloch (Heart of Midlothian) 38
1933–1934	Jimmy Smith (Rangers) 41
1932–1933	Willie McFadden (Motherwell) 45
1931–1932	Willie McFadden (Motherwell) 52
1930–1931	Barney Battles (Heart of Midlothian) 44
1929–1930	Benny Yorston (Aberdeen) 38
1928–1929	Evelyn Morrison (Falkirk) 43
1927–1928	Jimmy McGrory (Celtic) 47
1926–1927	Jimmy McGrory (Celtic) 49
1925–1926	Willie Devlin (Cowdenbeath) 40
1924–1925	Willie Devlin (Cowdenbeath) 33
1923–1924	David Halliday (Dundee) 38
1922–1923	John White (Heart of Midlothian) 30
1921–1922	Duncan Walker (St Mirren) 45
1920–1921	Hugh Ferguson (Motherwell) 43
1919–1920	Hugh Ferguson (Motherwell) 33
1918–1919	David McLean (Rangers) 29
1917–1918	Hugh Ferguson (Motherwell) 35
1916–1917	Bert Yarnall (Airdrieonians) 39
1915–1916	James McColl (Celtic) 34
1914–1915	Tom Gracie (Heart of Midlothian) 29 James Richardson (Ayr) 29
1913–1914	James Reid (Airdrieonians) 27
1912–1913	James Reid (Airdrieonians) 30
1911–1912	Willie Reid (Rangers) 33
1910–1911	Willie Reid (Rangers) 38
1909–1910	Jimmy Quinn (Celtic) 24 John Simpson (Falkirk) 24
1908–1909	John Hunter (Dundee) 29
1907–1908	John Simpson (Falkirk) 32
1906–1907	Jimmy Quinn (Celtic) 29
1905–1906	Jimmy Quinn (Celtic) 20
1904–1905	Robert C Hamilton (Rangers) 19 Jimmy Quinn (Celtic) 19
1903–1904	Robert C Hamilton (Rangers) 28
1902–1903	David Reid (Hibernian) 14
1901–1902	William Maxwell (Third Lanark) 10
1900–1901	Robert C Hamilton (Rangers) 20
1899–1900	Robert C Hamilton (Rangers) 15 William Michael (Heart of Midlothian) 15
1898–1899	Robert C Hamilton (Rangers) 25
1897–1898	Robert C Hamilton (Rangers) 18

1896–1897	William Taylor (Heart of Midlothian) 12
1895–1896	Allan Martin (Celtic) 19
1894–1895	James Miller (Clyde) 12
1893–1894	Sandy McMahon (Celtic) 16
1892–1893	Sandy McMahon (Celtic) 11 John Campbell (Celtic) 11
1891–1892	John Bell (Dumbarton) 23
1890–1891	John Bell (Dumbarton) 20

* Not played 1940–1946 due to the Second World War.

LEAGUE OF WALES CHAMPIONS

2007–2008	Llanelli
2006–2007	TNS
2005–2006	TNS
2004–2005	TNS
2003–2004	Rhyl
2002–2003	Barry Town
2001–2002	Barry Town
2000–2001	Barry Town
1999–2000	TNS
1998–1999	Barry Town
1997–1998	Barry Town
1996–1997	Barry Town
1995–1996	Barry Town
1994–1995	Bangor City
1993–1994	Bangor City
1992–1993	Cwmbran Town

WELSH CUP*

2007–2008	Bangor City
2006–2007	Carmarthen Town
2005–2006	Rhyl
2004–2005	TNS
2003–2004	Rhyl
2002–2003	Barry Town
2001–2002	Barry Town
2000–2001	Barry Town
1999–2000	Bangor City
1998–1999	Inter Cardiff
1997–1998	Bangor City
1996–1997	Barry Town
1995–1996	Llansantffraid
1994–1995	Wrexham
1993–1994	Barry Town
1992–1993	Cardiff City
1991–1992	Cardiff City
1990–1991	Swansea City
1989–1990	Hereford United
1988–1989	Swansea City
1987–1988	Cardiff City
1986–1987	Merthyr Tydfil
1985–1986	Kidderminster Harriers
1984–1985	Shrewsbury Town
1983–1984	Shrewsbury Town
1982–1983	Swansea City
1981–1982	Swansea City
1980–1981	Swansea City
1979–1980	Newport County
1978–1979	Shrewsbury Town
1977–1978	Wrexham
1976–1977	Shrewsbury Town
1975–1976	Cardiff City
1974–1975	Wrexham
1973–1974	Cardiff City
1972–1973	Cardiff City
1971–1972	Wrexham
1970–1971	Cardiff City

Season	Champion
1969–1970	Cardiff City
1968–1969	Cardiff City
1967–1968	Cardiff City
1966–1967	Cardiff City
1965–1966	Swansea Town
1964–1965	Cardiff City
1963–1964	Cardiff City
1962–1963	Borough United
1961–1962	Bangor City
1960–1961	Swansea Town
1959–1960	Wrexham
1958–1959	Cardiff City
1957–1958	Wrexham
1956–1957	Wrexham
1955–1956	Cardiff City
1954–1955	Barry Town
1953–1954	Flint Town United
1952–1953	Rhyl
1951–1952	Rhyl
1950–1951	Merthyr Tydfil
1949–1950	Swansea Town
1948–1949	Merthyr Tydfil
1947–1948	Lovells Athletic
1946–1947	Chester
1939–1940	Wellington
1938–1939	South Liverpool
1937–1938	Shrewsbury Town
1936–1937	Crewe Alexandra
1935–1936	Crewe Alexandra
1934–1935	Tranmere Rovers
1933–1934	Bristol City
1932–1933	Chester
1931–1932	Swansea Town
1930–1931	Wrexham
1929–1930	Cardiff City
1928–1929	Connah's Quay
1927–1928	Cardiff City
1926–1927	Cardiff City
1925–1926	Ebbw Vale
1924–1925	Wrexham
1923–1924	Wrexham
1922–1923	Cardiff City
1921–1922	Cardiff City
1920–1921	Wrexham
1919–1920	Cardiff City
1914–1915	Wrexham
1913–1914	Wrexham
1912–1913	Swansea Town
1911–1912	Cardiff City
1910–1911	Wrexham
1909–1910	Wrexham
1908–1909	Wrexham
1907–1908	Chester
1906–1907	Oswestry
1905–1906	Wellington
1904–1905	Wrexham
1903–1904	Druids
1902–1903	Wrexham
1901–1902	Wellington
1900–1901	Oswestry
1899–1900	Aberystwyth
1898–1899	Druids
1897–1898	Druids
1896–1897	Wrexham
1895–1896	Bangor Town
1894–1895	Newtown
1893–1894	Chirk
1892–1893	Wrexham
1891–1892	Chirk
1890–1891	Shrewsbury Town
1889–1890	Chirk
1888–1889	Bangor City
1887–1888	Chirk
1886–1887	Chirk
1886–1886	Druids
1884–1885	Druids
1883–1884	Oswestry
1882–1883	Wrexham
1881–1882	Druids
1880–1881	Druids
1879–1880	Druids
1878–1879	Newtown
1877–1878	Wrexham

* Not played 1915–1919 due to the First World War and 1940–1946 due to the Second World War.

WALES: LEAGUE TOP SCORERS

Season	Top Scorer
2007–2008	Rhys Griffiths (Llanelli) 40
2006–2007	Rhys Griffiths (Llanelli) 30
2005–2006	Rhys Griffith (Llanelli) 28
2004–2005	Marc Lloyd–Williams (TNS) 34
2003–2004	Andy Moran (Rhyl) 27
2002–2003	Graham Evans (Caersws) 24
2001–2002	Marc Lloyd–Williams (Bangor City) 47
2000–2001	Graham Evans (Caersws) 25
1999–2000	Chris Summers (Cwmbran Town) 28
1998–1999	Eifion Williams (Barry Town) 28
1997–1998	Eifion Williams (Barry Town) 40
1996–1997	Tony Bird (Barry Town) 42
1995–1996	Ken McKenna (Conwy United) 38
1994–1995	Frank Mottram (Bangor City) 30
1993–199	David Taylor (Porthmadog) 43
1992–1993	Steve Woods (Ebbw Vale) 29

NORTHERN IRELAND: IRISH PREMIER LEAGUE***

2007–2008	Linfield
2006–2007	Linfield
2005–2006	Linfield
2004–2005	Glentoran
2003–2004	Linfield
2002–2003	Glentoran
2001–2002	Portadown
2000–2001	Linfield
1999–2000	Linfield
1998–1999	Glentoran
1997–1998	Cliftonville
1996–1997	Crusaders
1995–1996	Portadown
1994–1995	Crusaders
1993–1994	Linfield
1992–1993	Linfield
1991–1992	Glentoran
1990–1991	Portadown
1989–1990	Portadown
1988–1989	Linfield
1987–1988	Glentoran
1986–1987	Linfield
1985–1986	Linfield
1984–1985	Linfield
1983–1984	Linfield
1982–1983	Linfield
1981–1982	Linfield
1980–1981	Glentoran
1979–1980	Linfield
1978–1979	Linfield
1977–1978	Linfield
1976–1977	Glentoran
1975–1976	Crusaders
1974–1975	Linfield
1973–1974	Coleraine
1972–1973	Crusaders
1971–1972	Glentoran
1970–1971	Linfield
1969–1970	Glentoran
1968–1969	Linfield
1967–1968	Glentoran
1966–1967	Glentoran
1965–1966	Linfield
1964–1965	Derry City
1963–1964	Glentoran
1962–1963	Distillery
1961–1962	Linfield
1960–1961	Linfield
1959–1960	Glenavon
1958–1959	Linfield
1957–1958	Ards
1956–1957	Glenavon
1955–1956	Linfield
1954–1955	Linfield
1953–1954	Linfield
1952–1953	Glentoran
1951–1952	Glenavon
1950–1951	Glentoran
1949–1950	Linfield
1948–1949	Linfield
1947–1948	Belfast Celtic
1939–1940	Belfast Celtic
1938–1939	Belfast Celtic
1937–1938	Belfast Celtic
1936–1937	Belfast Celtic
1935–1936	Belfast Celtic
1934–1935	Linfield
1933–1934	Linfield
1932–1933	Belfast Celtic
1931–1932	Linfield
1930–1931	Glentoran
1929–1930	Linfield
1928–1929	Belfast Celtic
1927–1928	Belfast Celtic
1926–1927	Belfast Celtic
1925–1926	Belfast Celtic
1924–1925	Glentoran
1923–1924	Queen's Island
1922–1923	Linfield
1921–1922	Linfield
1920–1921	Glentoran
1919–1920	Belfast Celtic
1914–1915	Belfast Celtic
1913–1914	Linfield
1912–1913	Glentoran
1911–1912	Glentoran
1910–1911	Linfield
1909–1910	Cliftonville
1908–1909	Linfield
1907–1908	Linfield
1906–1907	Linfield
1905–1906	Cliftonville/Distillery (shared title)
1904–1905	Glentoran
1903–1904	Linfield
1902–1903	Distillery
1901–1902	Linfield
1900–1901	Distillery
1899–1900	Belfast Celtic
1898–1899	Distillery
1897–1898	Linfield
1896–1897	Glentoran
1895–1896	Distillery
1894–1895	Linfield
1893–1894	Glentoran
1892–1893	Linfield
1891–1892	Linfield
1890–1891	Linfield

* Known as the Irish Football League until 2003.
** Not played 1915–1919 due to the First World War and 1941–1947 due to the Second World War.

NORTHERN IRELAND: IRISH CUP

Season	Winner
2007–2008	Linfield
2006–2007	Linfield
2005–2006	Linfield
2004–2005	Portadown
2003–2004	Glentoran
2002–2003	Coleraine
2001–2002	Linfield
2000–2001	Glentoran
1999–2000	Glentoran
1998–1999	Portadown awarded cup after Cliftonville's disqualification
1997–1998	Glentoran
1996–1997	Glenavon
1995–1996	Glentoran
1994–1995	Linfield
1993–1994	Linfield
1992–1993	Bangor
1991–1992	Glenavon
1990–1991	Portadown
1989–1990	Glentoran
1988–1989	Ballymena
1987–1988	Glentoran
1986–1987	Glentoran
1985–1986	Glentoran
1984–1985	Glentoran
1983–1984	Ballymena United
1982–1983	Glentoran
1981–1982	Linfield
1980–1981	Ballymena United
1979–1980	Linfield
1978–1979	Cliftonville
1977–1978	Linfield
1976–1977	Coleraine
1975–1976	Carrick Rangers
1974–1975	Coleraine
1973–1974	Ards
1972–1973	Glentoran

1971–1972 Coleraine
1970–1971 Distillery
1969–1970 Linfield
1968–1969 Ards
1967–1968 Crusaders
1966–1967 Crusaders
1965–1966 Glentoran
1964–1965 Coleraine
1963–1964 Derry City
1962–1963 Linfield
1961–1962 Linfield
1960–1961 Glenavon
1959–1960 Linfield
1958–1959 Glenavon
1957–1958 Ballymena United
1956–1957 Glenavon
1955–1956 Distillery
1954–1955 Dundela
1953–1954 Derry City
1952–1953 Linfield
1951–1952 Ards I
1950–1951 Glentoran
1949–1950 Linfield
1948–1949 Derry City
1947–1948 Linfield
1946–1947 Belfast Celtic
1945–1946 Linfield
1944–1945 Linfield
1943–1944 Belfast Celtic
1942–1943 Belfast Celtic
1941–1942 Linfield
1940–1941 Belfast Celtic
1939–1940 United
1938–1939 Linfield
1937–1938 Belfast Celtic
1936–1937 Belfast Celtic
1935–1936 Linfield
1934–1935 Glentoran
1933–1934 Linfield
1932–1933 Glentoran
1931–1932 Glentoran
1930–1931 Linfield
1929–1930 Linfield
1928–1929 Ballymena United
1927–1928 Willowfield
1926–1927 Ards
1925–1926 Belfast Celtic
1924–1925 Distillery
1923–1924 Queen's Island
1922–1923 Linfield
1921–1922 Linfield
1920–1921 Glentoran
1919–1920 Shelbourne awarded cup after Belfast Celtic and Glentoran were expelled from the competition
1918–1919 Linfield
1917–1918 Belfast Celtic
1916–1917 Glentoran
1915–1916 Linfield
1914–1915 Linfield
1913–1914 Glentoran
1912–1913 Linfield
1911–1912 Linfield awarded cup after withdrawal of others
1910–1911 Shelbourne
1909–1910 Distillery
1908–1909 Cliftonville
1907–1908 Bohemians
1906–1907 Cliftonville

1905–1906 Shelbourne
1904–1905 Distillery
1903–1904 Linfield
1902–1903 Distillery
1901–1902 Linfield
1900–1901 Cliftonville
1899–1900 Cliftonville
1898–1899 Linfield
1897–1898 Linfield
1896–1897 Cliftonville
1895–1896 Distillery
1894–1895 Linfield
1893–1894 Distillery
1892–1893 Linfield
1891–1892 Linfield
1890–1891 Linfield
1889–1890 Gordon Highlanders
1888–1889 Distillery
1887–1888 Cliftonville
1886–1887 Ulster
1885–1886 Distillery
1884–1885 Distillery
1883–1884 Distillery
1882–1883 Cliftonville
1881–1882 Queen's Island
1880–1881 Moyola Park

NORTHERN IRELAND: LEAGUE TOP SCORERS

2007–2008 Peter Thompson (Linfield 29)
2006–2007 Gary Hamilton (Glentoran) 27
2005–2006 Peter Thompson (Linfield) 25
2004–2005 Chris Morgan (Glentoran) 19
2003–2004 Glenn Ferguson (Linfield) 25
2002–2003 Vinny Arkins (Portadown) 29
2001–2002 Vinny Arkins (Portadown) 30
2000–2001 Davy Larmour (Linfield) 17
1999–2000 Vinny Arkins (Portadown) 29
1998–1999 Vinny Arkins (Portadown) 19
1997–1998 Vinny Arkins (Portadown) 22
1996–1997 Garry Haylock (Portadown) 16
1995–1996 Garry Haylock (Portadown) 19
1994–1995 Glenn Ferguson (Glenavon) 27
1993–1994 Darren Erskine (Ards) 22
Stephen McBride (Glenavon) 22
1992–1993 Stevie Cowan (Portadown) 27
1991–1992 Harry McCourt (Omagh Town) 18
Stephen McBride (Glenavon) 18
1990–1991 Stephen McBride (Glenavon) 22
1989–1990 Martin McGaughey (Linfield) 19
1988–1989 Stephen Baxter (Linfield) 17
1987–1988 Martin McGaughey

(Linfield) 18
1986–1987 Ray McCoy (Coleraine) 14
Gary McCartney (Glentoran) 14
1985–1986 Trevor Anderson (Linfield) 14
1984–1985 Martin McGaughey (Linfield) 34
1983–1984 Martin McGaughey (Linfield) 15
Trevor Anderson (Linfield) 15
1982–1983 Jim Campbell (Ards) 15
1981–1982 Gary Blackledge (Glentoran) 18
1980–1981 Des Dickson (Coleraine) 18
Paul Malone (Ballymena United) 18
1979–1980 Jimmy Martin (Glentoran) 17
1978–1979 Tommy Armstrong (Ards) 21
1977–1978 Warren Feeney (Glentoran) 17
1976–1977 Ronnie McAteer (Crusaders) 20
1975–1976 Des Dickson (Coleraine) 23
1974–1975 Martin Malone (Portadown) 19
1973–1974 Des Dickson (Coleraine) 24
1972–1973 Des Dickson (Coleraine) 23
1971–1972 Peter Watson (Distillery) 15
Des Dickson (Coleraine) 15
1970–1971 Bryan Hamilton (Linfield) 18
1969–1970 Des Dickson (Coleraine) 21
1968–1969 Danny Hale (Derry City) 21
1967–1968 Sammy Pavis (Linfield) 30
1966–1967 Sammy Pavis (Linfield) 25
1965–1966 Sammy Pavis (Linfield) 28
1964–1965 Kenny Halliday (Coleraine) 19
Dennis Guy (Glenavon) 19
1963–1964 Trevor Thompson (Glentoran) 12
1962–1963 Joe Meldrum (Distillery) 27
1961–1962 Mick Lynch (Ards) 20
1960–1961 Trevor Thompson (Glentoran) 22
1959–1960 Jimmy Jones (Glenavon) 29
1958–1959 Jackie Milburn (Linfield) 26
1957–1958 Jackie Milburn (Linfield) 29
1956–1957 Jimmy Jones (Glenavon) 33
1955–1956 Jimmy Jones (Glenavon) 26
1954–1955 Fay Coyle (Coleraine) 20
1953–1954 Jimmy Jones (Glenavon) 32
1952–1953 Sammy Hughes (Glentoran) 28
1951–1952 Jimmy Jones (Glenavon) 27
1950–1951 Sammy Hughes (Glentoran) 23
Walter Allen (Portadown) 23

1949–1950 Sammy Hughes (Glentoran) 23
1948–1949 Billy Simpson (Linfield) 19
1947–1948 Jimmy Jones (Belfast Celtic) 28

FRANCE LEAGUE 1 CHAMPIONS*

2007–2008 Lyon
2006–2007 Lyon
2005–2006 Lyon
2004–2005 Lyon
2003–2004 Lyon
2002–2003 Lyon
2001–2002 Lyon
2000–2001 Nantes
1999–2000 Monaco
1998–1999 Bordeaux
1997–1998 Lens
1996–1997 Monaco
1995–1996 Auxerre
1994–1995 Nantes
1993–1994 Paris Saint–Germain
1992–1993 No winner (Marseille stripped of title)
1991–1992 Marseille
1990–1991 Marseille
1989–1990 Marseille
1988–1989 Marseille
1987–1988 Monaco
1986–1987 Bordeaux
1985–1986 Paris Saint–Germain
1984–1985 Bordeaux
1983–1984 Bordeaux
1982–1983 Nantes
1981–1982 Monaco
1980–1981 Saint–Étienne
1979–1980 Nantes
1978–1979 Strasbourg
1977–1978 Monaco
1976–1977 Nantes
1975–1976 Saint–Étienne
1974–1975 Saint–Étienne
1973–1974 Saint–Étienne
1972–1973 Nantes
1971–1972 Marseille
1970–1971 Marseille
1969–1970 Saint–Étienne
1968–1969 Saint–Étienne
1967–1968 Saint–Étienne
1966–1967 Saint–Étienne
1965–1966 Nantes
1964–1965 Nantes
1963–1964 Saint–Étienne
1962–1963 Monaco
1961–1962 Stade Reims
1960–1961 Monaco
1959–1960 Stade Reims
1958–1959 Nice
1957–1958 Stade Reims
1956–1957 Saint–Étienne
1955–1956 Nice
1954–1955 Stade Reims
1953–1954 Lille
1952–1953 Stade Reims
1951–1952 Nice
1950–1951 Nice
1949–1950 Bordeaux
1948–1949 Stade Reims
1947–1948 Marseille
1946–1947 CO Roubaix–Tourcoing

1945–1946	Lille
1938–1939	Sète
1937–1938	Sochaux
1936–1937	Marseille
1935–1936	RCF Paris
1934–1935	Sochaux
1933–1934	Sète
1932–1933	Lille

* Not played 1939–1945 due to the Second World War.

COUPE DE FRANCE (FRENCH CUP)

2008	Lyon
2007	Sochaux
2006	Paris Saint–Germain
2005	Auxerre
2004	Paris Saint–Germain
2003	Auxerre
2002	Lorient
2001	RC Strasbourg
2000	Nantes
1999	Nantes
1998	Paris Saint–Germain
1997	Nice
1996	Auxerre
1995	Paris Saint–Germain
1994	Auxerre
1993	Paris Saint–Germain
1992	Not played due to Furiani Stadium disaster in Bastia
1991	Monaco
1990	Montpellier
1989	Marseille
1988	Metz
1987	Girondins
1986	Girondins
1985	Monaco
1984	Metz
1983	Paris Saint–Germain
1982	Paris Saint–Germain
1981	Bastia
1980	Monaco
1979	Nantes
1978	AS Nancy
1977	Saint–Étienne
1976	Marseille
1975	Saint–Étienne
1974	Saint–Étienne
1973	Lyon
1972	Marseille
1971	Rennes
1970	Saint–Étienne
1969	Marseille
1968	Saint–Étienne
1967	Lyon
1966	RC Strasbourg
1965	Rennes
1964	Lyon
1963	Monaco
1962	Saint–Étienne
1961	CS Sedan
1960	Monaco
1959	Le Havre
1958	Stade Reims
1957	Toulouse FC (1937)
1956	CS Sedan

1955	Lille
1954	Nice
1953	Lille
1952	Nice
1951	Strasbourg
1950	Stade Reims
1949	RCF Paris
1948	Lille
1947	Lille
1946	Lille
1945	RCF Paris
1944	ÉF Nancy–Lorraine
1943	Marseille
1942	Red Star
1941	Girondins
1940	RCF Paris
1939	RCF Paris
1938	Marseille
1937	Sochaux
1936	RCF Paris
1935	Marseille
1934	Sète
1933	Excelsior AC Roubaix
1932	Cannes
1931	Club Français
1930	Sète
1929	Montpellier
1928	Red Star
1927	Marseille
1926	Marseille
1925	CASG Paris
1924	Marseille
1923	Red Star
1922	Red Star
1921	Red Star
1920	CA Paris
1919	CASG Paris
1918	Olympique de Paris

FRANCE: LEAGUE TOP SCORERS*

2007–2008	Karim Benzema (Lyon) 20
2006–2007	Pauleta (Paris Saint–Germain) 15
2005–2006	Pauleta (Paris Saint–Germain) 21
2004–2005	Alexander Frei (Rennes) 20
2003–2004	Djibril Cissé (Auxerre) 26
2002–2003	Shabani Nonda (Monaco) 26
2001–2002	Djibril Cissé (Auxerre) 22 Pauleta (Bordeaux) 22
2000–2001	Sonny Anderson (Lyon) 22
1999–2000	Sonny Anderson (Lyon) 23
1998–1999	Sylvain Wiltord (Bordeaux) 22
1997–1998	Stéphane Guivarc'h (Auxerre) 21
1996–1997	Stéphane Guivarc'h (Rennes) 22
1995–1996	Sonny Anderson (Monaco) 21
1994–1995	Patrice Loko (Nantes) 22
1993–1994	Youri Djorkaeff (Monaco) 20 Roger Boli (Lens) 20 Nicolas Ouédec (Nantes) 20

1992–1993	Alen Boksic (Marseille) 22
1991–1992	Jean–Pierre Papin (Marseille) 27
1990–1991	Jean–Pierre Papin (Marseille) 23
1989–1990	Jean–Pierre Papin (Marseille) 30
1988–1989	Jean–Pierre Papin (Marseille) 22
1987–1988	Jean–Pierre Papin (Marseille) 19
1986–1987	Bernard Zénier (Metz) 18
1985–1986	Jules Bocandé (Metz) 23
1984–1985	Vahid Halilhodzic (Nantes) 28
1983–1984	Patrice Garande (Auxerre) 21 Delio Onnis (Sporting Toulon Var) 21
1982–1983	Vahid Halilhodzic (Nantes) 27
1981–1982	Delio Onnis (Tours) 29
1980–1981	Delio Onnis (Tours) 24
1979–1980	Delio Onnis (Monaco) 21 Erwin Kostedde (Stade Laval) 21
1978–1979	Carlos Bianchi (Paris Saint–Germain) 27
1977–1978	Carlos Bianchi (Paris Saint–Germain) 37
1976–1977	Carlos Bianchi (Stade Reims) 28
1975–1976	Carlos Bianchi (Stade Reims) 34
1974–1975	Delio Onnis (Monaco) 30
1973–1974	Carlos Bianchi (Stade Reims) 30
1972–1973	Josip Skoblar (Marseille) 26
1971–1972	Josip Skoblar (Marseille) 30
1970–1971	Josip Skoblar (Marseille) 44
1969–1970	Hervé Revelli (Saint–Étienne) 28
1968–1969	André Guy (Lyon) 25
1967–1968	Étienne Sansonetti (AC Ajaccio) 26
1966–1967	Hervé Revelli (Saint–Étienne) 31
1965–1966	Philippe Gondet (Nantes) 36
1964–1965	Jacques Simon (Nantes) 24
1963–1964	Ahmed Oudjani (Lens) 30
1962–1963	Serge Masnaghetti (Valenciennes) 35
1961–1962	Sékou Touré (Montpellier HSC) 25
1960–1961	Roger Piantoni (Stade Reims) 28
1959–1960	Just Fontaine (Stade Reims) 28
1958–1959	Tadeusz Cisowski (RCF Paris) 30
1957–1958	Just Fontaine (Stade Reims) 34
1956–1957	Tadeusz Cisowski (RCF Paris) 33
1955–1956	Tadeusz Cisowski (RCF Paris) 31

1954–1955	René Bliard (Stade Reims) 30
1953–1954	Édouard Kargulewicz (Bordeaux) 27
1952–1953	Gunnar Andersson (Marseille) 35
1951–1952	Gunnar Andersson (Marseille) 31
1950–1951	Roger Piantoni (FC Nancy) 28
1949–1950	Jean Grumellon (Rennes) 24
1948–1949	Jean Baratte (Lille) 26 Jozef Humpal (Sochaux) 26
1947–1948	Jean Baratte (Lille) 31
1946–1947	Pierre Sinibaldi (Stade Reims) 33
1945–1946	René Bihel (Lille) 28
1938–1939	Roger Courtois (Sochaux) 27 Désiré Koranyi (Sète) 27
1937–1938	Jean Nicolas (Rouen) 26
1936–1937	Oskar Rohr (Strasbourg) 30
1935–1936	Roger Courtois (Sochaux) 34
1934–1935	André Abbeglen (Sochaux) 30
1933–1934	István Lukacs (Sète) 28
1932–1933	Robert Mercier (Club Français) 15 Walter Kaiser (Rennes) 15

* Not played 1939–1945 due to the Second World War.

ITALY: SERIE A CHAMPIONS*

2007–2008	Internazionale
2006–2007	Internazionale
2005–2006	Internazionale (Juventus stripped of title)
2004–2005	Not awarded (Juventus stripped of title)
2003–2004	AC Milan
2002–2003	Juventus
2001–2002	Juventus
2000–2001	Roma
1999–2000	Lazio
1998–1999	AC Milan
1997–1998	Juventus
1996–1997	Juventus
1995–1996	AC Milan
1994–1995	Juventus
1993–1994	AC Milan
1992–1993	AC Milan
1991–1992	AC Milan
1990–1991	Sampdoria
1989–1990	Napoli
1988–1989	Internazionale
1987–1988	AC Milan
1986–1987	Napoli
1985–1986	Juventus
1984–1985	Hellas Verona
1983–1984	Juventus
1982–1983	Roma
1981–1982	Juventus
1980–1981	Juventus
1979–1980	Internazionale

1978–1979	AC Milan
1977–1978	Juventus
1976–1977	Juventus
1975–1976	Torino
1974–1975	Juventus
1973–1974	Lazio
1972–1973	Juventus
1971–1972	Juventus
1970–1971	Internazionale
1969–1970	Cagliari
1968–1969	Fiorentina
1967–1968	AC Milan
1966–1967	Juventus
1965–1966	Internazionale
1964–1965	Internazionale
1963–1964	Bologna
1962–1963	Internazionale
1961–1962	AC Milan
1960–1961	Juventus
1959–1960	Juventus
1958–1959	AC Milan
1957–1958	Juventus
1956–1957	AC Milan
1955–1956	Fiorentina
1954–1955	AC Milan
1953–1954	Internazionale
1952–1953	Internazionale
1951–1952	Juventus
1950–1951	AC Milan
1949–1950	Juventus
1948–1949	Torino
1947–1948	Torino
1946–1947	Torino
1945–1946	Torino
1942–1943	Torino
1941–1942	Roma
1940–1941	Bologna
1939–1940	Ambrosiana–Inter
1938–1939	Bologna
1937–1938	Ambrosiana–Inter
1936–1937	Bologna
1935–1936	Bologna
1934–1935	Juventus
1933–1934	Juventus
1932–1933	Juventus
1931–1932	Juventus
1930–1931	Juventus
1929–1930	Ambrosiana–Inter
1928–1929	Bologna
1927–1928	Torino
1926–1927	Not awarded (Torino stripped of title)
1925–1926	Juventus
1924–1925	Bologna
1923–1924	Genoa
1922–1923	Genoa
1921–1922	Pro Vercelli (awarded by the CCI federation) US Novese (awarded by the FIGC federation)
1920–1921	Pro Vercelli
1919–1920	Internazionale
1914–1915	Genoa
1913–1914	AS Casale
1912–1913	Pro Vercelli
1911–1912	Pro Vercelli
1910–1911	Pro Vercelli
1909–1910	Internazionale
1909	Pro Vercelli
1908	Pro Vercelli

1907	AC Milan
1906	AC Milan
1905	Juventus
1904	Genoa
1903	Genoa
1902	Genoa
1901	AC Milan
1900	Genoa
1899	Genoa
1898	Genoa

* Not played 1915–1919 due to the First World War and 1943–1945 due to the Second World War.

COPPA ITALIA (ITALIAN CUP)

2007–2008	Roma
2006–2007	Roma
2005–2006	Internazionale
2004–2005	Internazionale
2003–2004	Lazio
2002–2003	AC Milan
2001–2002	Parma
2000–2001	Fiorentina
1999–2000	Lazio
1998–1999	Parma
1997–1998	Lazio
1996–1997	Vicenza
1995–1996	Fiorentina
1994–1995	Juventus
1993–1994	Sampdoria
1992–1993	Torino
1991–1992	Parma
1990–1991	Roma
1989–1990	Juventus
1988–1989	Sampdoria
1987–1988	Sampdoria
1986–1987	Napoli
1985–1986	Roma
1984–1985	Sampdoria
1983–1984	Roma
1982–1983	Juventus
1981–1982	Internazionale
1980–1981	Roma
1979–1980	Roma
1978–1979	Juventus
1977–1978	Internazionale
1976–1977	AC Milan
1975–1976	Napoli
1974–1975	Fiorentina
1973–1974	Bologna
1972–1973	AC Milan
1971–1972	AC Milan
1970–1971	Torino
1969–1970	Bologna
1968–1969	Roma
1967–1968	Torino
1966–1967	AC Milan
1965–1966	Fiorentina
1964–1965	Juventus
1963–1964	Roma
1962–1963	Atalanta
1961–1962	Napoli
1960–1961	Fiorentina
1959–1960	Juventus
1958–1959	Juventus
1957–1958	Lazio
1942–1943	Torino
1941–1942	Juventus
1940–1941	Venezia
1939–1940	Fiorentina

1938–1939	Internazionale
1937–1938	Juventus
1936–1937	Genoa
1935–1936	Torino
1923–1935	Not played
1922	Vado

ITALY: LEAGUE TOP SCORERS*

2007–2008	Alessandro Del Piero (Juventus) 21
2006–2007	Francesco Totti (Roma) 26
2005–2006	Luca Toni (Fiorentina) 31
2004–2005	Cristiano Lucarelli (Livorno) 24
	Alberto Gilardino (Parma) 24
2003–2004	Andriy Shevchenko (AC Milan) 24
2002–2003	Christian Vieri (Internazionale) 24
2001–2002	David Trézéguet (Juventus) 24
	Dario Hubner (Piacenza) 24
2000–2001	Hernán Crespo (Lazio) 26
1999–2000	Andriy Shevchenko (AC Milan) 24
1998–1999	Márcio Amoroso (Udinese) 22
1997–1998	Oliver Bierhoff (Udinese) 27
1996–1997	Filippo Inzaghi (Atalanta) 24
1995–1996	Giuseppe Signori (Lazio) 24 Igor Protti (Bari) 24
1994–1995	Gabriel Batistuta (Fiorentina) 26
1993–1994	Giuseppe Signori (Lazio) 23
1992–1993	Giuseppe Signori (Lazio) 26
1991–1992	Marco van Basten (AC Milan) 25
1990–1991	Gianluca Vialli (Sampdoria) 17
1989–1990	Marco van Basten (AC Milan) 19
1988–1989	Aldo Serena (Internazionale) 22
1987–1988	Diego Maradona (Napoli) 15
1986–1987	Pietro Paolo Virdis (AC Milan) 17
1985–1986	Roberto Pruzzo (Roma) 19
1984–1985	Michel Platini (Juventus) 18
1983–1984	Michel Platini (Juventus) 20
1982–1983	Michel Platini (Juventus) 16
1981–1982	Roberto Pruzzo (Roma) 15
1980–1981	Roberto Pruzzo (Roma) 18
1979–1980	Roberto Bettega (Juventus) 16
1978–1979	Bruno Giordano (Lazio) 19
1977–1978	Paolo Rossi (Vicenza) 24
1976–1977	Francesco Graziani (Torino) 21
1975–1976	Paolino Pulici (Torino) 21
1974–1975	Paolino Pulici (Torino) 18
1973–1974	Giorgio Chinaglia (Lazio) 24
1972–1973	Paolino Pulici (Torino) 17 Gianni Rivera (AC Milan) 17 Giuseppe Savoldi (Bologna) 17
1971–1972	Roberto Boninsegna (Internazionale) 22

1970–1971	Roberto Boninsegna (Internazionale) 24
1969–1970	Gigi Riva (Cagliari) 21
1968–1969	Gigi Riva (Cagliari) 20
1967–1968	Pierino Prati (AC Milan) 15
1966–1967	Gigi Riva (Cagliari) 18
1965–1966	Luis Vinicio (Vicenza) 25
1964–1965	Sandro Mazzola (Internazionale) 17 Alberto Orlando (Fiorentina) 17
1963–1964	Harald Nielsen (Bologna) 21
1962–1963	Pedro Manfredini (Roma) 19 Harald Nielsen (Bologna) 19
1961–1962	José Altafini (AC Milan) 22 Aurelio Milani (Fiorentina) 22
1960–1961	Sergio Brighenti (Sampdoria) 27
1959–1960	Omar Sivori (Juventus) 27
1958–1959	Antonio Valentin Angelillo (Internazionale) 33
1957–1958	John Charles (Juventus) 28
1956–1957	Dino Da Costa (Roma) 22
1955–1956	Gino Pivatelli (Bologna) 29
1954–1955	Gunnar Nordahl (AC Milan) 27
1953–1954	Gunnar Nordahl (AC Milan) 23
1952–1953	Gunnar Nordahl (AC Milan) 26
1951–1952	John Hansen (Juventus) 30
1950–1951	Gunnar Nordahl (AC Milan) 34
1949–1950	Gunnar Nordahl (AC Milan) 35
1948–1949	Stefano Nyers (Internazionale) 26
1947–1948	Giampiero Boniperti (Juventus) 27
1946–1947	Valentino Mazzola (Torino) 29
1945–1946	Eusebio Castigliano (Torino) 13
1942–1943	Silvio Piola (Lazio) 21
1941–1942	Aldo Boffi (AC Milan) 22
1940–1941	Ettore Puricelli (Bologna) 22
1939–1940	Aldo Boffi (AC Milan) 24
1938–1939	Aldo Boffi (AC Milan) 19 Ettore Puricelli (Bologna) 19
1937–1938	Giuseppe Meazza (Internazionale) 20
1936–1937	Silvio Piola (Lazio) 21
1935–1936	Giuseppe Meazza (Internazionale) 25
1934–1935	Enrico Guaita (Roma) 28
1933–1934	Felice Borel (Juventus) 31
1932–1933	Felice Borel (Juventus) 29
1931–1932	Pedro Petrone (Fiorentina) 25 Angelo Schiavio (Bologna) 25
1930–1931	Rodolfo Volk (Roma) 29
1929–1930	Giuseppe Meazza (Internazionale) 31

* Not played 1943–1945 due to the 2nd World War.

GERMANY: BUNDELIGA CHAMPIONS

2007–2008	Bayern Munich

Season	Champion
2006–2007	VfB Stuttgart
2005–2006	Bayern Munich
2004–2005	Bayern Munich
2003–2004	Werder Bremen
2002–2003	Bayern Munich
2001–2002	Borussia Dortmund
2000–2001	Bayern Munich
1999–2000	Bayern Munich
1998–1999	Bayern Munich
1997–1998	Kaiserslautern
1996–1997	Bayern Munich
1995–1996	Borussia Dortmund
1994–1995	Borussia Dortmund
1993–1994	Bayern Munich
1992–1993	Werder Bremen
1991–1992	VfB Stuttgart
1990–1991	Kaiserslautern
1989–1990	Bayern Munich
1988–1989	Bayern Munich
1987–1988	Werder Bremen
1986–1987	Bayern Munich
1985–1986	Bayern Munich
1984–1985	Bayern Munich
1983–1984	VfB Stuttgart
1982–1983	Hamburg
1981–1982	Hamburg
1980–1981	Bayern Munich
1979–1980	Bayern Munich
1978–1979	Hamburg
1977–1978	Köln
1976–1977	Borussia Mönchengladbach
1975–1976	Borussia Mönchengladbach
1974–1975	Borussia Mönchengladbach
1973–1974	Bayern Munich
1972–1973	Bayern Munich
1971–1972	Bayern Munich
1970–1971	Borussia Mönchengladbach
1969–1970	Borussia Mönchengladbach
1968–1969	Bayern Munich
1967–1968	Nürnberg
1966–1967	Eintracht Braunschweig
1965–1966	1860 Munich
1964–1965	Werder Bremen
1963–1964	Köln

GERMANY: DFB–POKAL (GERMAN CUP)

2008	Bayern Munich
2007	Nürnberg
2006	Bayern Munich
2005	Bayern Munich
2004	Werder Bremen
2003	Bayern Munich
2002	Schalke
2001	Schalke
2000	Bayern Munich
1999	Werder Bremen
1998	Bayern Munich
1997	VfB Stuttgart
1996	Kaiserslautern
1995	Borussia Mönchengladbach
1994	Werder Bremen

Year	
1993	Bayer Leverkusen
1992	Hannover 96
1991	Werder Bremen
1990	Kaiserslautern
1989	Borussia Dortmund
1988	Eintracht Frankfurt
1987	Hamburg
1986	Bayern Munich
1985	Bayer Uerdingen
1984	Bayern Munich
1983	Köln
1982	Bayern Munich
1981	Eintracht Frankfurt
1980	Fortuna Düsseldorf
1979	Fortuna Düsseldorf
1978	Köln
1977	Köln
1976	Hamburg
1975	Eintracht Frankfurt
1974	Frankfurt
1973	Borussia Mönchengladbach
1972	Schalke
1971	Bayern Munich
1970	Kickers Offenbach
1969	Bayern Munich
1968	Köln
1967	Bayern Munich
1966	Bayern Munich
1965	Borussia Dortmund
1964	1860 Munich
1963	Hamburg
1962	Nürnberg
1961	Werder Bremen
1960	Borussia Mönchengladbach
1959	Schwarz–Weiss Essen
1958	Stuttgart
1957	Bayern Munich
1956	Karlsruher
1955	Karlsruher
1954	VfB Stuttgart
1953	Rot–Weiss Essen
1944–1952	Not played
1943	First Vienna
1942	1860 Munich
1941	Dresdner SC
1940	Dresdner SC
1939	Nürnberg
1938	Rapid Vienna
1937	Schalke
1936	VfB Leipzig
1935	Nürnberg

GERMANY: TOP SCORERS

Season	Player
2007–2008	Luca Toni (Bayern Munich) 24
2006–2007	Theofanis Gekas (VfL Bochum) 20
2005–2006	Miroslav Klose (Werder Bremen) 25
2004–2005	Marek Mintál (Nürnberg) 24
2003–2004	Ailton (Werder Bremen) 28
2002–2003	Thomas Christiansen (VfL Bochum) 21
	Giovane Elber (Bayern Munich) 21
2001–2002	Márcio Amoroso (Borussia Dortmund) 18
	Martin Max (1860 Munich) 18
2000–2001	Sergej Barbarez (Hamburg) 22
	Ebbe Sand (Schalke) 22
1999–2000	Martin Max (1860 Munich) 19
1998–1999	Michael Preetz (Hertha Berlin) 23
1997–1998	Ulf Kirsten (Bayer Leverkusen) 22
1996–1997	Ulf Kirsten (Bayer Leverkusen) 22
1995–1996	Fredi Bobic (VfB Stuttgart) 17
1994–1995	Mario Basler (Werder Bremen) 20
	Heiko Herrlich (Borussia Mönchengladbach) 20
1993–1994	Stefan Kuntz (Kaiserslautern) 18
	Tony Yeboah (Eintracht Frankfurt) 18
1992–1993	Ulf Kirsten (Bayer Leverkusen) 20
	Tony Yeboah (Eintracht Frankfurt) 20
1991–1992	Fritz Walter (VfB Stuttgart) 22
1990–1991	Roland Wohlfarth (Bayern Munich) 21
1989–1990	Jørn Andersen (Eintracht Frankfurt) 18
1988–1989	Thomas Allofs (Köln) 17
	Roland Wohlfarth (Bayern Munich) 17
1987–1988	Jürgen Klinsmann (VfB Stuttgart) 19
1986–1987	Uwe Rahn (Borussia Mönchengladbach) 24
1985–1986	Stefan Kuntz (VfL Bochum) 22
1984–1985	Klaus Allofs (Köln) 26
1983–1984	Karl–Heinz Rummenigge (Bayern Munich) 26
1982–1983	Rudolf Völler (Werder Bremen) 23
1981–1982	Horst Hrubesch (Hamburg) 27
1980–1981	Karl–Heinz Rummenigge (Bayern Munich) 29
1979–1980	Karl–Heinz Rummenigge (Bayern Munich) 26
1978–1979	Klaus Allofs (Fortuna Düsseldorf) 22
1977–1978	Dieter Müller (Köln) 24
	Gerd Müller (Bayern Munich) 24
1976–1977	Dieter Müller (Köln) 34
1975–1976	Klaus Fischer (Schalke) 29
1974–1975	Jupp Heynckes (Borussia Mönchengladbach) 27
1973–1974	Gerd Müller (Bayern Munich) 30
	Jupp Heynckes (Borussia Mönchengladbach) 30
1972–1973	Gerd Müller (Bayern Munich) 36
1971–1972	Gerd Müller (Bayern Munich) 40
1970–1971	Lothar Kobluhn (Rot–Weiß Oberhausen) 24
1969–1970	Gerd Müller (Bayern Munich) 38
1968–1969	Gerd Muller (Bayern Munich) 30
1967–1968	Johannes Löhr (Köln) 27
1966–1967	Lothar Emmerich (Borussia Dortmund) 28
	Gerd Müller (Bayern Munich) 28
1965–1966	Lothar Emmerich (Borussia Dortmund) 31
1964–1965	Rudolf Brunnenmeier (1860 Munich) 24
1963–1964	Uwe Seeler (Hamburg) 30

NETHERLANDS: EREDIVISIE CHAMPIONS

Season	Champion
2007–2008	PSV Eindhoven
2006–2007	PSV Eindhoven
2005–2006	PSV Eindhoven
2004–2005	PSV Eindhoven
2003–2004	Ajax
2002–2003	PSV Eindhoven
2001–2002	Ajax
2000–2001	PSV Eindhoven
1999–2000	PSV Eindhoven
1998–1999	Feyenoord
1997–1998	Ajax
1996–1997	PSV Eindhoven
1995–1996	Ajax
1994–1995	Ajax
1993–1994	Ajax
1992–1993	Feyenoord
1991–1992	PSV Eindhoven
1990–1991	PSV Eindhoven
1989–1990	Ajax
1988–1989	PSV Eindhoven
1987–1988	PSV Eindhoven
1986–1987	PSV Eindhoven
1985–1986	PSV Eindhoven
1984–1985	Ajax
1983–1984	Feyenoord
1982–1983	Ajax
1981–1982	Ajax
1980–1981	AZ Alkmaar
1979–1980	Ajax
1978–1979	Ajax
1977–1978	PSV Eindhoven
1976–1977	Ajax
1975–1976	PSV Eindhoven
1974–1975	PSV Eindhoven
1973–1974	Feyenoord
1972–1973	Ajax
1971–1972	Ajax
1970–1971	Feyenoord
1969–1970	Ajax
1968–1969	Feyenoord
1967–1968	Ajax
1966–1967	Ajax
1965–1966	Ajax
1964–1965	Feyenoord
1963–1964	DWS

1962–1963	PSV Eindhoven
1961–1962	Feyenoord
1960–1961	Feyenoord
1959–1960	Ajax
1958–1959	Sparta Rotterdam
1957–1958	DOS
1956–1957	Ajax
1955–1956	Rapid JC
1954–1955	Willem II
1953–1954	FC Eindhoven
1952–1953	RCH
1951–1952	Willem II
1950–1951	PSV Eindhoven
1949–1950	Limburgia
1948–1949	SVV
1947–1948	BVV
1946–1947	Ajax
1945–1946	HFC Haarlem
1943–1944	Volewijckers
1942–1943	ADO Den Haag
1941–1942	ADO Den Haag
1940–1941	Heracles
1939–1940	Feyenoord
1938–1939	Ajax
1937–1938	Feyenoord
1936–1937	Ajax
1935–1936	Feyenoord
1934–1935	PSV Eindhoven
1933–1934	Ajax
1932–1933	Go Ahead
1931–1932	Ajax
1930–1931	Ajax
1929–1930	Go Ahead
1928–1929	PSV Eindhoven
1927–1928	Feyenoord
1926–1927	Heracles
1925–1926	Sportclub Enschede
1924–1925	HBS
1923–1924	Feyenoord
1922–1923	RCH
1921–1922	Go Ahead
1920–1921	NAC Breda
1919–1920	Be Quick
1918–1919	Ajax
1917–1918	Ajax
1916–1917	Go Ahead
1915–1916	Willem II
1914–1915	Sparta Rotterdam
1913–1914	Kon HVV
1912–1913	Sparta Rotterdam
1911–1912	Sparta Rotterdam
1910–1911	Sparta Rotterdam
1909–1910	Kon HVV
1908–1909	Sparta Rotterdam
1907–1908	Quick
1906–1907	Kon HVV
1905–1906	Kon HBS
1904–1905	Kon HVV
1903–1904	HBS
1902–1903	Kon HVV
1901–1902	Kon HVV
1900–1901	Kon HVV
1899–1900	Kon HVV
1898–1899	RAP
1897–1898	RAP

KNVB CUP (DUTCH CUP)

2007–2008	Feyenoord
2006–2007	Ajax
2005–2006	Ajax
2004–2005	PSV Eindhoven
2003–2004	Utrecht
2002–2003	Utrecht
2001–2002	Ajax
2000–2001	FC Twente
1999–2000	Roda JC
1998–1999	Ajax
1997–1998	Ajax
1996–1997	Roda JC
1995–1996	PSV Eindhoven
1994–1995	Feyenoord
1993–1994	Feyenoord
1992–1993	Ajax
1991–1992	Feyenoord
1990–1991	Feyenoord
1989–1990	PSV Eindhoven
1988–1989	PSV Eindhoven
1987–1988	PSV Eindhoven
1986–1987	Ajax
1985–1986	Ajax
1984–1985	Utrecht
1983–1984	Feyenoord
1982–1983	Ajax
1981–1982	AZ Alkmaar
1980–1981	AZ Alkmaar
1979–1980	Feyenoord
1978–1979	Ajax
1977–1978	AZ Alkmaar
1976–1977	FC Twente
1975–1976	PSV Eindhoven
1974–1975	FC Den Haag
1973–1974	PSV Eindhoven
1972–1973	NAC Breda
1971–1972	Ajax
1970–1971	Ajax
1969–1970	Ajax
1968–1969	Feyenoord
1967–1968	ADO Den Haag
1966–1967	Ajax
1965–1966	Sparta Rotterdam
1964–1965	Feyenoord
1963–1964	Fortuna Sittard
1962–1963	Willem II
1961–1962	Sparta Rotterdam
1960–1961	Ajax
1959–19660	Not played
1958–1959	VVV
1957–1958	Sparta Rotterdam
1956–1957	Fortuna Sittard
1950–1956	Not played
1949–1950	PSV Eindhoven
1948–1949	Quick
1947–1948	Wageningen
1944–1947	Not played
1943–1944	Willem II
1942–1943	Ajax
1939–1942	Not played
1938–1939	Wageningen
1937–1938	VSV
1936–1937	FC Eindhoven
1935–1936	Roermond
1934–1935	Feyenoord
1933–1934	Groningen
1932–1933	Not played
1931–1932	DFC
1930–1931	Not played
1929–1930	Feyenoord
1928–1929	Not played
1927–1928	RCH
1926–1927	VUC

1925–1926	LONGA
1924–1925	ZFC
1923–1924	Not played
1922–1923	Not played
1921–1922	Not played
1920–1921	Schoten
1919–1920	CVV
1918–1919	Not played
1917–1918	RCH
1916–1917	Ajax
1915–1916	Quick
1914–1915	HFC
1913–1914	DFC
1912–1913	HFC
1911–1912	Haarlem
1910–1911	Quick
1909–1910	Quick
1908–1909	Quick
1907–1908	HBS
1906–1907	VOC
1905–1906	Concordia
1904–1905	VOC
1903–1904	HFC
1902–1903	HVV
1901–1902	Haarlem
1900–1901	HBS
1899–1900	Velocitas Breda
1898–1899	RAP

NETHERLANDS: LEAGUE TOP SCORERS

2007–2008	Klaas-Jan Huntelaar (Ajax) 33
2006–2007	Afonso Alves (SSC Heerenveen) 34
2005–2006	Klaas-Jan Huntelaar (SC Heerenveen and Ajax) 33
2004–2005	Dirk Kuyt (Feyenoord) 29
2003–2004	Mateja Kežman (PSV Eindhoven) 31
2002–2003	Mateja Kežman (PSV Eindhoven) 35
2001–2002	Pierre van Hooijdonk (Feyenoord) 24
2000–2001	Mateza Kežman (PSV Eindhoven) 24
1999–2000	Ruud van Nistelrooy (PSV Eindhoven) 29
1998–1999	Ruud van Nistelrooy (PSV Eindhoven) 29
1997–1998	Nikos Machlas (Vitesse) 34
1996–1997	Luc Nilis (PSV Eindhoven) 21
1995–1996	Luc Nilis (PSV Eindhoven) 21
1994–1995	Ronaldo (PSV Eindhoven) 30
1993–1994	Jari Litmanen (Ajax) 26
1992–1993	Dennis Bergkamp (Ajax) 26
1991–1992	Dennis Bergkamp (Ajax) 22
1990–1991	Romário (PSV Eindhoven) 25 Dennis Bergkamp (Ajax) 25
1989–1990	Romário (PSV Eindhoven) 23
1988–1989	Romário (PSV Eindhoven) 19
1987–1988	Wim Kieft (PSV Eindhoven) 29
1986–1987	Marco van Basten (Ajax) 31
1985–1986	Marco van Basten (Ajax) 37
1984–1985	Marco van Basten (Ajax) 22
1983–1984	Marco van Basten (Ajax) 28
1982–1983	Peter Houtman (Feyenoord) 30
1981–1982	Wim Kieft (Ajax) 32

1980–1981	Ruud Geels (Sparta Rotterdam) 22
1979–1980	Kees Kist (AZ Almaar) 27
1978–1979	Kees Kist (AZ Alkmaar) 34
1977–1978	Ruud Geels (Ajax) 30
1976–1977	Ruud Geels (Ajax) 34
1975–1976	Ruud Geels (Ajax) 29
1974–1975	Ruud Geels (Ajax) 30
1973–1974	Willy van der Kuijlen (PSV Eindhoven) 27
1972–1973	Cas Janssens (NEC) 18 Willy Brokamp (MVV Maastricht) 18
1971–1972	Johan Cruyff (Ajax) 25
1970–1971	Ove Kindvall (Feyenoord) 24
1969–1970	Willy van der Kuijlen (PSV Eindhoven) 26
1968–1969	Dick van Dijk (FC Twente) 30 Ove Kindvall (Feyenoord) 30
1967–1968	Ove Kindvall (Feyenoord) 28
1966–1967	Johan Cruyff (Ajax) 33
1965–1966	Willy van Kuijlen (PSV Eindhoven) 23 Piet Kruiver (Feyenoord) 23
1964–1965	Frans Geurtsen (DWS) 23
1963–1964	Frans Geurtsen (DWS) 28
1962–1963	Pierre Kerkhofs (PSV Eindhoven) 22
1961–1962	Dick Tol (Volendam) 27
1960–1961	Henk Groot (Ajax) 41
1959–1960	Henk Groot (Ajax) 38
1958–1959	Leon Canjels (NAC Breda) 34
1957–1958	Leo Canjels (NAC Breda) 32
1956–1957	Coen Dillon (PSV Eindhoven) 43

SPAIN: LA LIGA CHAMPIONS

2007–2008	Real Madrid
2006–2007	Real Madrid
2005–2006	Barcelona
2004–2005	Barcelona
2003–2004	Valencia
2002–2003	Real Madrid
2001–2002	Valencia
2000–2001	Real Madrid
1999–2000	Deportivo La Coruña
1998–1999	Barcelona
1997–1998	Barcelona
1996–1997	Real Madrid
1995–1996	Atlético Madrid
1994–1995	Real Madrid
1993–1994	Barcelona
1992–1993	Barcelona
1991–1992	Barcelona
1990–1991	Barcelona
1989–1990	Real Madrid
1988–1989	Real Madrid
1987–1988	Real Madrid
1986–1987	Real Madrid
1985–1986	Real Madrid
1984–1985	Barcelona
1983–1984	Athletic Bilbao
1982–1983	Athletic Bilbao
1981–1982	Real Sociedad
1980–1981	Real Sociedad
1979–1980	Real Madrid
1978–1979	Real Madrid

Season	Champion
1977–1978	Real Madrid
1976–1977	Atlético Madrid
1975–1976	Real Madrid
1974–1975	Real Madrid
1973–1974	Barcelona
1972–1973	Atlético Madrid
1971–1972	Real Madrid
1970–1971	Valencia
1969–1970	Atlético Madrid
1968–1969	Real Madrid
1967–1968	Real Madrid
1966–1967	Real Madrid
1965–1966	Atlético Madrid
1964–1965	Real Madrid
1963–1964	Real Madrid
1962–1963	Real Madrid
1961–1962	Real Madrid
1960–1961	Real Madrid
1959–1960	Barcelona
1958–1959	Barcelona
1957–1958	Real Madrid
1956–1957	Real Madrid
1955–1956	Athletic Bilbao
1954–1955	Real Madrid
1953–1954	Real Madrid
1952–1953	Barcelona
1951–1952	Barcelona
1950–1951	Atlético Madrid
1949–1950	Atlético Madrid
1948–1949	Barcelona
1947–1948	Barcelona
1946–1947	Valencia
1945–1946	Sevilla
1944–1945	Barcelona
1943–1944	Valencia
1942–1943	Athletic Bilbao
1941–1942	Valencia
1940–1941	Atlético Madrid
1939–1940	Atlético Madrid
1936–1939	Not played due to the Spanish Civil War
1935–1936	Athletic Bilbao
1934–1935	Real Betis
1933–1934	Athletic Bilbao
1932–1933	Real Madrid
1931–1932	Real Madrid
1930–1931	Athletic Bilbao
1929–1930	Athletic Bilbao
1928–1929	Barcelona

SPAIN: COPA DEL REY (SPANISH CUP)

2008	Valencia
2007	Sevilla
2006	Espanyol
2005	Real Betis
2004	Real Zaragoza
2003	Mallorca
2002	Deportivo La Coruña
2001	Real Zaragoza
2000	Espanyol
1999	Valencia
1998	Barcelona
1997	Barcelona
1996	Atlético Madrid
1995	Deportivo La Coruña
1994	Real Zaragoza
1993	Real Madrid
1992	Atlético Madrid
1991	Atlético Madrid
1990	Barcelona
1989	Real Madrid
1988	Barcelona
1987	Real Sociedad
1986	Real Zaragoza
1985	Atlético Madrid
1984	Athletic Bilbao
1983	Barcelona
1982	Real Madrid
1981	Barcelona
1980	Real Madrid
1979	Valencia
1978	Barcelona
1977	Real Betis
1976	Atlético Madrid
1975	Real Madrid
1974	Real Madrid
1973	Athletic Bilbao
1972	Atlético Madrid
1971	Barcelona
1970	Real Madrid
1969	Athletic Bilbao
1968	Barcelona
1967	Valencia
1966	Real Zaragoza
1965	Atlético Madrid
1964	Real Zaragoza
1963	Barcelona
1962	Real Madrid
1961	Atlético Madrid
1960	Atlético Madrid
1959	Barcelona
1958	Athletic Bilbao
1957	Barcelona
1956	Athletic Bilbao
1955	Athletic Bilbao
1954	Valencia
1953	Barcelona
1952	Barcelona
1951	Barcelona
1950	Athletic Bilbao
1949	Valencia
1948	Sevilla
1947	Real Madrid
1946	Real Madrid
1945	Athletic Bilbao
1944	Athletic Bilbao
1943	Athletic Bilbao
1942	Barcelona
1941	Valencia
1940	Espanyol
1939	Sevilla
1938	Not played due to the Spanish Civil War
1937	Not played due to the Spanish Civil War
1936	Real Madrid
1935	Sevilla
1934	Real Madrid
1933	Athletic Bilbao
1932	Athletic Bilbao
1931	Athletic Bilbao
1930	Athletic Bilbao
1929	Espanyol
1928	Barcelona
1927	Real Unión
1926	Barcelona
1925	Barcelona
1924	Real Unión
1923	Athletic Bilbao
1922	Barcelona
1921	Athletic Bilbao
1920	Barcelona
1919	Arenas de Getxo
1918	Real Unión
1917	Real Madrid
1916	Athletic Bilbao
1915	Athletic Bilbao
1914	Athletic Bilbao
1913	Racing Irún
1913	Barcelona
1912	Barcelona
1911	Athletic Bilbao
1910	Barcelona
1910	Athletic Bilbao
1909	Ciclista (later Real Sociedad)
1908	Real Madrid
1907	Real Madrid
1906	Real Madrid
1905	Real Madrid
1904	Not played, Athletic Bilbao awarded the trophy
1903	Athletic Bilbao
1902	Club Vizcaya (later Athletic Bilbao)

SPAIN: LEAGUE TOP SCORERS

Season	Scorer
2007–2008	Dani Güiza (Mallorca) 27
2006–2007	Ruud van Nistelrooy (Real Madrid) 25
2005–2006	Samuel Eto'o (Barcelona) 26
2004–2005	Diego Forlán (Villareal) 25
2003–2004	Ronaldo (Real Madrid) 24
2002–2003	Roy Makaay (Deportivo La Coruña) 29
2001–2002	Diego Tristán (Deportivo La Coruña) 21
2000–2001	Raúl (Real Madrid) 24
1999–2000	Salva Ballesta (Racing Santander) 27
1998–1999	Raúl (Real Madrid) 23
1997–1998	Christian Vieri (Atlético Madrid) 24
1996–1997	Ronaldo (Barcelona) 34
1995–1996	Juan Antonio Pizzi (Tenerife) 31
1994–1995	Iván Zamorano (Real Madrid) 27
1993–1994	Romário (Barcelona) 30
1992–1993	Bebeto (Deportivo La Coruña) 29
1991–1992	Manolo Sánchez (Atlético Madrid) 27
1990–1991	Emilio Butragueño (Real Madrid) 19
1989–1990	Hugo Sánchez (Real Madrid) 38
1988–1989	Baltazar (Atlético Madrid) 35
1987–1988	Hugo Sánchez (Real Madrid) 29
1986–1987	Hugo Sánchez (Real Madrid) 34
1985–1986	Hugo Sánchez (Atlético Madrid) 22
1984–1985	Hugo Sánchez (Atlético Madrid) 19
1983–1984	Jorge da Silva (Real Valladolid) 17
	Juanito (Real Valladolid) 17
1982–1983	Poli Rincón (Real Betis) 20
1981–1982	Quini (Barcelona) 26
1980–1981	Quini (Barcelona) 20
1979–1980	Quini (Sporting Gijón) 24
1978–1979	Hans Krankl (Barcelona) 29
1977–1978	Mario Kempes (Valencia) 28
1976–1977	Mario Kempes (Valencia) 24
1975–1976	Quini (Sporting Gijón) 18
1974–1975	Carlos (Athletic Bilbao) 19
1973–1974	Quini (Sporting Gijón) 20
1972–1973	Marianín (Real Oviedo) 19
1971–1972	Enrique Porta (Granada) 20
1970–1971	José Eulogio Gárate (Atlético Madrid) 17
	Carles Rexach (Barcelona) 17
1969–1970	Amancio (Real Madrid) 16
	Luis Aragonés (Atlético Madrid) 16
	José Eulogio Gárate (Atlético Madrid) 16
1968–1969	Amancio (Real Madrid) 14
	José Eulogio Gárate (Atlético Madrid) 14
1967–1968	Fidel Uriarte (Athletic Bilbao) 22
1966–1967	Waldo (Valencia) 24
1965–1966	Vavá (Elche) 19
1964–1965	Cayetano Ré (Barcelona) 25
1963–1964	Ferenc Puskás (Real Madrid) 20
1962–1963	Ferenc Puskás (Real Madrid) 26
1961–1962	Juan Seminario (Real Zaragoza) 25
1960–1961	Ferenc Puskás (Real Madrid) 27
1959–1960	Ferenc Puskás (Real Madrid) 26
1958–1959	Alfredo di Stéfano (Real Madrid) 23
1957–1958	Manuel Badenes (Real Valladolid) 19
	Alfredo di Stéfano (Real Madrid) 19
	Ricardo (Valencia) 19
1956–1957	Alfredo di Stéfano (Real Madrid) 31
1955–1956	Alfredo di Stéfano (Real Madrid) 24
1954–1955	Juan Arza (Sevilla) 28
1953–1954	Alfredo di Stéfano (Real Madrid) 27
1952–1953	Telmo Zarra (Athletic Bilbao) 24
1951–1952	Pahiño (Real Madrid) 28
1950–1951	Telmo Zarra (Athletic Bilbao) 38
1949–1950	Telmo Zarra (Athletic

Bilbao) 25

Season	Top scorer
1948–1949	César (Barcelona) 28
1947–1948	Pahiño (Celta Vigo) 23
1946–1947	Telmo Zarra (Athletic Bilbao) 34
1945–1946	Telmo Zarra (Athletic Bilbao) 24
1944–1945	Telmo Zarra (Athletic Bilbao) 19
1943–1944	Mundo (Valencia) 27
1942–1943	Mariano Martín (Barcelona) 32
1941–1942	Mundo (Valencia) 27
1940–1941	Pruden (Atlético Madrid) 30
1939–1940	Victor Unamuno (Athletic Bilbao) 26
1936–1939	Not played due to Spanish Civil War
1935–1936	Isidro Lángara (Real Oviedo) 27
1934–1935	Isidro Lángara (Real Oviedo) 26
1933–1934	Isidro Lángara (Real Oviedo) 27
1932–1933	Manuel Olivares (Real Madrid) 16
1931–1932	Guillermo Gorostiza (Athletic Bilbao) 12
1930–1931	Bata (Athletic Bilbao) 27
1929–1930	Guillermo Gorostiza (Athletic Bilbao) 19
1928–1929	Paco Bienzobas (Real Sociedad) 14

BRAZIL: CAMPEONATO BRASILEIRO CHAMPIONS

Year	Champion
2007	São Paulo
2006	São Paulo
2005	Corinthians
2004	Santos
2003	Cruzeiro
2002	Santos
2001	Atlético Paranaense
2000	Not played
1999	Corinthians
1998	Corinthians
1997	Vasco da Gama
1996	Grêmio
1995	Botafogo
1994	Palmeiras
1993	Palmeiras
1992	Flamengo
1991	São Paulo
1990	Corinthians
1989	Vasco da Gama
1988	Bahia
1987	Sport Club Recife
1986	São Paulo
1985	Coritiba
1984	Fluminense
1983	Flamengo
1982	Flamengo
1981	Grêmio
1980	Flamengo
1979	Internacional
1978	Guarani
1977	São Paulo
1976	Internacional
1975	Internacional
1974	Vasco da Gama
1973	Palmeiras
1972	Palmeiras
1971	Atlético Mineiro

BRAZIL: COPA DO BRASIL (BRASILIAN CUP)*

2007	Fluminense
2006	Flamengo
2005	Paulista
2004	Santo André
2003	Cruzeiro
2002	Corinthians
2001	Grêmio
2000	Cruzeiro
1999	Juventude
1998	Palmeiras
1997	Grêmio
1996	Cruzeiro
1995	Corinthians
1994	Grêmio
1993	Cruzeiro
1992	Internacional
1991	Criciúma
1990	Flamengo
1989	Grêmio
1968	Botafogo
1967	Palmeiras
1966	Cruzeiro
1965	Santos
1964	Santos
1963	Santos
1962	Santos
1961	Santos
1960	Palmeiras
1959	Bahia

* Known as Taça Brasil 1959–1968.

BRAZIL: LEAGUE TOP SCORERS

Year	Top scorer
2007	Josiel (Paraná) 20
2006	Souza (Goiás) 17
2005	Romário (Vasco da Gama) 22
2004	Washington (Atlético Paranaense) 34
2003	Dimba (Goiás) 31
2002	Luís Fabiano (São Paulo) 19
	Rodrigo Fabri (Grêmio) 19
2001	Romário (Vasco da Gama) 21
2000	Dill (Goiás) 20
	Magno Alves (Fluminense) 20
	Romário (Vasco da Gama) 20
1999	Guilherme (Atlético Mineiro) 28
1998	Viola (Santos) 21
1997	Edmundo (Vasco da Gama) 29
1996	Paulo Nunes (Grêmio) 16
	Renaldo (Atlético Mineiro) 16
1995	Túlio (Botafogo) 23
1994	Márcio Amoroso (Guarani) 19
1993	Guga (Santos) 15
1992	Bebeto (Vasco da Gama) 18
1991	Paulinho McLaren (Santos) 15
1990	Charles (Bahia) 11
1989	Túlio (Goiás) 11
1988	Nilson (Internacional) 15
1987	Muller (São Paulo) 10
1986	Careca (São Paulo) 25
1985	Edmar (Guarani) 20
1984	Roberto Dinamite (Vasco da Gama) 16
1983	Serginho (Santos) 22
1982	Zico (Flamengo) 20
1981	Nunes (Flamengo) 16
1980	Zico (Flamengo) 21
1979	César (América) 13
1978	Paulinho (Vasco da Gama) 19
1977	Reinaldo (Atlético Mineiro) 28
1976	Dario (Internacional) 16
1975	Flávio (Internacional) 16
1974	Roberto Dinamite (Vasco da Gama) 16
1973	Ramón (Santa Cruz) 21
	Túlio (Botafogo) 19
1972	Dario (Atlético Mineiro) 17
	Pedro Rocha (São Paulo) 17
1971	Dario (Atlético Mineiro) 15

ARGENTINA: PRIMERA DIVISION CHAMPIONS*

Year	Champion
2007A	Lanús
2007C	San Lorenzo
2006A	Estudiantes
2006C	Boca Juniors
2005A	Boca Juniors
2005C	Vélez Sársfield
2004A	Newell's Old Boys
2004C	River Plate
2003A	Boca Juniors
2003C	River Plate
2002A	Independiente
2002C	River Plate
2001A	Racing Club
2001C	San Lorenzo
2000A	Boca Juniors
2000C	River Plate
1999A	River Plate
1999C	Boca Juniors
1998A	Boca Juniors
1998C	Vélez Sársfield
1997A	River Plate
1997C	River Plate
1996A	River Plate
1996C	Vélez Sársfield
1995A	Vélez Sársfield
1995C	San Lorenzo
1994A	River Plate
1994C	Independiente
1993A	River Plate
1993C	Vélez Sarsfield
1992A	Boca Juniors
1992C	Newell's Old Boys
1991A	River Plate
1990–1991	Newell's Old Boys
1989–1990	River Plate
1988–1989	Independiente
1987–1988	Newell's Old Boys
1986–1987	Rosario Central
1985–1986	River Plate
1985N	Argentinos Juniors
1984N	Ferro Carril Oeste
1984M	Argentinos Juniors
1983N	Estudiantes
1983M	Independiente
1982N	Ferro Carril Oeste
1982M	Estudiantes
1981M	Boca Juniors
1981N	River Plate
1980M	River Plate
1980N	Rosario Central
1979M	River Plate
1979N	River Plate
1978M	Quilmes
1978N	Independiente
1977M	River Plate
1977N	Independiente
1976M	Boca Juniors
1976N	Boca Juniors
1975M	River Plate
1975N	River Plate
1974M	Newell's Old Boys
1974N	San Lorenzo
1973M	Huracán
1973N	Rosario Central
1972M	San Lorenzo
1972N	San Lorenzo
1971M	Independiente
1971N	Rosario Central
1970M	Independiente
1970N	Boca Juniors
1969M	Chacarita Juniors
1969N	Boca Juniors
1968M	San Lorenzo
1968N	Vélez Sársfield
1967M	Estudiantes
1967N	Independiente
1966	Racing Club
1965	Boca Juniors
1964	Boca Juniors
1963	Independiente
1962	Boca Juniors
1961	Racing Club
1960	Independiente
1959	San Lorenzo
1958	Racing Club
1957	River Plate
1956	River Plate
1955	River Plate
1954	Boca Juniors
1953	River Plate
1952	River Plate
1951	Racing Club
1950	Racing Club
1949	Racing Club
1948	Independiente
1947	River Plate
1946	San Lorenzo
1945	River Plate
1944	Boca Juniors
1943	Boca Juniors
1942	River Plate
1941	River Plate
1940	Boca Juniors
1939	Independiente
1938	Independiente
1937	River Plate
1936	River Plate
1935	Boca Juniors
1934	Boca Juniors
1933	San Lorenzo
1932	River Plate
1931	Boca Juniors

* In 1999 the championship was split into two tournaments: Apertura (August to December) and Clausura (February to June).

Championship was previously split into two tournaments in 1967–1986: Metropolitano (open only to teams afiliated to the national association) and Nacional (open to teams from the provinces).

ARGENTINA: LEAGUE TOP SCORERS

Year	Top scorer
2007A	German Denis (Independiente) 18

(Independiente) 16

2002C Fernando Cavenaghi (River Plate) 15

2001A Martín Cardetti (River Plate 17)

2001C Bernardo Romeo (San Lorenzo) 15

2000A Juan Pablo Ángel (River Plate) 13

2000C Esteban Fuertes (Colón) 17

1999A Javier Saviola (River Plate) 15

1999C José Luis Calderon (Independiente) 17

1998A Martín Palermo (Boca Juniors) 20

1998C Roberto Sosa (Gimnasia) 17

1997A Rubén Da Silva (Rosario Central) 15

1997C Sergio Martínez (Boca Juniors) 15

1996A Gustavo Reggi (Ferro Carril Oeste) 11

1996C Ariel López (Lanús) 12

1995A José Luis Calderon (Estudiantes) 13

1995C José Oscar Flores (Vélez Sársfield) 14

1994A Enzo Francescoli (River Plate) 12

1994C Hernán Crespo (River Plate) 11

Marcelo Espina (Platense) 11

1993A Sergio Martínez (Boca Juniors) 12

1993C Rubén Da Silva (River Plate 13

1992A Alberto Acosta (San Lorenzo) 12

1992C Diego Latorre (Boca Juniors) 9

1991A Ramón Angel Díaz (River Plate) 14

1990–1991 Esteban González (Vélez Sársfield) 18

1989–1990 Ariel Cozzoni (Newell's Old Boys) 23

1988–1989 Oscar Dertycia (Argentinos Juniors) 20

Néstor Raúl Gorosito (San Lorenzo) 20

1987–1988 José Luis Rodriguez (Deportivo Español) 18

1986–1987 Omar Palma (Rosario Central) 20

1985–1986 Enzo Francescoli (River Plate) 25

1985N Jorge Comas (Vélez Sársfield) 12

1984N Pedro Pablo Pasculli (Argentinos Juniors) 9

1984M Enzo Francescoli (River Plate) 24

1983N Armando Husillos (Loma Negra) 11

1983M Víctor Ramos (Newell's

Old Boys) 30

1982N Miguel Juárez (Ferro Carril Oeste) 22

1982M Carlos Manuel Morete (Independiente) 20

1981M Raúl Chaparro (Instituto) 20

1981N Carlos Bianchi (Vélez Sársfield) 15

1980M Diego Maradona (Argentinos Juniors) 25

1980N Diego Maradona (Argentinos Juniors) 17

1979M Diego Maradona (Argentinos Juniors) 14

Sergio Fortunato (Estudiantes) 14

1979N Diego Maradona (Argentinos Juniors) 12

1978M Diego Maradona (Argentinos Juniors) 22

Luis Andreucci (Quilmes) 22

1978N José Omar Reinaldi (Talleres) 18

1977M Carlos Álvarez (Argentinos Juniors) 27

1977N Alfredo Letanu (Estudiantes) 13

1976M Mario Kempes (Rosario Central) 21

1976N Norberto Eresuma (San Lorenzo de Mar del Plata) 12

Luis Ludueña (Talleres) 12

Víctor Marchetti (Atlético Unión) 12

1975M Héctor Scotta (San Lorenzo) 32

1975N Héctor Scotta (San Lorenzo) 28

1974M Carlos Manuel Morete (River Plate) 18

1974N Mario Kempes (Rosario Central) 25

1973M Oscar Más (River Plate) 17

Hugo Curioni (Boca Juniors) 17

Ignacio Peña (Estudiantes) 17

1973N Juan Gómez Voglino (Atlanta) 18

1972M Miguel Ángel Brindisi (Huracán) 21

1972N Carlos Manuel Morete (River Plate) 14

1971M Carlos Bianchi (Vélez Sársfield) 36

1971N Alfredo Obberti (Newell's Old Boys) 10

José Luñis (Juventud Antoniana) 10

1970M Oscar Más (River Plate) 16

1970N Carlos Bianchi (Vélez Sársfield) 14

1969M Walter Machado (Racing Club) 14

1969N Rodolfo Fischer (San Lorenzo) 14

Carlos Bulla (Platense) 14

1968M Alfredo Obberti (Los

Andes) 13

1968N Omar Wehbe (Vélez Sársfield) 13

1967M Bernardo Acosta (Lanús) 18

1967N Luis Artime (Independiente) 11

1966 Luis Artime (Independiente) 23

1965 Juan Carlos Carone (Vélez Sársfield) 19

1964 Héctor Rodolfo Viera (San Lorenzo) 17

1963 Luis Artime (River Plate) 25

1962 Luis Artime (River Plate) 25

1961 José Sanfilippo (San Lorenzo) 26

1960 José Sanfilippo (San Lorenzo) 34

1959 José Sanfilippo (San Lorenzo) 31

1958 José Sanfilippo (San Lorenzo) 28

1957 Roberto Zarate (River Plate) 22

1956 Juan Alberto Castro (Rosario Central) 17

Ernesto Grillo (Independiente) 17

1955 Oscar Massei (Rosario Central) 21

1954 Ángel Berni (San Lorenzo) 19

Norberto Conde (Vélez Sársfield) 19

José Borello (Boca Juniors) 19

1953 Juan José Pizzuti (Racing Club) 22

Juan Benavidez (San Lorenzo) 22

1952 Eduardo Ricagni (Huracán) 28

1951 Santiago Vernazza (River Plate) 22

1950 Mario Papa (San Lorenzo) 24

1949 Llamil Simes (Racing Club) 26

Juan José Pizzuti (Banfield) 26

1948 Benjamín Santos (Rosario Central) 21

1947 Alfredo di Stéfano (River Plate) 27

1946 Mario Boye (Boca Juniors) 24

1945 Ángel Labruna (River Plate) 25

1944 Atilio Mellone (Huracán) 26

1943 Luis Arrieta (Lanús) 23

Ángel Labruna (River Plate) 23

1942 Raúl Frutos (Platense) 23

Rinaldo Martino (San Lorenzo) 25

1941 José Canteli (Newell's Old Boys) 30

1940 Delfín Benitez (Racing Club) 33

Isidro Langara (San Lorenzo) 33

1939 Arsenio Erico (Independiente) 40

1938 Arsenio Erico (Independiente) 43

1937 Arsenio Erico (Independiente) 47

1936 Evaristo Barrera (Racing Club) 32

1935 Agustín Cosso (Vélez Sársfield) 33

1934 Evaristo Barrera (Racing Club) 34

1933 Francisco Varallo (Boca Juniors) 34

1932 Bernabé Ferreyra (River Plate) 43

1931 Alberto Zozaya (Estudiantes) 33

USA: NORTH AMERICAN SOCCER LEAGUE CHAMPIONS

1984 Chicago Sting
1983 Tulsa Roughnecks
1982 New York Cosmos
1981 Chicago Sting
1980 New York Cosmos
1979 Vancouver Whitecaps
1978 New York Cosmos
1977 New York Cosmos
1976 Toronto Metros–Croatia
1975 Tampa Bay Rowdies
1974 Los Angeles Aztecs
1973 Philadelphia Atoms
1972 New York Cosmos
1971 Dallas Tornado
1970 Rochester Lancers
1969 Kansas City Spurs
1968 Atlanta Chiefs

NORTH AMERICAN SOCCER LEAGUE TOP SCORERS

1984 Steve Zungul (Golden Bay Earthquakes) 20
1983 Roberto Cabanas (New York Cosmos) 25
1982 Ricardo Alonso (Jacksonville Tea Men) 21
1981 Giorgio Chinaglia (New York Cosmos) 29
1980 Giorgio Chinaglia (New York Cosmos) 32
1979 Giorgio Chinaglia (New York Cosmos) 26
1978 Giorgio Chinaglia (New York Cosmos) 34
1977 Steve David (Los Angeles Aztecs) 26
1976 Derek Smethurst (Tampa Bay Rowdies) 20
1975 Steve David (Miami Toros) 23
1974 Paul Child (San Jose Earthquakes) 15
1973 Warren Archibald (Miami Toros) 12
Ilija Mitic (Dallas Tornado) 12
1972 Randy Horton (New York Cosmos) 9
1971 Carlos Metidieri (Rochester

1981	Giorgio Chinaglia (New York Cosmos) 29
1980	Giorgio Chinaglia (New York Cosmos) 32
1979	Giorgio Chinaglia (New York Cosmos) 26
1978	Giorgio Chinaglia (New York Cosmos) 34
1977	Steve David (Los Angeles Aztecs) 26
1976	Derek Smethurst (Tampa Bay Rowdies) 20
1975	Steve David (Miami Toros) 23
1974	Paul Child (San Jose Earthquakes) 15
1973	Warren Archibald (Miami Toros) 12
	Ilija Mitic (Dallas Tornado) 12
1972	Randy Horton (New York Cosmos) 9
1971	Carlos Metidieri (Rochester Lancers) 19
1970	Kirk Apostolidis (Dallas Tornado) 16
1969	Kaiser Motaung (Atlanta Apollos) 16
1968	John Kowalik (Chicago Mustangs) 30
	Cirilo Fernandez (San Diego Toros) 30

USA: MAJOR LEAGUE SOCCER CHAMPIONS – MLS CUP

2007	Houston Dynamo
2006	Houston Dynamo
2005	Los Angeles Galaxy
2004	DC United
2003	San Jose Earthquakes
2002	Los Angeles Galaxy
2001	San Jose Earthquakes
2000	Kansas City Wizards
1999	DC United
1998	Chicago Fire
1997	DC United
1996	DC United

MLS TOP SCORERS

2007	Luciano Emilio (DC United) 20
2006	Jeff Cunningham (Real Salt Lake) 16
2005	Taylor Twellman (New England Revolution) 17
2004	Brian Ching (San Jose Earthquakes) 12
2003	Carlos Ruiz (Los Angeles Galaxy) 15
2002	Carlos Ruiz (Los Angeles Galaxy) 24
2001	Alex Pineda Chacón (Miami Fusion) 19
2000	Mamadou Diallo (Tampa Bay Mutiny) 26
1999	Jason Kreis (Dallas Burn) 18
1998	Stern John (Columbus Crew) 26
1997	Jaime Moreno (DC United) 16
1996	Roy Lassiter (Tampa Bay Mutiny) 27

JAPAN: J-LEAGUE CHAMPIONSHIP

2007	Kashima Antlers
2006	Urawa Red Diamonds
2005	Gamba Osaka

2004	Yokohama F. Marinos
2003	Yokohama F. Marinos
2002	Júbilo Iwata
2001	Kashima Antlers
2000	Kashima Antlers
1999	Júbilo Iwata
1998	Kashima Antlers
1997	Júbilo Iwata
1996	Kashima Antlers
1995	Yokohama Marinos
1994	Verdy Kawasaki
1993	Verdy Kawasaki

JAPAN: ALL-JAPAN FOOTBALL CHAMPIONSHIP*

1991–1992	Yomiuri
1990–1991	Yomiuri
1989–1990	Nissan
1988–1989	Nissan
1987–1988	Yamaha Motors
1986–1987	Yomiuri
1985–1986	East Furukawa
1984	Yomiuri
1983	Yomiuri
1982	Mitsubishi Motors
1981	Fujita
1980	Yanmar Diesel
1979	Fujita
1978	Mitsubishi Motors
1977	Fujita
1976	East Furukawa
1975	Yanmar Diesel
1974	Yanmar Diesel
1973	Mitsubishi Motors
1972	Hitachi
1971	Yanmar Diesel
1970	Toyo Kogyo
1969	Mitsubishi Motors
1968	Toyo Kogyo
1967	Toyo Kogyo
1966	Toyo Kogyo
1965	Toyo Kogyo

* Amateur tournament played until the formation of the J-League. Amateur league was highest level of the sport in Japan until 1992.

JAPAN: EMPEROR'S CUP*

2007	Kashima Antlers
2006	Urawa Reds
2005	Urawa Reds
2004	Tokyo Verdy 1969
2003	Júbilo Iwata
2002	Kyoto Purple Sanga
2001	Shimizu S-Pulse
2000	Kashima Antlers
1999	Nagoya Grampus Eight
1998	Yokohama Flügels
1997	Kashima Antlers
1996	Verdy Kawasaki
1995	Nagoya Grampus Eight
1994	Bellmare Hiratsuka
1993	Yokohama Flügels
1992	Yokohama Marinos
1991	Nissan
1990	Matsushita
1989	Nissan
1988	Nissan
1987	Yomiuri

1986	Yomiuri
1985	Nissan
1984	Yomiuri Club
1983	Nissan
1982	Yamaha
1981	NKK
1980	Mitsubishi Heavy Industries
1979	Fujita Industries
1978	Mitsubishi Heavy Industries
1977	Fujita Industries
1976	Furukawa Electric
1975	Hitachi
1974	Yanmar Diesel
1973	Mitsubishi Heavy Industries
1972	Hitachi
1971	Mitsubishi Heavy Industries
1970	Yanmar Diesel
1969	Toyo Industries
1968	Yanmar Diesel
1967	Toyo Industries
1966	Waseda University
1965	Toyo Industries
1964	Title shared between Yawata Steel and Furukawa Electric
1963	Waseda University
1962	Chuo University
1961	Furukawa Electric
1960	Furukawa Electric
1959	Kwangaku
1958	Kwangaku
1957	Chuo University
1956	Keio BRB
1955	All Kwangaku
1954	Keio BRB
1953	Kwangaku
1952	All Keio University
1951	Keio BRB
1950	All Kwangaku
1949	Tokyo University LB
1946	Tokyo University
1940	Keio BRB
1939	Keio BRB
1938	Waseda University
1937	Keio University
1936	Keio BRB
1935	Seoul Shukyu-dan
1933	Tokyo Old Boys 4
1932	Keio
1931	Tokyo University
1930	Kwangaku
1929	Kwangaku
1928	Waseda University WMW
1927	Kobe-Ichi Junior High School
1925	Rijo Shukyu-dan
1924	Rijo
1923	Astra
1922	Nagoya Shukyu-dan
1921	Tokyo Shukyu-dan

* Not played 1926 due to Emperor Taisho's death; not played 1934 due to East Asian Games; not played 1941–1945 due to the Second World War; not played 1947–1948 due to post Second World War disorder.

JAPAN LEAGUE TOP SCORERS

2007	Juninho (Kawasaki Frontale) 22
2006	Washington (Urawa Red Diamonds) 26
	Magno Alves (Gamba Osaka) 26
2005	Araújo (Gamba Osaka) 33

2004	Emerson (Urawa Reds) 27
2003	Ueslei (Nagoya Grampus Eight) 22
2002	Naohiro Takahara (Júbilo Iwata) 26
2001	Will (Consadole Sapporo) 24
2000	Masashi Nakayama (Júbilo Iwata) 20
1999	Hwang Sun-Hong (Cerezo Osaka) 24
1998	Masashi Nakayama (Júbilo Iwata) 36
1997	Patrick Mboma (Gamba Osaka) 25
1996	Kazuyoshi Miura (Verdy Kawasaki) 23
1995	Masahiro Fukuda (Urawa Reds) 32
1994	Frank Ordenewitz (JEF United Ichihara) 30
1993	Ramón Díaz (Yokohama Marinos) 28

AUSTRALIA: A-LEAGUE*

2007–2008	Newcastle Jets
2006–2007	Melbourne Victory
2005–2006	Sydney FC
2004–2005	Not played
2003–2004	Perth Glory
2002–2003	Perth Glory
2001–2002	Olympic Sharks
2000–2001	Wollongong City Wolves
1999–2000	Wollongong City Wolves
1998–1999	South Melbourne
1997–1998	South Melbourne
1996–1997	Brisbane Strikers
1995–1996	Melbourne Knights
1994–1995	Melbourne Knights
1993–1994	Adelaide City
1992–1993	Marconi Fairfield
1991–1992	Adelaide City
1990–1991	South Melbourne Hellas
1989–1990	Olympic UTS
1989	Marconi Fairfield
1988	Marconi Fairfield
1987	Apia Leichhardt
1986	Adelaide City
1985	Brunswick Juventus
1984	South Melbourne Hellas
1983	Budapest St. George
1982	Sydney City Hakoah
1981	Sydney City Hakoah
1980	Sydney City Hakoah
1979	Marconi Fairfield
1978	West Adelaide Hellas
1977	Sydney City Hakoah

* Known as Australian National Soccer League and played under a different format until 2004.

AUSTRALIA A-LEAGUE TOP SCORERS

2007–2008	Joel Griffiths (Newcastle Jets) 12
2006–2007	Daniel Allsopp (Melbourne Victory) 11
2005–2006	Alex Brosque (Queensland Roar) 8
	Bobby Despotovski (Perth Glory) 8
	Archie Thompson (Melbourne Victory) 8
	Stewart Petrie (Central Coast Mariners) 8

GLOSSARY

AGGREGATE
When a fixture is played over two legs, the aggregate is the scores of both matches added together.

ASSISTANT REFEREES
The flag-carrying officials positioned on either touchline who help the referee.

AWAY GOALS
In matches played over two legs, goals scored in the away match count extra if the aggregate score is tied.

BENCH
A bench at the side of the pitch to seat players who are waiting their chance to play or who have been been removed from play due to injury or other reasons. A substitute is often referred to as being 'on the bench'.

CAP
An appearance for an international team. The term originated in England, where players were once presented with a white silk cap every time they played for their country.

CENTRE SPOT
The point in the centre of the pitch where the match starts and re-starts after a goal.

CHIP
A pass or shot in which the bottom of the ball is struck with a short stabbing motion with no follow through.

CORNER FLAG
A flag marking the corner arc.

CORNER KICK
An attacking dead ball situation arising when the defending team puts the ball over their own goal line, between the corner flag and the goalpost.

CROSS
To kick or pass the ball across the pitch, usually into the penalty area to create a goalscoring opportunity.

CRUYFF TURN
A deceptive turn named after the world-famous Dutch footballer of the 1970s, Johan Cruyff, who perfected it.

DEAD BALL
A break in play, often due to a free kick or throw in.

DISTRIBUTION
Passing the ball to team mates. Good distribution is making the right type of pass at the best moment.

DIVE
An attempt by a player to convince the referee (falsely) that a foul has been committed against them by diving to the ground. This is against the Laws of the Game.

DRAG-BACK
When a player drags the ball behind him and executes a quick turn and change of direction.

DRIBBLE
Moving the ball with lots of small, quick kicks, usually with both feet.

DUMMY
To deceive an opponent by pretending to pass or shoot in one direction and then moving the opposite way.

EIGHTEEN-YARD BOX
The larger marked area around the goal, in which a penalty may be given.

EXTRA TIME
Additional period of time played at the end of a match that has resulted in a draw to try to decide the winner. Extra time is usually only played in a knockout competition where a winner must be decided.

FAR POST
The goal post furthest away from the point of attack.

FIELD OF PLAY
The football pitch; the surface on which the game is played and its markings.

FOURTH OFFICIAL
A match official who assists the referee in a number of different tasks. The fourth official may also be called on to replace any other official who cannot continue in a match.

FOUL
An infringement of the laws of football, such as when a player trips kicks or pushes an opponent (accidentally or deliberately).

FREE KICK
When play is stopped by the referee and a kick awarded to the opposing side, usually due to a foul or infringement.

FREE TRANSFER
When a player transfers from one team to another after their contract has expired, so that no transfer fee is paid. It is also known as the Bosman ruling.

FRIENDLY GAME
A match where there is no trophy, prize or ranking dependent on the result. This is sometimes called an exhibition match.

GOAL
1. The nets supported by two posts and a crossbar at each end of the pitch, where the goalkeepers stand.
2. When the ball crosses the line into the goal area and a team scores.

GOAL KICK
A kick awarded to the defending team when the ball has crossed the goal line last touched by an attacking player, but no goal has been scored.

GOAL LINE
The line linking the corner flags with the goal posts.

GOLDEN BOOT
Award given to the top scoring player in a particular football competition.

GOLDEN GOAL
A way of deciding the winner when a match in a knock-out contest ends in a draw. The first goal scored in extra time, known as a 'golden goal', wins the match instantly. If there is no Golden Goal in 30 minutes of extra time, a penalty shoot-out decides the match.

HALFWAY LINE
The marked-out line that separates one half of the pitch from the other.

HANDBALL
A type of foul. It is illegal for an outfield player to touch the ball with his or her hand in open play.

HAT-TRICK
Three goals scored by the same player in one match. When a player scores two goals in one match it is sometimes referred to as 'a brace'.

INFRINGEMENT
To break one of the laws of football.

INTERCEPT
To steal possession of or get in the way of an opponent's pass.

INJURY TIME
Time added at the end of a match to allow for time lost due to injuries, substitutions or other stoppages. The fourth official notifies the teams how much time has been added.

KICK-OFF
The way of starting each half of a football match. The kick-off is the first kick off the half which sets the ball in play. It is taken from the centre spot. The kick which restarts play after a goal is scored is also known as a kick-off.

KIT
The clothing worn by a player during a match, including shorts, shirt, socks, boots and shin pads.

LEG
One game of a match between two teams that is played over two individual games. The winner is the team with the better aggregate score.

LOCAL DERBY
A match between two local rival teams.

MAN OF THE MATCH
Award given to the player judged to be the most outstanding in a particular match.

MARK
To position yourself close to an opponent so that it is difficult for him to receive or pass the ball.

MATCH
A competitive game, usually comprising two halves of 45 minutes.

NEAR POST
The goal post nearest to the point of attack.

NUTMEG
To kick the ball through an opponent's legs and then collect it on the other side. The word is thought to originate from the Victorian term 'to nutmeg', meaning 'to trick'.

OFFSIDE
When an attacker has moved beyond the second last defender as the ball is played forward.

ONE-TWO
A quick back-and-forth pass between two players, also known as a wall pass.

OWN GOAL
A goal scored accidentally by a player into his own net.

PASS
When a player passes the ball to another member of his team during a match.

PENALTY
A specific kind of free kick awarded when an attacker is fouled in the penalty area.

PENALTY SHOOT-OUT
A way of deciding the winner in a knockout competition where the match ends in a draw. The teams take turn to shoot at goal from the penalty spot. Usually the best of five wins, however if the teams are level after five penalties they play until one team misses.

PENALTY SPOT
The place from where the penalty is taken.

PITCH
The field of play.

PHYSIO
Short for a physiotherapist, a health worker who treats injuries during a match and helps players to recover from long term injuries.

PLAYMAKER
A player who creates attacking moves and opportunities for his team to score.

POSSESSION
To have the ball.

QUARTER-FINALS
In a knockout competition, the four matches that decide which four of the eight remaining teams will play in the semi-finals.

READING THE GAME
Playing the game intelligently e.g. using tactical knowledge to improve positioning, passing, tackling and intercepting.

RED CARD
A player is shown this after an extremely serious foul or infringement, or after receiving two yellow cards in a match. They usually receive a suspension.

REFEREE
The official in charge of the match, who checks that the laws of football are not broken.

REPLAY
A match played between two teams for a second time at a later date, because the first match resulted in a draw.

ROUND-ROBIN
A competition where all teams play each other in turn and the team with the highest points score is the winner. In some other competitions, the first round has the teams split into groups who then play round-robins to decide which will go through to later rounds. The rest of the tournament is played as knockout rounds.

RUNNERS-UP
The team who finish in second place in a competition.

SCORE
To get a goal.

SEMI-FINALS
In a knockout competition, the two matches that decide which two of the four remaining teams will play in the final.

SENT OFF
When a player receives a red card and is sent from the field of play.

SHIN PADS
Protective shields for the shins and ankles, usually worn underneath the socks.

SHOOT
To aim a kick or pass at the goal.

SILVER GOAL
A way of deciding the winner when a match in a knockout contest ends in a draw. The team leading after a fifteen-minute period of extra time win the match, with the goal that gives them the lead known as a 'silver goal'. If the score is level, another fifteen-minute period is played. If the score is still level, the match is decided by a penalty shoot-out.

SIX-YARD BOX
The small marked-out area around the goal.

STOP TURN
A way of changing direction quickly by stopping the ball at speed.

SUBSTITUTE
A player who replaces another player during a match, either for tactical reasons or because the first player is injured or not playing well. Up to three substitutes are allowed in most matches.

SWERVE
To kick or strike across the back of the ball so that it bends in the opposite direction.

TACKLE
To fairly challenge a player for the ball. A tackle can be block or sliding.

THROW-IN
A throw from the touchline awarded by the referee when the opposition have kicked the ball out of play.

TOUCHLINES
The two lines running down the length of the pitch

TRANSFER
The movement of a player under contract from one team to another team.

TRANSFER FEE
When a player transfers from one team to another, the team he is joining pay a sum of money, known as a transer fee, to the team he is leaving.

VOLLEY
To kick the ball before it touches the ground, usually as a shot on goal.

WALL
A line of two or more players defending their goal against a free kick.

WARM-DOWN
Period of gradual decrease in physical activity after a match or training session. Warming down allows the body to transition smoothly to a resting state.

WARM-UP
Preparation for a match or training session by gradual increase in physical activity. Warming up properly reduces the risk of injury and improves performance.

YELLOW CARD
This is shown by the referee for a serious offence or persistant offending.

ACKNOWLEDGEMENTS

THE PUBLISHER WOULD LIKE TO THANK THE FOLLOWING FEDERATIONS AND CLUBS FOR THEIR KIND PERMISSION TO REPRODUCE THEIR LOGOS OR TEAM BADGES:

M.L.S. properties courtesy of Major League Soccer, L.L.C.

Accra Hearts of Oak Sporting Club, ADO Den Haag, All India Football Federation, Amsterdamsche Football Club Ajax, Arbil Football Club, Arsenal Football Club, ASEC Mimosas, AS Monaco Football Club, AS Nancy-Lorraine, Asociación Paraguaya de Fútbol, AZ Alkmaar, Bayer 04 Leverkusen, Blackpool Football Club, Bolton Football Club, Borussia Dortmund, Bulgarian Football Union, Canadian Soccer Association, Cantera Puma, Chelsea Football Club, Club Atlético Osasuna, Corporación Deportiva Once Caldas, Cotonsport Garoua, Croatian Football Federation, Dalian Shide, Danish Football Association, Federación Costarricense de Fútbol, Federación Mexicana de Fútbol Asociación, Fédération Camerounaise de Football, FC Basel 1893, FC Bayern Munich, FC Dallas, FC de Metz, FC Dynamo Kiev, FC Eintracht, FC Girondins de Bordeaux, FC Groningen, FC Lorient Bretagne Sud, FC Twente, Football Association of Wales, Football Federation Australia, Fulham Football Club, Galatasaray S.K., Go Ahead Eagles, Hamburger SV, Hanover 96, Hertha BSC Berlin, Invincible Eleven, Irish Football Association (www.irishfa.com), Israel Football Association, Japan Football Association, Jubilo Iwata Yamaha Football Club, Kazier Chiefs, Korea Football Association, Le Mans Union Club 72, Levante Unión Deportiva, Liberia Football Association, Middlesbrough Football Club, N.E.C., Newcastle United Football Club, New Zealand Football, Nottingham Forest Football Club, OGC Nice, Panathinaikos Football Club, Paris Saint-Germain Football Club, Portsmouth Football Club, Racing Club de Lens, Racing Club de Strasbourg, Real Madrid Club de Fútbol, Real Murcia, Real Racing Club de Santander, Real Valladolid Club de Fútbol, Real Zaragoza, Romanian Football Federation, Royal Netherlands Football Association, Royal Sporting Club Anderlecht, Royal Standard de Liège, Saudi Arabia Football Federation, Scottish Football Association, Singapore Armed Forces Football Club, SK Slavia Praha, SM Caen, Sparta Rotterdam, Sport Club Corinthians Paulista, Stade Rennais Football Club, Suwon Samsung Bluewings Football Club, Toulouse Football Club, UEFA, U.S. Soccer Federation, Vitesse, VVV-Venlo, Werder Bremen, Willem II Tilburg, Wolverhampton Wanderers Football Club.

THE PUBLISHER WOULD LIKE TO THANK THE FOLLOWING FOR THEIR KIND PERMISSION TO REPRODUCE THEIR PHOTOGRAPHS:

(Key: a-above; b-below/bottom; c-centre; f-far; l-left; r-right; t-top)

Action Images: 11cl, 11fbl, 15tc, 12bc, 30br, 38bl, 38crb, 40-41ca, 42br, 47tl, 57ca, 57ftl (friedel), 88cr, 125cl, 126fbr, 126tr, 127tl, 129bl; Reuters / Thomas Bohlen 124br; Andrew Budd 126br; Reuters/Claro Cortes IV WC 127cr; Jean Marie Hervio / Flash Press 102cb; Reuters / Enrique Marcarian 126ftl, 127ftr; Alex Morton 67c, 124ftr; John Sibley 127ftl; Sporting Picture 37br; Sporting Pictures 40cr, 124ftl, 125cr, 127tr; Barcelona FC 127rc; Boogertman + Partners Architects (Pty) Ltd: 63fcrb; Corbis: Toni Albir/epa 1; Jose L. Argueta/isiphotos.com 14bc; Yannis Behrakis / Reuters 2-3; Sandor Bojar/epa 45cb; Joao Luiz Bulcao 6-7; P. Caron/Corbis Sygma 148bl; Daniel Dal Zennaro/epa 36-37; Michael Dalder/Reuters 19tr, 126c; Tim De Waele 50c; Marcos Delgado/epa 90b; Duomo 122-123; Carlo Ferraro/epa 105crb; Andrew Fox 80-81; Marc Francotte/TempSport 39tc; Maurizio Gambarini/epa 82-83; Mast Irham/epa 89b; Michael Janosz/isiphotos.com 11br; Youri Kochetkov/epa 46cb; Andres Kudacki 4-5, 59ca; C. Liewig/Corbis Sygma 35br; Christian Liewig 18-19, 96bl; Christian Liewig / Tempsport 69bl; Christian Liewig/TempSport 45bl, 110clb, 110-111 (b/g); Neil Marchand/Liewig Media Sports 60bl; Stefan Matzke/NewSport 37bc; Tannen Maury/epa 56crb, 91br; Thierry Orban 45cl; Gerry Penny/epa 94-95; Jerome Prevost / TempSport 103cr; Jerome Prevost/TempSport 86bl; Ben Radford 22br; Stephane Reix/For Picture 39l, 46bl; Reuters 54bl, 71bl; Reuters/Juan Carlos Ulate 90cl; Reuters/Kim Kyung-Hoon 18tr; Reuters/Marcelo Del Pozo 97cl; Jean-Yves Ruszniewski/TempSport 28bl, 52-53; Ruben Sprich/Reuters 44cb; Darren Staples/Reuters 11tr, 16tl; John Todd/ISI 19br; Underwood & Underwood 10bl; Horacio Villalobos 51tc; Jens Wolf/epa 35c; Wu Xiaoling/Xinhua Press 26clb; Getty Images: 37tl, 104cl, 104-105 (b/g), 106r, 106-107 (background), 107clb, 107tr, 109crb, 116c, 116r, 117cb, 123clb, 125fcl, 126cl, 126fbl, 126tl, 127fbl, 127fbr; AFP 34bl, 53br, 68cra, 83tl, 86tl, 114cb, 114crb, 115cr, 115tc, 120c, 121clb, 126ftr; AFP Photo / Timothy A. Clary 57ftl (keller); AFP Photo/Alfredo Estrella 99bl; Arif Ali / AFP 121tc; Allsport UK 91ca; Allsport UK/Allsport 11c; Vanderlei Almeida/AFP 98br; Odd Andersen / AFP 66br; Torsten Blackwood / AFP 77b; Bagu Blanco 111tc; Bongarts 122l, 124bl, 124cl; Lutz Bongarts 72clb; Shaun Botterill 35tl, 74br, 118tr; Shaun Botterill/Allsport 90cr; Shaun Botterill/Allsport Uk 87tl; Simon Bruty/Allsport 97; Gerard Burkhart/AFP 99cl; David Cannon/Allsport 32cb, 34cl, 38br, 101tr; Central Press/Hulton Archive 42cl; Denis Charlet / AFP 103cl; Phil Cole 27clb; Jonathan Daniel 56-57; Stephane De Sakutin / AFP 102cl, 102-103 (Background); Adrian Dennis 79br; Adrian Dennis/AFP 27tr; Khaled Desouki / AFP 118br, 119r; Denis Doyle 43fcrb; Stephen Dunn 57br; Stephen Dunn/Allsport 91bl; Evening Standard/Hulton Archive 61bl, 75br; Evening Standard/Stringer/Hulton Archive 10cb; Franck Fife/AFP 16fcrb; Stu Forster 41tc, 59bc; Stu Forster/Allsport 62cr; Fox Photos 100cb; Fox Photos/Hulton Archive 12cl; Gallo Images 118clb; Bru Garcia/AFP 111crb; John Gurzinski/AFP 99cb; Martyn Harrison/AFP 93cl; Alexander Hassenstein/Bongarts 63bc; Patrick Hertzog/AFP 34cr; Mike Hewitt 96cb; Tobias Heyer/Bongarts 46br; Hulton Archive 58cl, 98cb; isifa/Filip Singer 113crb; Karim Jaafar / AFP 121cr; Jose Jordan/AFP 111cra; Keystone/Hulton Archive 34clb, 42c; Saeed Khan / AFP 78cr; Toshifumi Kitamura / AFP 79bl; Pornchai Kittiwongsakul / AFP 78tl; James Knowler 93tr; Natalia Kolesnikova/AFP 112c; Dima Korotayev/Epsilon 112; David Leah/Allsport 35bl, Alex Livesey 87bl; Pierre-Philippe Marcou/AFP 13bl; Marty Melville 120cl; Rabih Moghrabi / AFP 66cl; Dean Mouhtaropoulos 112cr; Peter Muhly/AFP 43bl; Guang Niu 76bc; Mark Nolan 120r; Ralph Orlowski 49tr; Ryan Pierse 100cl; Steve Powell/Allsport 36cl; Gary M. Prior 26br; Gary M. Prior/Allsport 65bc; Ben Radford 67clb, 72cr; Mark Ralston /AFP 121cra; Cesar Rangel/AFP 110r; Andreas Rentz / Bongarts 76cr; Holm Roehner/Bongarts 13tl; Martin Rose/Bongarts 39c; Evaristo Sa/AFP 13br; Issouf Sanogo/Afp 11bl; Roberto Schmidt/AFP 42bl; Antonio Scorza/AFP 90c, 98bl; Michael Steele 43cl; Chung Sung-Jun 24c; Henri Szwarc / Stringer / Bongarts 66bl; Mark Thompson/Allsport 62cl; Mirek Towski/Time Life Pictures 51br; Pius Utomi Ekpei / AFP 119c, 119cla; Friedemann Vogel/Bongarts 113cl; Wirelmage 117tl, 117tr; Toru Yamanaka 121cla; Mary Evans Picture Library: 9bl, 9r, 9t, 10tl, 10cl, 10cr; Central Press/Stringer/Hulton Archive 10br; The National Soccer Hall of Fame, Oneonta, NY: 10fcr, 56bl; PA Photos: 50bl, 79tl, 83cr; Abaca Abaca Press 125br; Africa Visuals 62bl, 63tc; AP Photo/ Claudio Cruz 99br; AP Photo/Anja Niedringhaus 92l; AP Photo/Ariel Schalit 88br, 88c; AP Photo/Ben Curtis 88bl; AP Photo/Carlo Fumagalli 52bl; AP Photo/Eugene Hoshiko 92cr; AP Photo/Fernando Llano 51l; AP Photo/Hans Punz 59br; AP Photo/Jae C. Hong 93br; AP Photo/Jon Super 101c; AP Photo/Massimo Pinca 105tc; AP Photo/Nasser Nasser 64br, 64c; AP Photo/Roberto Candia 58r; AP Photo/Vincent Thian 89ca; Bernat Armangue/AP25clb; Matthew Ashton / EMPICS Sport 66cr, 73cla; Matthew Ashton/Empics Sport 13ca, 32br, 75cl, 75cr, 82tl, 89cl, 91cl, 127br; Mark Baker / AP 77clb; Barratts 78bl, 82cra, 125ftr, 127fcl; Gregorio Borgia/AP 27br; Bruno Press 109tr; Jon Buckle/Empics Sport 54tr; Jon Buckle/Empics Sport/ 12bl; Buzzi 36cra, 105tl; Liewig Christian/Abaca 53c; Barry Coombs/EMPICS Sport 125tr; Cordon Press 111cla; Bas Czerwinski/AP 108cr; David Davies/PA Archive 83ftr; Adam Davy / Empics Sport 72tr; Adam Davy/Empics Sport 12r, 46fcla, 62br, 63l; Adam Davy/Empics Sport/ 21tl; Sean Dempsey/PA Archive 108cb; DPA 36bl, 38cl, 39br, 127cl, 150-151; DPA Deutsche Press-Agentur 44c, 124tl; Mike Egerton / EMPICS Sport 77; Mike Egerton/EMPICS Sport 21br, 24cr, 28clb, 14r, 33bl, 47c, 51bc, 59cb, 75bl, 126cr; Mike Egerton/Empics Sport/ 24bl; Empics Sport 20fbr, 23cl, 54c, 64cr, 65bl, 74c, 77cl; Christophe Ena/AP 20cr; Nigel French/EMPICS Sport 108-109; Nigel French/Empics Sport/ 65crb; Simon Galloway/Empics Sport 44fcra; Petros Giannakouris/AP 86cl; Gouhier-Hahn-Orban/Cameleon/abacapress.com 24tl; Laurence Griffiths/EMPICS Sport 125tl; Janerik Henriksson/Scanpix 123br; Torbjorn Jakobsson/Scanpix 13tr; Petr David Josek / AP 41br; Jasper Juinen/AP 18bl; Keystone/Hulton Archive 83fcr; Ross Kinnaird/EMPICS Sport 125fcr; Christian Liewig 68cla, 68clb; David Mariuz/AP 29cl; Tony Marshall / EMPICS Sport 41bc, 67crb, 72bc, 76cl; Tony Marshall/Empics Entertainment 45cr; Tony Marshall/EMPICS Sport 21c, 21tc, 21tr, 30bl, 52tl, 53bc, 55br, 55tr, 65cl, 104cr, 106clb, 126fcl; Tony Marshall/Empics Sport/ 74bl; Clive Mason 25c; Ricardo Mazalan 41c; Taamallah Mehdi / ABACA 102-103; Peter Morrison/AP 47bc; Steve Morton/Empics Sport 55tc; Daniel Motz 83tr; Rebecca Naden/PA Wire 100cr; PA Archive 32cr, 40bl, 125bl, 125ftl; PA Wire 33br; PA/PA Archive 32bl; Photocome 89cr; Nick Potts/Empics Sport 96br; Presse Sports 50fbr, 86cr; Michael Probst/AP 27tl; Rangers FC 96ca; Brian Rasmussen/Scanpix 46tc; Michael Regan/Empics Sport 45tr; Martin Rickett/PA Archive 32-33; Martin Rickett/PA Wire 97br; Peter Robinson / Empics Sport 40br, 67br; Peter Robinson/Empics Sport 36br, 38cr, 45tl, 47tc, 52c, 52cb, 74cr, 87cr, 124cr, 124fbl, 125fbl, 126fcr; Peter Robinson/Empics Sport/ 83c; S&G 126bl; Popperfoto 127bc; Jorge Saenz/AP 75clb; Marcio Jose Sanchez / AP 76tr; Neal Simpson / EMPICS Sport 103tl; Neal Simpson/EMPICS Sport 37ca, 57clb, 97bc, 125fbr; SMG 55bl, 96cr, 98cra; Howard Smith/International Sports Images 123tr; Michael Sohn/AP 16l, 19r, 46c; Jon Super/AP 18tr; Topham Picturepoint 50crb, 124fbr; Marcel Van Hoorn/AP 108cl, 108-109 (background); Geert Vanden Wijngaert/AP 22c; John Walton/Empics Sport 16cb; Aubrey Washington/EMPICS Sport 124tr; Haydn West 44br; Panapress: MAXPPP 69ca, 93bc; Reuters: 33c, 57ftl (howard), 99c, 107tl, 113tr, 114ca, 116clb, 131br; Sporting Pictures (UK) Ltd: 92br, 103cb; Wikipedia, The Free Encyclopedia: 8cla

Front Endpapers: Varley Picture Agency; Back Endpapers: Varley Picture Agency

Jacket images: Back: Corbis: Andy Rain/epa.

All other images © Dorling Kindersley
For further information see: www.dkimages.com